Praise for
Following Atticus

"Tom Ryan's lyrical narrative recounts the epic White Mountain adventures he's shared with Atticus M. Finch, his stalwart miniature schnauzer. During one amazing winter Ryan and Finch attempted to hike ninety-six snow-draped peaks in just ninety days. This unlikely duo traversed hundreds of miles through the rugged terrain of the Whites, home of 'the world's worst weather,' battling snow, cold, and wind and looking upon scenes of unspeakable beauty. This tale alone ensures that *Following Atticus* will delight dog lovers and mountain enthusiasts alike. But the book also takes the reader on a spiritual journey, as man and dog face unforeseen challenges with grace, courage, and love."

—Steven D. Smith and Mike Dickerman, authors of
The 4,000-Footers of the White Mountains

"Animals come into our lives prepared to teach, if only those of us on the human side of the bond would be humble enough to learn. Tom Ryan has obviously been paying close attention as he generously shares the wisdom and humanity of his remarkable dog, taking us on a noble quest. Atticus M. Finch is the four-legged mentor all dog lovers will crave."

—Dr. Nick Trout, author of *Tell Me Where It Hurts*

"Exceptionally evocative writing and [an] engaging story . . . this is a book that can be read more than once. Inspirational and heart-warming."

—*Library Journal*

following atticus

FORTY-EIGHT HIGH PEAKS, ONE LITTLE DOG, AND AN EXTRAORDINARY FRIENDSHIP

TOM RYAN

WILLIAM MORROW

An Imprint of HarperCollins*Publishers*

HarperCollins books may be purchased for educational, business, or sales promotional use. For information please write: Special Markets Department, HarperCollins Publishers, 10 East 53rd Street, New York, NY 10022.

A hardcover edition of this book was published in 2011 by William Morrow, an imprint of HarperCollins Publishers.

FIRST WILLIAM MORROW PAPERBACK EDITION PUBLISHED 2012.

Designed by Lisa Stokes

The Library of Congress has cataloged the hardcover edition as follows:

Ryan, Tom.
  Following Atticus : forty-eight high peaks, one little dog, and an extraordinary friendship / Tom Ryan.
    p. cm.
  ISBN 978-0-06-199710-5
  1. Ryan, Tom. 2. Mountaineers—United States—Biography. 3. Dogs—Anecdotes. 4. Dog owners—Anecdotes. 5. Human-animal relationships—Anecdotes. I. Title.
  GV199.92.R93A3 2011
  796.522092—dc22
  [B]
                                                                      2011005118

ISBN 978-0-06-199711-2 (pbk.)

13 14 15 16 OV/RRD 10 9 8 7

For R.R.—always in my heart

"There's no sense in going further—it's the edge of cultivation,"
So they said, and I believed it . . .

Till a voice, as bad as Conscience, rang interminable changes
On one everlasting Whisper day and night repeated—so:
"Something hidden. Go and find it. Go and look behind the Ranges—
Something lost behind the Ranges. Lost and waiting for you. Go!"

—RUDYARD KIPLING, "THE EXPLORER"

We must be willing to get rid of the life we've planned, so as to have
the life that is waiting for us.

—JOSEPH CAMPBELL

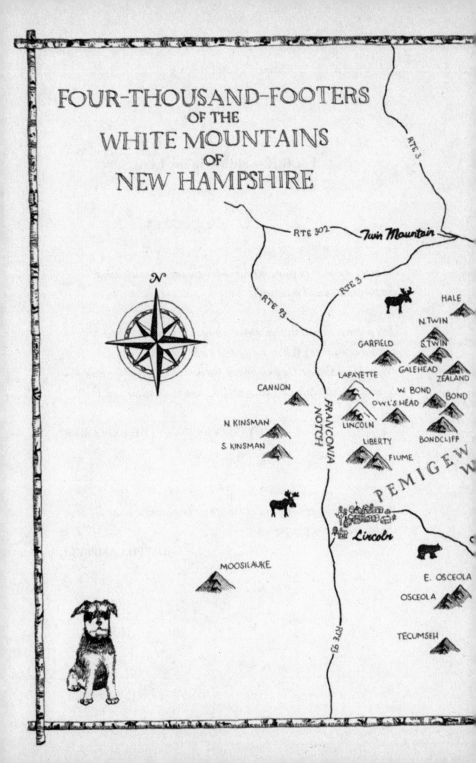

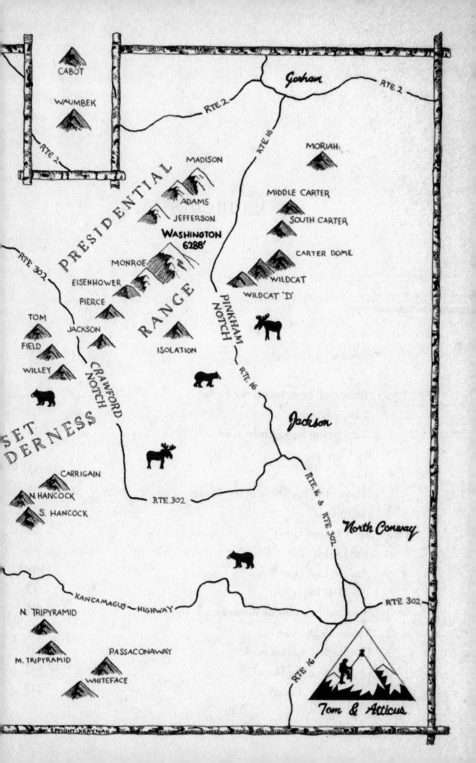

Contents

Prologue   x

Part I | Innocence Lost, Innocence Found
  1 | A Door Opens   3
  2 | "Carry Him Everywhere You Go"   24
  3 | Big Changes   38
  4 | A Gift   53
  5 | "People Die Up There in the Winter"   65
  6 | For the Kids   84
  7 | The Greatest Quest   93
  8 | The Little Giant   99
  9 | Stars to Light the Way   108
 10 | The M. Is Important   115
 11 | "Our Faith Comes in Moments . . ."   121
 12 | Atticus in Disguise   127
 13 | The Spell of Agiocochook   131
 14 | Five Astounding Days   142
 15 | "Thank You, Friend"   147

Part II | Light over Dark

16 | A Heartrending Turn of Events 155

17 | "I'm Not Leaving Him Alone" 165

18 | The Friends of Atticus 169

19 | Soul Work 175

20 | Bread Crumbs 183

21 | Dinner with Frank Capra 189

22 | The Promise 194

Part III | Full Circle

23 | A New Quest 203

24 | The Witch 207

25 | Magic Is Where You Find It 214

26 | Death on Franconia Ridge 219

27 | My Last Letter Home 228

28 | Those Eyes, Those Beautiful Eyes 235

29 | Mount Washington 243

30 | Good-bye 247

31 | Heartache 253

32 | The Great Art of Sauntering 261

33 | Paige 266

34 | Home 271

Acknowledgments 274

Prologue

October 8, 2006

Dear Dad,

    I have a new favorite photo. I took it on Saturday while walking down the Polecat Ski Trail on Wildcat Mountain.

    Off in the distance—stately, proud, and jagged—stands the gigantic duo of Mount Adams and Mount Madison. Sloping down from their craggy summits and from the low shoulder of Mount Washington spreads an infinite army of trees stationed by rank. Highest are the evergreens, those hardy trees that never change throughout the seasons. They extend up to tree line, just below the summits, and slope downward until they mingle with the deciduous trees in their October war paint. An infantry of red, orange, and yellow that rolls forward like a great wave from an ocean swell. By the colors and the undulating hills at the foot of the mountains, you can almost see the trees pulsing, like an army ready to charge into battle.

    This army flows ever onward toward the camera until it forms a battle line both tense and even, ready for the order from high above to advance.

    In front of the trees there is a field—a mixture of faded yellow and green, flattened through the years, as if many battles have taken place there. In the foreground, separated from the front lines by yards of grass, sitting with his back to the camera, is a small, solitary figure looking at the legions of trees as they stretch on mile after mile.

The lone figure sits erect, ready for the wave to break, ready for whatever the world is about to unleash upon him. He is serene (or perhaps resigned to the coming test), humble and undaunted because he has faith that he will find a way.

He is Frodo Baggins; he is Don Quixote; he is Huck Finn. He is every unlikely hero who ever took a step out the door and found himself swept up in adventure.

Looking at the photo, I think of what the poet William Irwin Thompson wrote: "When we come to an edge we come to a frontier that tells us that we are now about to become more than we have been before."

For there he sits, alone in that field, facing an edge, facing a frontier, facing a wilderness that dwarfs him. And yet he sits. Facing it. Not turning away. Not running away.

The little fellow in the photograph is my hiking partner, Atticus M. Finch, named for yet another humble and unlikely literary hero.

Since May 21 of last year, he has been kind enough to put up with me as I've flung the two of us into our mountain adventures. Up until then we weren't all that active. We mostly sat around Newburyport. We took little walks in the woods or on the beach, but never too far because I was too heavy and out of shape. Then, last year, after being introduced to the four-thousand-footers, we immediately fell head over heels for them and hiked all forty-eight peaks in eleven weeks. We so rushed through them all that I decided to do them again throughout this spring, summer, and fall—and this time we took our time to enjoy them more.

Watching Atticus gazing upon those trees was when I started to celebrate this round of the forty-eight, but more than that I celebrated this curious little dog. How lucky I am to have him as a hiking partner. Come wind, sun, snow, or rain he has been with me every step of the way. Most of the time it's just the two of us, and our tight bond has grown even stronger.

When I saw him sitting, facing that wilderness, I thought of all those unlikely heroes in literature who have faced unimagined challenges and come out seasoned and strangely different. In the end they became more than they'd ever been, and you just knew that through sadness and joy, through good days and bad, no matter what happened next, after the story ended and they walked off into the sunset, they could handle all the trials and tribulations that life had in store for them. But while knowing that, I also knew the sadness that comes with the closing of a book, in saying good-bye to my favorite characters. I often mourn the end of an adventure for that very reason. I have come to judge a good story as one that makes me feel as if I'm losing a friend when I read the final page, close the book, and put it down for the last time.

Luckily for me, this is not the end of a book but merely a chapter. Atticus and I have many adventures to go before our days are done. As a matter of fact, the next one starts in just a couple of months, and that will be a story unto itself, I'm sure.

While walking farther down the ski slope through the shaded green grass and between sun-soaked golden trees, I took note of everything I was feeling, absorbed the beauty like a sponge, and looked upon Atticus with the same wonder I have for these mountains and for the trees and for the wind that knows them both. In watching him bounce down the slope in his carefree style, I smiled. How could I not?

Looking at this little dog, who weighs twenty pounds after a good meal, I find myself loving him as much as I do because, like all those unlikely literary heroes, there's more to him than meets the eye. And I am lucky enough to count him not only as a hiking partner but also a friend.

There are some days that are perfect, not so much for what is accomplished as for what is felt and will always be remembered. Yesterday was one of those perfect days, when two friends finished one chapter and went off in search of another.

Love,
Tom

Part I

Innocence Lost, Innocence Found

*May your trails be crooked, winding, lonesome,
dangerous, leading to the most amazing view. May
your mountains rise into and above the clouds.*

—EDWARD ABBEY

A Door Opens

I led a most unusual life. Some would even say it was exciting. I was the editor, publisher, and lone employee of my own newspaper. In it I chronicled the life and times of Newburyport, a small city on the North Shore of Massachusetts. I was poor but influential, happy but stressed, fulfilled in my work but not in my life. I was making a difference, but at the same time I felt like there was something missing.

Most of my nights were spent covering meetings at city hall, and after those meetings I'd get the stories behind the stories when I'd chat with city officials for hours on end. I filled my days conversing with characters from all walks of life and listening as they told me the secrets of Newburyport. In a city of seventeen thousand, everyone had a story to tell—and typically several more about their neighbors. Every two weeks my paper hit the streets filled with those stories, and nearly every issue sold out. It was a must-read, for as the typical Newburyporter saw it, the world revolved around our little city where the Merrimack River meets the Atlantic Ocean.

I stayed up late at night and got up early each morning. There was no need for an alarm clock, however. I lived alone on the third floor of the old Grand Army Building in the heart of the downtown, and I slept on a couch. The sun rose out of the Atlantic, and daybreak spread across Plum Island, raced along the Merrimack, touched down on Joppa Flats, cast its early-morning shadows through the tightly knit historic neighborhoods of the South End, and when it reached the redbrick buildings in the downtown, it set them ablaze. The blinding orange glow reflected off that canyon of brick into my large, west-facing windows and told me it was time to get up.

But Tuesdays were different, especially in winter, when the days were shorter and the early mornings darker. I'd bolt upright, awakened by the cacophony of the trash truck making its way up State Street. The whine of the gears, the squeal of the brakes, the crash of garbage dumped into the truck, the compressor's heavy metallic thud. I'd rush out of bed, grab my trash, hurtle down two flights of stairs, and hope to beat the truck to the curb outside my back door on Charter Street. For five years I raced that trash truck, sometimes winning, sometimes not.

I never put my garbage out on Monday night the way my neighbors did. I was warned not to. This was Newburyport, after all, a city with long-held secrets. For as postcard-pretty as it was, it had a charmingly sinister side. Since I dealt in secrets, and those who shared them, I could not be too careful. But after five years I was tired of being paranoid and tired of racing the trash truck. One Monday night I put out four bags of trash. As fate would have it, it was the night my trash disappeared. It was the night my greatest adventure would begin.

My paper was called the *Undertoad*. The title came from John Irving's *The World According to Garp:* a reminder that there's always something lurking, beneath even the smoothest surface. It wasn't a typical name for a newspaper, but Newburyport was not your typical city. It was Norman Rockwell meets Alfred Hitchcock. It was townies and newcomers, straights and gays. It was old Yankees and the Irish and the Greeks. It was a city divided many times over.

Newburyport was the home of William Lloyd Garrison, the abolitionist who sharpened his pen locally before taking on slavery on the national stage with his paper the *Liberator*. It was the home of Andrew J. "Bossy" Gillis, the on-again, off-again bad-boy mayor from the wrong side of the tracks who was as colorful a political character as any this nation has ever seen. Bossy published his own paper to take on his political foes. He called it the *Asbestos*, because "it was too hot to handle." Newburyport was the home of John P. Marquand, a Pulitzer Prize–winning novelist who used the local gentry in many of his works. And for nearly a decade during the 1930s and '40s, Newburyport, with its rigid, antiquated class structure, was also the home of William Lloyd Warner, a Chicago anthropologist and sociologist, and his team of thirty researchers. Their study of Newburyport, *Yankee City*, is perhaps the longest-running study ever done of an American city.

I was compared to all of them, but most often I was considered a cross between Garrison and Gillis. As humbling as this was, I admitted to being more Gillis than Garrison. In the Newburyport I knew, you had to be a bit of a brawler if you were going to be writing about scoundrels. In my debut issue of the *'Toad*, I wrote about my desire to "shine light in the dark places, weed the garden, and poison the poisoners." But I was no mere muckraker; I was a romantic who regularly invoked the words of Emerson, Thoreau, and other existentialists. I uncovered the dirt, but I also had high hopes for where the city could go and what it could be.

Once, when a new reporter came to work for the *Newburyport Daily News*, she sought me out, even though I was the competition, and asked, "So what's it like here?"

"It's like nothing you've ever seen," I told her.

She wasn't impressed. "I hear the same thing about every town I go to."

A year later she left the paper to work for a Boston television station. I asked her, "So what was it like?"

"It was like nothing I've ever seen!"

The city was filled with characters and character. It had a history of fishing, then of shipbuilding and shipping, then of textile mills and shoe factories. In the fifties and sixties, after the mills and factories folded or moved elsewhere, Newburyport was left to rot. The most heavy-handed politician in town at the time led the charge to demolish the great Federal-style buildings of the downtown and replace them with strip malls and parking lots. A group of citizens came together, hired an architect to show what the downtown could look like if it were saved, and went to court to stop the demolition. They won, and Newburyport became the first city in the country to use HUD money to restore instead of demolish a blighted downtown. This brought about a great restoration, but to many of the locals it brought about an even greater bitterness. For once newcomers saw how beautiful a place it was, they started moving in, and gentrification washed away much of the old and the familiar. Locals no longer saw it as their city and bemoaned the loss of the stores they'd grown up with as one by one they were replaced by upscale boutiques.

Through all its changes, the one constant in Newburyport was the rough-and-tumble political scene. Politics was king and, more often than not, dirty. Those who had power did whatever they had to do to hold on to it. It wasn't just native against newcomer; it was also native against native. Some called the town "Cannibal City." Others referred to the locals as crabs in a bucket—when one climbs up, the others try to pull him down. It was full of incest and infighting at their most vicious—and about the most wonderful place in the world for a new writer.

I'd arrived on the scene during a perfect political storm. Power had been wrested from the good-old-boy network by a mayor who had been in the city for only three years. To add insult to injury, it just so happened that this newcomer was also a woman and a lesbian. She was a breath of fresh air for a stuffy provincial city that took itself far too seriously. The mayor was coming to the end of her first two-year term, and the good old boys not only wanted to drive her from the corner office, they wanted her out of town.

I had no thought of getting involved in politics or starting a newspaper. But I was so shocked by the way they bullied this young mayor, mostly with rumor and innuendo, that I couldn't help myself, and I jumped into the fray. I wrote letters to the editor of the daily and weekly papers. Without realizing it, I was following in the footsteps of Garrison and Gillis by naming names, something not typically done in Newbury-port. In a wild and raucous election, the incumbent won a close battle against a former mayor who had served five straight terms long before. Although I was new to town, my letters were credited with helping bring about the victory. A year later the *Undertoad* was born, and it wasn't long before the *Boston Globe* referred to my paper as "the insider's guide to the underside of Newburyport."

Depending on where you stood in town, whom you were related to or were friends with, I was either a muckraker or a reformer. I took on the good old boys, refused to worship the long-existing sacred cows that the *Daily News* protected, and was helped in part because I didn't know the first thing about journalism. Instead I paid more attention to what ordinary people had to say and thought about what I didn't like about newspapers and then did just the opposite. My headlines were sensational and color-ful but factual. My reporting was intimate and included as many names in each issue as possible. I realized that people didn't care too much about organizations or city boards because they couldn't relate to them. But in a small city where everyone knew your name, they could relate to a city official they saw at the health club, who was the coach of their son's Little League team, or who managed a local restaurant. Articles ran the gamut of emotions.

I chastised native-born city councilors for attempting to block the mayor's every move simply because she was a newcomer, and I spent many issues highlighting the clearly defined lines between the natives and newcomers holding political office. I'd often find the richest stories at various board meetings that weren't always attended by reporters from the other papers. I caught board members doing favors for friends or business associates when they should have recused themselves from the hearing, and I'd send information to the state's ethics commission. On more than one occasion, board members chose to resign.

I would often sit shocked as city councilors or other community leaders lied in some televised meeting and thought nothing of it. When I'd report it, they'd act as though I were the one who had crossed the line—and in some ways they were right, I had. I refused to let business happen as it always had happened.

Their lies knew no bounds. My favorite was when one seething city councilor who was friendly with many local developers argued against the city's buying several acres of open space that were slated for development. He pointed out that he should care about the land more than anyone else because his brother was buried in the adjoining cemetery. The cemetery was on a hill, and conservationists feared that development of the land would cause the historic burial ground to shift, the land to erode, and some of the graves to crumble. The problem was that the city councilor's brother was dead, all right, but he was buried elsewhere.

No one was above criticism, least of all any of the mayors I covered. They offered the best grist for my paper, whether it came to appointing an ethically challenged person to one of the city's boards—someone whose only qualification was having worked on the mayor's campaign and helped him or her get elected—or attempting to slide through a land deal for a supporter. The mayors didn't stick around very long during the *Undertoad* years. It was usually one two-year term and out.

But my paper wasn't all negative. It couldn't be. While pointing out what was wrong with the city, I also showed what was right with it. I'd support a courageous vote by a councilor or a stance by a mayor. I applauded the better members of the various city boards and commissions and deserving city employees. In a regular column titled "Ten Things to Love About Newburyport," I listed ten people who were doing good things. It could be a developer who believed in historic preservation, a librarian who took great pride in her work and loved books and the people who read them, or a cashier at the local supermarket who never missed a day of work and greeted nearly every customer by name. Each December I named at least one Person of the Year. There were activists, business leaders, courageous police offers, teachers, and coaches. One year Pete Daigle, the city-hall custodian, won the award because of his gentle nature, his hard work, and his ability to keep his head while others all around him in city government were losing theirs.

As for my qualifications as a journalist, I had none. I didn't go to school for journalism, and the only writing I'd ever done was a handful of letters to the editor. I knew little about politics but knew what I didn't like about politicians. My only background came from my father's romanticized view of the Kennedys and the Founding Fathers—he thought theirs and not his was the greatest generation.

My father, Jack Ryan, was politically active, and he conscripted each of his nine children into working for Democratic candidates for any office, national or local. It didn't matter that we didn't know a candidate or didn't want to get involved and would much rather have been out playing with our friends. We were forced to canvass the neighborhoods in our hometown of Medway, Massachusetts, passing out campaign brochures. On weekends we'd have to stand for hours holding signs supporting his favorite candidates. But, like all my brothers and sisters, once I moved away from home, I got as far from politics as I could. I'd had my fill.

As for Jack Ryan's political beliefs—they were a bit confusing. He was the liberal Archie Bunker. He believed in equal rights, as long as a minority wasn't going to be living next door to us in little Medway.

One summer, while I was working as a student athletic trainer at the University of Iowa and had the chance to spend time with the trainer of the Harlem Globetrotters and some of the players, my father advised me, "Watch your wallet."

"Dad, they're millionaires. I'm making fifty dollars a week and room and board—they don't need my money."

"Doesn't matter. It's in their blood."

When I was in the seventh grade, I had a crush on the only black girl in town. She stood out as striking and exotic in our lily-white town. I told my father about her at dinner one night, and he told me I shouldn't even think about dating her. It wasn't a threat, it was just that he thought if we ended up getting married, being half white and half black wouldn't be fair to our kids. But I was only in seventh grade!

I can remember him giving me a strange look the night I told him one of my friends in high school was Norman Finkelstein. "You're friends with a Jew?"

"Yeah, I like him. What's wrong with Jews?"

He shrugged. "I just never knew an Irishman who was friends with a Jew. Usually the Jews stay to themselves."

Toward the end of his life, when my father grew too old to take care of himself, I was thrilled by my brother David's choice of attorney to handle his estate. Even if he could have thought clearly, I'm not sure Dad would have known quite what to think. His name was Ryan Swartz. I couldn't decide whether Jack Ryan would be pleased by the name Ryan or put off by the Jewish-sounding name of Swartz. David suggested that Dad would be happy, since he believed in the stereotype that a man with a Jewish-sounding last name would definitely be good with money. The only caveat, I'm sure, had he his wits, would have been, "Good choice. Just keep an eye on him."

And yet throughout all of this, if my father saw someone who was black or Asian or Puerto Rican or Jewish, or any minority, being attacked, he would come to his or her defense.

He was a hard man to figure out. I chalk it all up to his generation and to his growing up in the poorest Irish Catholic section of Boston and coming of age during the Great Depression.

If I told him about a friend who had an Italian last name, he would ask, "Italian?" And if I'd say, "Italian and Jewish," he would say something like, "Really? A Jew married an Italian?" He'd then get a puzzled look on his face as he tried to figure out how such a thing could possibly have happened in the world he grew up in.

In the end I didn't take too much of his guff and laughed off such nonsense, but when I was younger, I thought his opinions were vile. Maturity taught me to make light of his prejudices, with the slightest twist of my own knife. Whenever I was leaving, I'd lean forward to say good-bye and kiss him. Of course he'd squirm when I did this, because he was a homophobe. But that's partially why I did it. (He once cringed when I told him I was reading Oscar Wilde—"That fag?" You can just imagine how he thought I'd completely lost it when I went to see Michael Feinstein—a gay Jew—in concert! I lied when I told him, "Not to worry, Dad, he's going to sing 'Danny Boy.'" But oddly enough, that made it okay.)

Then again, this was the man who cried when Jack and Bobby Kennedy were shot, teared up when Hubert H. Humphrey lost to Nixon, and brought us to Gettysburg and was proud of the Union Army and what it fought for. When he saw how prisoners of George W. Bush's war on terror were being treated at Abu Ghraib, he said it was the first time in his life he was embarrassed to be an American. And yet he opened bank accounts for all his grandchildren except my sister's adopted girl, who had "inferior stock" because of the Hispanic blood running through her veins.

In Jack Ryan's world, there was only one thing worse than being a gook, a Polack, a guinea, a 'Rican, or a nigger—and that was a Republican.

My father's prejudices were only one of the reasons we often went years without speaking. As puzzling as his politics were, they paled in comparison to his conflicting relationships with his children. I don't doubt that he loved us, even though he never said it and it was often hard to see. But I also believed he resented us.

I was the youngest of nine children, and by the time I came on the scene, life had pretty much worn my father down. He was mostly a stranger to me; he was that way with all of us. We'd rarely see his tender side. He preferred instead to build walls that would keep us out, and he believed in tough love and frequent beatings. He was often angry and bitter and felt as if life had passed him by.

He wasn't always that way, however. When he was a boy, he read book after book that gave wings to his imagination and led to dreams of the exotic lands he would visit and how the world would reveal her secrets to him. He thought of the riches he'd make and how he'd be famous one day. But his first adventure landed him in North Africa, France, and Italy during World War II, and none of the tales from his childhood had prepared him for the horror. He saw arms and legs blown off of men and faces torn apart by bullets, and had too many friends die in his arms. Worse than that were his memories of the people he had killed.

When the war was over, he came home and married my mother. Less than nine months later, my sister Joanne was born. Then came John, Claire, Eddie, Nancy, David, Jeff, Stephen, and, finally, me. He'd gone from being a young man with big plans to a father in his forties with nine children, married to a wife who ended up wheelchair-bound with multiple sclerosis.

I was seven years old when my mother died, and I don't remember her at all, although I can't help but believe that my father saw her death as life's latest cruel joke. For a while he did his best to keep the family together. It couldn't have been easy. He helped us with our homework, read to us in bed, spoiled us every Christmas and on our birthdays, and took us on vacations each year. But the older he grew, the more difficult it all became, and his bitterness always won out.

In the years following my mother's death, the beatings lessened but he often looked at us with antipathy, and he invented new ways to be disappointed by us and let us know we wouldn't amount to much. As the youngest, I watched as one by one my brothers and sisters left the house. They didn't fly from the nest with high expectations but rather limped from it, their wings clipped. When it was only the two of us remaining at home, he simply had nothing left to give. That's when I realized that there was something more painful than his beatings and belittlings: his indifference. There would be days, even weeks, when he wouldn't say a word to me. I couldn't understand it, but what fifteen-year-old could?

When he did speak, it was often to criticize me, saying I was too much of a dreamer; that my hopes were too high and I would crash and burn. But hopes and dreams were all I had in those days, and I hung on to them ferociously. And so began a tug-of-war that would last for decades. It was a battle that defined the rest of my life.

When I left the house, I wasn't sure what I wanted to do with my life; I just knew I didn't want to be Jack Ryan, and I didn't want to settle into the half-lives my brothers and sisters had accepted. Don't get me wrong, they weren't bad people; they were simply sad people, and I wanted something more. So I set out on an odyssey to find my purpose. The journey often seemed futile, and I became a modern-day gypsy, going from college to college, from job to meaningless job. I wasn't quite sure what I was looking for; I only knew I'd recognize it when I found it. My relationships were equally aimless. I was seeking something through the women I dated, but I couldn't find it. I was like Tarzan swinging through the jungle, from vine to vine, from woman to woman, holding on just long enough to find someone new, until at last I met Alexis, an interior designer who offered me all the comforts of love and home. However, she cared more about how things looked, while I cared more about how things felt, and the only thing we did well was fight. Ultimately things didn't work out between us, but we lasted long enough for Alexis to bring me to Newburyport. When we split up, I decided to stay. The city was different from anyplace I'd ever been. For the first time in my life, I felt like I was home.

Throughout my decade and a half as a wanderer, my father and I often went years without speaking. Occasionally there would be a peace treaty, but none of them ever lasted very long. And yet with all we'd been through—the hurt, anger, and frustration—I learned to have compassion for my father, and strangely enough, I even loved him. Down deep, I believed he did the best he could with the hand he was dealt. But that didn't change who we were, and we continued to fight.

When I started the *Undertoad*, he and I weren't speaking—but when we reconnected a few years later, he was more than a little pleased, even though he wouldn't admit it. You see, my father had a habit of writing letters to the editor of the local paper in which he would criticize or support politicians. My brothers and sisters and I were all mortified by his letters. So you can imagine how he must have felt when I made a living out of doing just that—publishing an editorial journal.

What my father probably wouldn't have understood was my reason for starting the *'Toad* in the first place—to defend the honor of a lesbian mayor. It was one thing to come to the aid of an underdog; it was something entirely different to base your livelihood on it.

Within a year of that mayor's reelection, the 'Toad was born, and at first it was free. I was able to quickly raise the price to fifty cents, then a dollar, and finally a dollar and a half. I made a living, albeit a small one, on the sales at newsstands and from subscriptions and advertisements. Sometimes I could even pay my bills. Whenever I thought about quitting, folks in town would do their best to put me out of business and motivate me to continue. They'd boycott my advertisers or they'd spread rumors about me: I was a pedophile, a deadbeat dad, a wife beater, a con artist. At first I was horrified by the rumors, but over time I learned that the best way to handle them was simply to print them on the front page. That's when the death threats started. These were anonymous and were either mailed to me or placed on the windshield of my car. As for my poor car, my tires were slashed so often that a local garage kept extra tires on hand just for me. My exhaust pipe was once filled with spray insulation foam.

I never reported the death threats to the police, because I feared that cops might have been the ones writing them. The police department in Newburyport had a long, controversial history, and most politicians were afraid of them, and because of that the officials looked the other way. It was suggested I do the same. This advice came from one of the more influential and controversial members of the police department.

It was late at night, and we were outside city hall. He said to me, "How about we form an uneasy alliance—you and me? I won't go after you if you don't go after me."

"But there's nothing to go after me for," I told him, trying to keep my voice from shaking.

"Who says we need something to go after? Besides, everyone's got something to hide." And then he winked and stalked off into the shadows of the night.

I didn't write about the police after that—not for another year and a half. But my readers wanted to know why, when there was so much to report. The truth is, I was afraid. Eventually, though, the day came when I decided that they were the only bullies in town I hadn't taken on. And when it came, it was like I'd swung a baseball bat at a hornet's nest. I used information from the minority of policemen who refused to go along to get along. My paper was filled with the misdeeds of the department, and I sold more copies than ever.

My readers loved it when I poked fun at a police officer who was caught stealing a bicycle. They found it even more entertaining when one of the department's expensive new cold-water skin-diving suits went missing. When the officer who took it was discovered, he said he'd borrowed it to fix a crack in his swimming pool. The only problem was that it went missing in the middle of winter.

Then there was the acting marshal (Newburyport's version of a police chief) who was appointed to help clean up the troubled department. But it didn't take long for everyone to realize he wasn't the answer when I printed a time sheet in the *'Toad* that showed him paying himself when he was actually out playing golf.

I was criticized a great deal for one story because I refused to print the name of the officer who was cheating on his wife on duty while I named times and places when he was supposed to be working but was throwing himself at another woman. I chose not to print his name in the paper because he and his wife had two small children in school and I didn't think it would be fair to them. His wife put together the pieces, though, and divorced him.

Once I started writing about the police, they were in nearly every issue of my paper.

Writing about local politics was one thing, but taking on the police upped the stress level in my life immeasurably. I was warned not to talk on a cordless phone, because members of the department could park near my apartment and try to listen in on my conversations on their radios. There wasn't a day when I didn't fear I might be arrested on some mysterious charge while walking down the street. But the more they came after me, the more intent I was on not giving in. It was the Irish in me, I suppose.

Officers who were believed to be my sources for stories were ostracized by their brethren. Some were disciplined. One even had charges brought up against him, and they attempted to send him to jail even though he and his wife were expecting their fourth child. Luckily, a judge saw through the accusations and dismissed the case.

The war raged on. I had many supporters, but I was on the front lines by myself. I began keeping a baseball bat in my car for protection. Elderly friends sometimes rode shotgun when I delivered the *'Toad* overnight to make sure no harm came to me.

I may have been public enemy number one, but I was saved because I was dealing with bullies who weren't all that bright. They were, to borrow a term from Jimmy Breslin, "the gang that couldn't shoot straight." Each time they came after me, they'd stumble and trip. It was the Road Runner versus Wile E. Coyote, and a community was watching and often laughing. I received numerous traffic tickets, and there was something outrageous about every one of them. I even received one for driving with worn tire-tread depth. It was written by a cross-eyed police officer who had been driving in the opposite direction. On the day my car insurance lapsed and my registration became invalid, the police were waiting for me with their version of a dragnet, and an officer was assigned to catch me driving. During the morning when several officers extended their breakfast at a local restaurant just so they could do their best to intimidate me at the next table, a bank was robbed on the other side of town. The crooks probably wouldn't have gotten away had the officers not been busy glowering at me while I ate my bacon and egg sandwich. At a city council meeting, all but four members of the department marched into the council chambers armed and in uniform—bringing to mind a police state—and presented the councilors a letter of complaint against me and my paper. Thirty uniformed and armed officers' attempt at intimidation was televised, and it backfired. People began taking public stands against the troubled department. A rally of several hundred citizens took place outside city hall in front of the statue of William Lloyd Garrison to decry the behavior of members of the department. Suddenly people weren't as afraid as they'd once been. The mayor at the time was forced to hire an independent consultant to look at the department. The consultant's report backed up the years' worth of stories I had written and even talked about how some local business owners admitted they were concerned that police officers might not protect them because they advertised in or sold the '*Toad*.

That's what was going on in my life when my trash was taken.

I returned from a meeting at city hall, and something looked different. And suddenly it hit me. All the rest of the trash on the street was still there waiting for the trash truck the next morning, but mine was missing. I thought it was curious, but a lot of curious things took place in Newburyport. I made light of it and shared the story with a few friends, one of them a police officer.

The next night I would learn that it was the police who had my trash. Two detectives were sifting through it in search of the sordid details of my life. I can't be certain what they were looking for, but it was believed they were searching for anything that would tarnish me: drug paraphernalia, child pornography, or perhaps something even more valuable to them—notes that would lead them to the informants within their department who were blowing the whistle on them. But alas, while my life might have seemed exciting to some, I was a boring, albeit overweight, fellow, and what they mostly found were too many Twinkie wrappers, Big Mac containers, and empty pints of Ben & Jerry's.

Having the police go through my trash shouldn't have shocked me. I had learned to be prepared for anything. And from the moment I published my first opinions on Newburyport politics, I'd led a controversial life. But it was the missing trash that got to me more than anything else. I felt violated. The very people who were sworn to protect my rights were digging through my personal life to find any way possible to hurt me. In the days that followed, I became paranoid. I'd done nothing wrong, but I half expected the police to break down my door at any moment and haul me away. I stopped sleeping and became increasingly edgy.

I had reached my breaking point.

A couple of weeks later, I received a seemingly harmless e-mail from Nancy Noyes, a member of the city's Zoning Board of Appeals. She sent it to everyone in her address book. There was a dog in need of a home. His original owner decided she no longer wanted him, and he'd been passed on to a family member who couldn't really take care of him, then to another, who was allergic to dogs. That's when Nancy intervened. Her plea was simple: "Can anyone give Max, an older miniature schnauzer, a home? If we can't find him a place, he may be dropped off at the pound, where, because of his age, he most likely won't be adopted and he will be put down."

I sat down to write Nancy and let her know that I would run a free ad in the *Undertoad* trying to find Max a home. As I got ready to type, my mind wandered. I'd always loved dogs, and I thought about getting one again someday. *But not now.* The time wasn't right. I was too busy with my paper, and besides, my landlord didn't allow pets. I wasn't sure what a miniature schnauzer was, but I figured it was a small yapper you'd see wearing a sweater knitted by the little old lady he lived with. When the time came for me to get a dog, it would be a real dog—a black Lab. Now, that was a man's dog—handsome, regal, strong, and loyal. The best dog I'd ever had was a black Lab named Seamus, so I knew something about them.

I then thought about how I had read somewhere that if you're bad at relationships, take a break from them. (And Lord knows I needed a break from them. I wasn't good in intimate relationships in the first place. What was worse, I had the unfortunate trait of choosing women who were even worse in relationships than I was.) After a while, get a plant. If the plant does well, try a pet. If you do okay with a pet, try another relationship. I looked at the plants turning to dust on my windowsill, and as if in a drugged state I inexplicably typed, "If no one else takes him, I will." It wasn't until I pushed the "send" button that I woke up from my daze. I instantly regretted my decision and thought about e-mailing Nancy back. But there were so many people on her e-mail list, one of them would surely provide a home for an unwanted dog.

When Nancy did write back, she said, "Thank you, Tom! That's great! The two of you will be very happy together."

What had I done? Where were all those good-hearted people who were going to take him so that I didn't have to?

A dog meant commitment, and I didn't want commitment. My life was too crazy for a pet. I tried to think of ways to back out of it. In the meantime I went online to see what a miniature schnauzer looked like.

Oh, my God, it was one of those little yappers!

The next afternoon I was told Max was ready for me to pick him up. So soon? No. Impossible. *I* wasn't ready, hadn't yet told my landlord (did I mention he didn't allow pets?), and hadn't even had time to prepare for a dog in my life or to dogproof my apartment. I delayed by a day and was told I could pick him up the following afternoon. He would be at a local groomer's, where he'd been washed but not cut.

I showed up without a leash, a collar, or a clue. While waiting for the groomer to make her appearance, I made my way around the room look-ing in each crate and thinking, *That dog doesn't look too bad*, or *I hope that's him*. What I didn't see was anything resembling a miniature schnauzer. Things were seeming hopeful—out of all the dogs in the place, there was only one I wouldn't want. It was a miserable-looking fellow or gal. Frankly, I couldn't tell its sex, since it looked more like a sheep overdue for shearing than a dog. While the other dogs were attentive to me when I paused at their crates, the little gray sheep didn't move. It lay there, uninterested, and for all I knew it was deaf, dumb, and blind. *Poor thing*, I thought. I pitied the owner of such a little beast and pictured someone just as unkempt and listless.

A moment later the groomer appeared. She was a heavyset woman who breezed in looking like she was in a hurry to get rid of a problem child. After some small talk, I asked, "Is Max in the other room?"

"No," she said. "He's right there."

I glanced behind me. She was pointing at the sheep.

I thought about making a break for it, but she was already unlatching the crate. The lump of hair wobbled out and over to me. I shifted my weight to my back foot, still thinking of running. The sheep came closer.

The groomer hurried us to the door as I protested that I wasn't prepared. "I don't even have a leash or a collar. . . ."

"You'll be fine," she said. The "fine" part came just before she slammed and locked the door behind us.

I walked over to my waiting car. The sheep followed.

I've had only one blind date in my life. The fact that I have had only one should tell you how it went. I opened the passenger door that day to let Max in much as I'd opened it for my blind date so many years earlier—with regret. I had the same feeling on both occasions: hope that neither date nor dog would get in. In both instances they hopped happily into the car. In both instances my stomach sank.

On the drive to my apartment, I occasionally glanced over at Max, wondering what he was doing. He was simply sitting up glancing back at me through the shag of gray hair covering his eyes. We did that a lot that first day, each of us looking at the other. I don't know how long we sat in silence, but I figure we were both thinking the same thing: *What the hell did I get myself into here?*

That night I went to a party and didn't want to leave the little sheep alone, so I enlisted the help of Doug and Barbara Cray, a couple of eighty-something friends who missed having a family dog. I was gone for only a couple of hours, but when I returned, I was greeted not by a little sheep but by a happy dog. Barbara told me that since I'd left, he hadn't budged from the door. He sat waiting for me to return. It was if he knew we belonged together. Somehow on that very first day, the sheep no one wanted and the man afraid of commitment had already bonded.

Plain old "Max" soon went through a metamorphosis. He got a haircut and finally looked like a dog, and then I changed his name. He became Maxwell Garrison Gillis. Max was just too common, hence Maxwell. Garrison was short for William Lloyd Garrison, and Gillis came from Bossy Gillis. What better names to attach to the dog of the city's latest independent newspaperman than two of my predecessors'?

Soon he would become known around the downtown and people would greet him by name. Even my landlord, who "just this once" allowed a pet into one of his apartments, snuck him treats.

Since I worked from home, I spent all my time in the front of my studio apartment, either sitting at my desk or sleeping on the couch. Max chose to sleep in the kitchenette. No coaxing would get him to stay in the main room with me, and that would never change. The only time he came to where I was sitting was when he needed to go out.

However, in the world outside my apartment, it was an entirely different story. We were inseparable. Maxwell G. Gillis became as regular a presence downtown as any other local character. Readers of my paper came to know him through my most popular column, "A Letter Home." It was an actual letter to my dad, and Max often appeared in it. When I delivered the *'Toad* overnight, he would come with me and was delighted by the number of subscribers who left treats out for him. He was a regular at city hall and even attended a mayoral inauguration. He got used to walking next to me without a leash and made his way in and out of various stores for treats.

Max was finally living the life all dogs should live. Unfortunately, that would not last.

I had him for less than a year and a half before the seizures started. John Grillo, our vet, told me with a sad shrug, "He's old." I knew this to mean he wouldn't last much longer. I just didn't realize how quickly the end would come.

Two days later, after a particularly violent set of seizures, I decided I would bring him to Dr. Grillo's the next day. That night Maxwell G. Gillis and I sat in front of Caffe di Siena and held court as city officials, business leaders, and a handful of good cops stopped by the coffee shop to pay their last respects. As people came and went, there weren't many dry eyes when they patted his head for the final time.

Later that night, Max once again refused to come into the main living area, so I took my bedding and went to the kitchen where he was lying on his dog bed and lay down with him. I was determined that the little dog who'd been unwanted would not spend his last night alone. And so I curled up with him, felt his weak heart beating, felt his chest rise and fall, felt him fold his back into me like a dog who finally knew what it was like to be loved. The last thing I heard before I fell asleep that night was his peaceful sigh.

The next morning we woke up as we had fallen asleep, and for a little while Max looked just fine, as if he'd never been sick. I was hopeful. Then a seizure struck. He convulsed and collapsed in exhaustion. Another came, and then another. I made the call to Dr. Grillo's office.

On his final day, we made the rounds one more time and shopkeepers said their good-byes to the dog with the distinguished name who no longer looked like a sheep. It was a difficult day for many, but none more than me. After saying his last good-bye, I carried Max to the car and put him in the passenger seat, and he sat up the way he did that very first day, as if it were the most natural thing in the world to do. But there was something different about it this time, at least for me. From the very beginning, he was comfortable with me, as if he knew he had a purpose in my life and that I needed him more than he needed me. While he had once seemed like the awkward blind date I couldn't shake, this time I didn't want to say good-bye.

We took a final drive around Newburyport from Maudslay State Park out to Plum Island, where he loved to romp on the beach. He gazed out the front window and watched Newburyport fly by. With a mile to go, Kenny Loggins's song "Whenever I Call You Friend" came on the radio, and it took all I had to be strong for the dog who was a friend when I needed one most.

I stayed with Maxwell G. Gillis and held him while two shots were given and life left him, his body flattening out on the metal table as if his soul had escaped and was now as free as it always should have been. I had a hard time leaving him there by himself, and I stayed for quite some time holding his lifeless body.

For the next couple of days, I mostly kept to myself. When I finally ventured out, it was late at night when no one else was around, and when I walked by the stores where Max got his treats, I was stunned to see that several of them had hung signs in their windows paying tribute to Maxwell Garrison Gillis.

NEWBURYPORT LOST A GOOD DOG TODAY.

WE'LL NEVER FORGET YOU, MAXWELL GARRISON GILLIS.

NEWBURYPORT WAS BETTER BECAUSE OF YOU, MAX.

And there were more. Many more.

When I went to my post-office box over the next few days, I would find more than fifty sympathy cards, some from people I didn't know. They told me how they already missed seeing Max around town.

The once-unwanted dog had become a most-loved dog, and not just by me. In the end he got to die with the dignity and the love he didn't know before we met.

During the time we spent together, he not only found a home, he also gave me one. That was something I hadn't counted on. When I rescued him, I didn't realize that I was taking the first steps toward rescuing myself.

J. M. Barrie, who wrote *Peter Pan*, said, "We never understand how little we need in this world until we know the loss of it." The loss of my friend made me understand just that. His coming and then leaving were both gifts that reminded me that there was much more to this world than the corruption and wrongdoing I wrote about in my paper.

Maxwell Garrison Gillis had opened a door, and Atticus Maxwell Finch was about to walk through it.

2

"Carry Him Everywhere You Go"

The best advice I received about raising a puppy didn't come from a book or a class but over the phone from a gritty voice with a southern twang. Paige Foster, Atticus's breeder, suggested I carry him with me everywhere we went during the first month we were together. I stretched it to two.

"And don't let anyone else hold him during that time," she added. "He needs to know you're his family. Y'all will bond that way."

I owe much to Paige. Buying a puppy from her meant having the freedom to pick her brain, no matter how often I called—calls that in the beginning were more frequent than she bargained for, I'm sure, and were typically panic-driven. I liked her style. She shot straight from the hip and preached common sense with a touch of earthy mysticism. During our conversations, which were always lengthy, I came to think of her as intuitive, and I trusted her in every way. By following Paige's advice, Atticus and I were able to forgo obedience school, much to the chagrin of various self-proclaimed dog experts we met through the years.

Once, upon seeing Atticus sitting up next to me on a park bench without a leash or collar on, one such expert marveled at how well behaved he was. She had a stern voice that made me feel as if I should be sitting up straight, too. She asked what kind of training I put him through, listing various intimidating words and phrases that sounded to my ear to be Germanic in root and I took to be the schools of thought for serious dog trainers.

I shrugged. "None, really. We just hang out together."

This did not sit well with her. She sized me up as a rube and gave me a look that fell halfway between pity and a scold before marching off in search, I imagined, of a music store where she could purchase some Wagner.

For as long as I can remember, people have commented on Atticus's peaceful demeanor. Then, as was almost always the case, they'd ask him to give them his paw. He wouldn't. Instead he just looked at them, not even bothering to cock his head.

They'd ask again. Again he just studied them.

Then it typically went this way:

"Does he know how to give his paw?"

"I don't know, never asked him."

"But didn't you teach him that?"

"No. I didn't teach him anything."

I never saw the point in teaching Atticus tricks. What I wanted from him was for him to be his own dog as much as I was my own man. The things I wanted him to learn were basic things that made going through life safe and easy. I know many who tell me that by teaching their dog tricks they worked on their relationship together. The dogs, I was told, liked the task and then the reward. I can't argue against any of that, but it wasn't for us.

All I wanted was for Atticus to fit in as much as he needed to so he wouldn't be a bother or get into trouble, but I also didn't think it was up to me to decide what he would become. That was up to him. As long as he could walk with me off leash, feel comfortable in public settings, and understand that he should never feel self-conscious anywhere, I was fine with it.

My carrying the little puppy in the length of my arm from wrist to elbow for two months, like a running back with a football, went a long way toward forging our relationship and deciding how things would be for years to come.

I first encountered Paige Foster through the Internet. I was looking for a new puppy to replace Maxwell G. Gillis, and I entered information into an online database. I was so impressed by Max that I wanted another miniature schnauzer.

Breeders from around the country responded to the information I supplied by sending e-mail photo after e-mail photo of *miniature* miniature schnauzers, five to eight weeks old, and the dates of their availability. None of them looked quite right to me. The truth is, they all looked *too* right and *too* stately in their perfect poses. They reminded me first of puppies a Stepford Wife might own and then of those poor overly processed little girls who are entered into beauty pageants by their parents. What they didn't resemble were puppies. Most important, they didn't remind me a bit of my dearly departed Maxwell G. Gillis, who was anything but perfect. He was rough around the edges, much like me, but he was real and I loved him.

For whatever the reason, of all the breeders who responded, it was Paige I started exchanging e-mails with. She'd send photos of puppies and I'd tell her, "No, they're not quite right." Then she'd send more and I'd tell her the same thing.

Finally she asked, "Just what are you looking for?"

I wrote to her about Max, going into depth about his personality and what we shared. I cannot remember exactly what I wrote, but I remember telling her I wanted a dog who would be cool to just hang out with. I wanted a dog who would sit with me, whether on the beach, on a bench in the center of town, or at a sidewalk café, and watch the world go by. I was looking for a thoughtful dog, more of a philosopher than an athlete. I wanted a dog who was independent, but not so independent as to be stubborn or troublesome. I wanted a friend.

Paige e-mailed back with a disclaimer. She had one last dog, but he was "different," so different that he was going to be the only dog she raised that she was going to keep for herself. When she sent along some photos, I saw a puppy unlike any of the perfect puppies I'd seen. He wasn't sitting up with a straight spine, preening for the camera. He was lying down, his head weighing heavily on top of one paw, eyes looking askance at the photographer, with a sigh that said, *Get this over with, will you?* He was unimpressed by the attention.

Max had been silver. This puppy looked nothing like him. He was black, except for his paws, nose, chest, and butt—they were white—and what mostly caught my eye were two bushy, snow-white eyebrows that looked like they belonged on an old fisherman.

The deal was done. I chose the puppy that didn't look like the others. In my mind I suppose I went with the one that didn't fit in because I felt like I didn't fit in either. I was also intrigued by the fact that he was the only pup in his litter. He was all alone in the world, and that's exactly how I felt.

Paige's initial advice, to carry Atticus wherever we went, worked well on several different levels. Yes, it helped us bond, and I earned his trust, but it did something more for me, something I did not anticipate. I felt somewhat guilty about moving forward so quickly to get another dog. It was something I thought I would never do, but there I was holding this little breathing creature in my arms just weeks after Max's death. He was tiny and vulnerable, and he needed me. It didn't take me long to realize I needed him, too.

Paige's advice was perfect for an only puppy and a solitary man with a broken heart. Man and dog grew together starting that very first day. But I would take time to remember Max. Our first stop after picking up Atticus at the airport was Plum Island. I carried Atticus onto the beach and took a small plastic bag from my pocket and cast some of Max's ashes out into a breaking wave.

Our first weeks together went very well. Everything was going just as Paige had said it would. There were no complaints. That is, until a cool spring morning when I left Atticus in my car while I met with my regular Saturday breakfast group. I backed my hatchback up to the window we'd be sitting near so I could keep my eye on Atticus. He climbed over some boxes to the top of the backseat, on the flat panel just inside the glass of the rear window. It was the first time in the two weeks I'd had him that we'd been apart from each other, and from this vantage point he could keep his eye on me as well.

Breakfast went as all our weekly breakfasts went; we poked fun at one another, caught up on personal news, and shared political gossip about the tempests in the teapot of our little city. There was always good grist at breakfast for the next issue of the *Undertoad*. My companions were deeply rooted townies tapped into the community grapevine. When they told me something, I would spend the week verifying the facts of their stories, and they always checked out. Those breakfasts were, for this outsider, an insider's view of Newburyport.

It was in the middle of this jovial gabbing that one of the townies, a hard, red-faced fellow who worked for the city's water department by day and drank by night, nudged me and pointed out the window. Atticus was still on top of the panel above the backseat just inside the rear window, but he had turned away from us. He squatted and peered at me over his shoulder.

"What's he doing?"

"He's taking a shit," another fellow said.

And he was looking me right in the eye as he did so.

Atticus received a roar of approval from the townies. He fit right in with this group of men who believed that the best way to have a ball was by busting each other's balls. From that point on, he was forever deemed a valuable member of our group and a worthy dog to follow Max, whom they had all grown fond of and had visited at his "going-away party" the night before he was put to sleep.

Atticus wasn't finished. He stood up, turned to face us, and then used his paws to smear the feces around in the car. Within seconds I was outside, unlocking the door, but it was too late. The backseat and the windows looked as if a class of kindergartners had been finger-painting with mud.

There's nothing quite as toxic at the smell of puppy poop. I drove home with the windows wide open, but it didn't help much. Meanwhile, the little six-pound monster sitting in the front passenger seat looked quite pleased with himself, as if he didn't have a care in the world, gazing serenely out the window.

A couple of days later, we had a similar episode. I left him in my apartment when I met friends for lunch. I returned an hour later. Before I even opened the door, I was greeted by that same horrid stench. My little Picasso puppy had spread his artwork all over the white walls of the hallway just inside the door.

I called Paige in a panic.

Her southern twang was laced with laughter as her drawl split every syllable into two. "He's letting you know you broke the contract. From day one you two have spent every minute together, and now you're leaving him behind and he doesn't like it."

I was pissed. Paige was amused.

"What do I do? How do I get him to stop?"

She told me to get a small crate, one he couldn't move around in much, and leave him in that while I went out.

"He won't mess that up. Dogs refuse to mess up their space," she told me.

The next day I put him in the newly purchased tiny crate and went out to lunch. When I returned, the familiar stench filled my nostrils. All I could see were two serious eyes staring out at me from the crate from what looked like the body of a Tootsie Roll. Not only had he messed in the small space, he then rolled in it!

I brought him to the tub and held him in one hand. With my other hand, I held my nose. Shit swirled down the drain while I sloshed him gently in the warm water until the little tar baby was gone and Atticus had returned.

Another call to Paige. "The crate didn't work! He crapped, and *then* he rolled in it!"

During those first few weeks, Paige laughed a lot. She enjoyed my torment but was secretly pleased at how earnest I was in my puppy-rearing ways. Each time I called, no matter how panicked or frustrated or aggravated I sounded, she responded with mirthful laughter. I think this northern boy had become her favorite source of entertainment.

"He's showing you his will. Do the same thing again tomorrow. Let him know he can't do this when you go out. Let him know *you* are in charge. And don't worry, y'all will work it out."

The next day I put him in his crate, resolved to win the war of the wills. An hour later I came back to the same results. The little Tootsie Roll with eyes was awaiting me when I opened the crate. He was not happy, not unhappy, more matter-of-fact about the whole thing.

Another trip to the tub to decrap him. This time I didn't phone Paige. I was a man who called out dirty cops and politicians in print. I endured threats, both anonymous and not so anonymous. I was as tough as nails. But here I was being bullied by a six-pound puppy. It was embarrassing.

I decided on a different technique.

Imagine this scene if you will: At the time I was literally about fifty times Atticus's weight. I sat on the side of the tub and held his sopping-wet body up under his legs while his paws dangled over the water. I looked him in the eyes and told him that he was going to have to get over it and that we would be together nearly all the time, but there were days he was going to have to stay back in the apartment or in the car. He didn't look away out of shame or defiance. Instead he seemed to appraise me while I talked.

"Here's the deal. We'll compromise—I won't put you in the crate when I go out if you agree not to make a mess of things. I won't be gone long, and I'm always coming back."

The next day I went out. I left him sitting by the door with a dog biscuit. When I locked the door, I fought off the sound of his squeals and cries and kept on walking. I returned to see him sitting in the same spot where I'd left him, the biscuit still there. He lunged at me, rearing up on his hind legs, his front paws landing around my knee, his face beaming with excitement that I really had come back. There was no stink in the apartment. And it would stay that way. Whenever I left him behind, I left him with a cookie and he behaved, and when I returned, he was happy to see me. Only after we had greeted each other again would he pounce on his cookie as if it were prey he'd been stalking.

We had reached détente. Paige was right—we worked it out.

I waited a little while before calling her again so I could casually tell her that I'd broken Atticus of his protest pooping. But as soon as I heard her voice, I confessed to the entire process. She laughed and laughed and said, "That little boy . . . he sure got some spirit!"

Paige may have been off when it came to the crate, but she was right about nearly everything else, and nothing worked as well as did my carrying him.

If you've ever known a miniature schnauzer, you know they can be stubborn. We got beyond that tendency. Perhaps it was due to the trust we built up when I carried him around town. Or maybe it had something to do with my not forcing him to do much of anything.

There were few rules, but they were important ones. They were basic. Atticus was allowed to do whatever he wanted so long as he was not endangering himself, he showed respect for my possessions, and he didn't bother other people.

If I asked him to sit, he had to sit, but it didn't matter to me where he sat. If I asked him to lie down, he would lie down where he wanted to, and that was okay, too. I didn't want to control him; I simply wanted to set up boundaries that would protect him.

For all she was right about, there was one other thing Paige was wrong about. She suggested even in that first month when I carried him that whenever we went out, I put on his harness and leash so he would associate them with going out and think of them in a positive way. But from the beginning he hated them both. Whenever I went to put on the harness, or a collar when his neck grew strong enough to have one, he cringed.

When outside, I'd attach the leash to the harness and put him on the ground. The first thing he did was take three steps away from me, asserting his independence and his dislike for the leash.

This led us to another compromise. On the rare occasion I wasn't carrying him, I put the leash on him but then dropped it and let him walk beside me. He was still tiny, and it was a funny sight seeing him drag his leash over the redbrick sidewalks of the downtown, but there was no willful fighting. I picked up the leash, or him, only if need be.

It didn't take long for him to feel at home in Newburyport. People got to know him just as they grew to know Max, first in my "Letter Home" column to my father and then by seeing him around town. In the issue following Max's death, I announced that Atticus was coming to town, and when he arrived, people were ready for him. During his first few days, wherever we were, folks drove by beeping their horns and yelling out their windows, "Welcome to town, Atticus!" Shop owners who only a few weeks prior to that were bidding good-bye to Maxwell with tears in their eyes and signs in their storefront windows joyously welcomed Atticus.

The celebration was overwhelming, from the endless puppy gifts left at my door to the constant greetings directed at Newburyport's newest resident. Atticus grew up thinking that everyone knew his name. Those first days in his new city were charmed. Everywhere we went, people wanted to meet him. To some extent this would happen with any cute puppy, but with Atticus it was different—people were making trips especially to see him, driving into town or going out of their way by crossing the street or running out of a building, and each time, they greeted him by his name. Through the columns in my paper, they'd seen how Max had changed my life and felt as if they'd known him. Now they wanted to meet the dog who was chosen to follow him.

The hardest part was telling people they couldn't hold Atticus, but after I explained what Paige had said, they understood my reasons even if they didn't like them. Instead they'd reach into my arms and pet him, many with soft innocence in their eyes (even the roughest, toughest men), as if he were a newborn human baby, some saying things to him like, "You would have loved Maxwell G. Gillis."

There wasn't a place Atticus didn't feel comfortable. When he grew a little bigger, he'd make his way in and out of stores getting his cookies while I waited outside—just as I had with Max. I loved his independence.

A curious reader of my newspaper wanted to know why he was Atticus M. Finch and not Atticus M. Ryan. I told her I wanted him to have his own identity. We were a team, but it was important to me that he was allowed to be himself and not simply my dog. I did not want an accessory so much as a living, breathing, feeling entity to accompany me through life. Allowing him to have his own last name was part of that, no matter how small or silly it may have seemed. When I shared this with Paige, she sighed happily in approval and thanked me. "It's important for a dog to be himself," she said.

From his earliest days, Atticus made his way into city hall with me, first to cover a troubled and befuddled mayor who shouldn't have lasted too long—and didn't. (It had something to do with cronyism and being caught threatening a police officer, as well as the fact that he just wasn't a very good mayor.) The mayor would see me sitting in one chair and Atticus sitting in another awaiting our weekly meeting in his outer office and wouldn't know what to say. Meanwhile, his secretary and aide both did. They greeted Atticus as everyone else did, by name, and they'd say, "Mr. Ryan and Mr. Finch are here to see you, Mr. Mayor."

When the next election came and a new mayor took office, she was better suited for the job than the last fellow, but she didn't last long either. (It had a lot to do with the sexual e-mails she was caught exchanging with a teacher.) During our first meeting in her office, she arched an eyebrow as I sat in one chair facing her desk while Atticus, now a bit older, sat up in another listening to her every word.

"You allow him on the furniture?" she asked, clearly disapproving.

"Why not? You allow politicians to sit here, don't you?"

Eventually that mayor grew to welcome him, even on the furniture.

And so it came to be that Atticus was a fixture in the mayor's office and in the rest of city hall at various board and committee meetings, where he would sit beside me on the hard wooden benches, my fleece jacket underneath him. No matter the length of the meeting, he would sit and behave, paying attention and doing better at not falling asleep than most in the audience and even some of the city officials. Depending on what I had written in the latest issue of my paper, I was either celebrated or reviled. Atticus, on the other hand, was usually greeted warmly in the hallways, either as Atticus or Mr. Finch.

Even through those growing years, as he matured both physically and socially, I continued to carry him on occasion. We'd become accustomed to it and both found comfort in it. From time to time, I would find myself in a street-corner conversation from which he felt left out, so he would nudge my leg with his nose to pick him up, and I'd hold him while I continued chatting. It was clear he wanted to be part of it, to be on our level.

Firefighters, bank presidents, children, school principals, store clerks, trash collectors, and homeless men alike made sure he was greeted by name.

Atticus also became a fixture in some of the restaurants around town. There was one where he sat on a chair at a table inside and they would bring him chunks of chicken or turkey. At another he would have pizza or a bagel. In other restaurants I'd wait while he trotted back into the kitchen and I'd hear the chef or the owner exclaim, "There you are! Have I got something good for you today, Atticus!"

The irony is that while I already had an identity in Newburyport and Atticus was developing his own, over time the two merged and we became known as "Tom and Atticus," much as a husband and wife lose their own identity in public. It was understood that if I was invited to a dinner party, so was he. If I was invited to the opening of a new business, so was he. If not, we were no-shows.

When friends were sick in Anna Jaques, the local hospital, and I would go to see them, Atticus would come along, too, and sit right on the bed next to the ailing patient. Dogs weren't typically allowed in patients' rooms, but that all changed for Atticus the day I visited my friend Vicki Pearson, a well-loved businesswoman and community leader who had just been elected to the school board. Right after the election, Vicki was diagnosed with a horrible cancer that snaked up her spine like a killing vine. When I visited her room the first time, she asked that I bring her nephew into the hospital to visit with her.

I turned to the nurse and wondered quietly if Vicki had had too much morphine in her system, because I had no idea who her nephew was or where I'd find him. Vicki heard this and spoke weakly through dry, cracked lips. "Of course you do. You live with him." She then told the nurse, "My nephew's name is Atticus M. Finch."

In the following days, Atticus was a regular on her bed. She couldn't lift her arms, but she could move her fingers. She used them to feed Atticus treats, and when they were gone, her "nephew" would lie down next to her and rest his head on her thigh while she gently fluffed his floppy ears.

It was Vicki, before she was sick, who demanded we eat only at restaurants where Atticus was allowed to join us whenever we met for lunch. And it was Vicki who thought nothing of having him sit in a chair at the table while we both shared our lunches with him.

She'd call me up and say, "Lunch?"

"Great," I'd say. "Where do you want to go?"

"Oh, I don't know."

"What are you in the mood for?" I'd ask, even though I knew better. For we always ended up in the same place—the Purple Onion. Vicki loved their sandwich wraps and salads. But more important to her, they had a few tables outside so Atticus could join us.

Atticus loved those days when I delivered the *'Toad*, and he loved the preceding nights—driving along nearly every street in the city for the home delivery, discovering small (and sometimes big) packages of treats left out for him on stoops by little old ladies and men. When the morning arrived and the stores opened, we'd go store to store, dropping off copies of the paper, Atticus collecting greetings and treats.

On delivery night he sat placidly in the passenger seat even when I left my car door open, when I walked up to a house to deliver a paper. However, whenever we arrived at Vicki's house, usually around 11:00 P.M., he would follow me up to her front door even though he'd never been there to visit with her and no treats were ever left for him. Somehow he seemed to understand that this was where his friend lived.

In the first few years of his life, Atticus had become that rare breed known as a Newburyporter. It didn't matter that he was a dog, especially since no one treated him like one. People were excited to see him and excited to greet him. You can only imagine the looks on his friends' faces the day he surprised them in his new bicycle basket.

I bought a bicycle and special-ordered a large, reinforced steel basket to sit on the front handlebars. It was big and strong enough to hold him. I had every intention of taking my time getting him used to riding in the basket, lined with a fleece blanket to soften the ride. I expected it to take a couple of weeks.

My plan was to just sit him in it the first few days. The next few days, I would put him in it and push it around the parking lot. Eventually I would try pedaling with him in the basket. I have no doubt that Paige's suggestion that I carry him in the beginning was the reason he trusted me so much that first day I put him in that basket. He looked at me expectantly yet calmly, as if to say, *Well, what are you waiting for?* I then pushed him around the parking lot. He gave me the same look. What the heck. I got on the bike and pedaled. Much to my own surprise, he didn't bother to lie down but sat up much like E.T., the extraterrestrial. He was my hood ornament while I pedaled around town, his marvelous floppy ears catching the wind, his happy mouth open to swallow it whole. He appeared to be flying. Friends everywhere greeted him with glee whenever we pedaled by, and he soaked it all in.

Before long he learned the word "bump." If we were heading for a pothole or railroad tracks or a slight curb, I'd say "Bump" and he'd lower his center of gravity to absorb the shock and then sit right back up again after the turbulence passed.

Atticus and I had learned to trust each other. Little did I know how important that would be in the coming years. And the time would come when Atticus and I would need Paige more than anyone else. But, for now, Paige had been right when she told me, "Y'all will work it out."

We had.

3

Big Changes

From our first days together, Atticus and I had a morning routine. We rose with the sun and drove out to Plum Island for a walk on the beach. When we were done, we'd go out for breakfast at Mad Martha's, Kathy Ann's, or the Fish Tale. Sometimes I would eat with friends, while at other times I sat alone. Either way, people approached me to share news and gossip. After breakfast Atticus and I went to city hall and made the rounds to see what was going on. Then we worked our way through the downtown.

We had regular places we stopped at and favorite people to see. There was Bob Miller, a friend who was a financial adviser with an office right across the street from city hall. He was always upbeat, a man in perpetual motion who could keep many things going at once. Then it was over to see Steve Martin, a fiery retired marine who had an opinion about everything in town. He owned Ashley Barnes, an upscale furniture shop on Pleasant Street. We'd drop in on Esther Sayer at the Inn Street Barber Shop, and she always had gossip. Next we'd see Gilda Tunney at her card store and stop by Fowles News and hang out with Pat Simboli. Atticus would sit on Pat's desk, a six-pound paperweight on his pile of papers, and we'd both listen to him expound on what was wrong with the world. Only Pat could bitch and moan with a smile on his face and make you laugh no matter how bleak his forecast. After that it was off to say hello to Linda Garcia at Abraham's Bagels. She always welcomed Atticus inside, and on the day a customer complained that he shouldn't be inside because of health reasons and threatened to take his business elsewhere, Linda thanked him for doing just that. From there it was over to John Farley Clothiers to sit down with John Allison, who owned the store with his wife, Linda, and DeeDee McCarty, their tailor.

We usually stayed a little longer with John and DeeDee, because I'd never met any people as enthusiastic about their lives as these two were, and I enjoyed it when they regaled me with their latest endeavors. John had taken up mountain climbing in his fifties and DeeDee was always off skiing, running races, snowshoeing, or hiking. I was amazed at their energy and could listen to their stories for hours. They were both meticulously dressed, as you would expect of people who sold expensive clothing. John was a small man with a spring in his step. He had distinguished-looking short white hair and a neatly trimmed mustache, and he resembled, more than anyone else, the top-hatted fellow from the Monopoly game. DeeDee was tall and statuesque and could fill the room with her confidence. In the store they were polished and polite, but I saw a different side of them when there were no customers around and they talked of their latest physical exploits. They each had the breath of life to them, and it was clear that while they made a living at the store, their true passion could be found in the great outdoors. I envied them and eagerly awaited each new chapter.

From Farley's we walked down Water Street to the Tannery, a collection of unique shops that had once been an actual tannery in the era when mills thrived in Newburyport. It was owned by David Hall, the rare developer who was environmentally conscious. He was a businessman who looked to make money, but not at the expense of the community. My friend Vicki Pearson worked for David, and whenever we came in, she made time for us. It didn't matter what she was doing—and she was always busy doing something—she'd put it aside. I was smart enough to know that this wasn't because of me but because of Atticus. In Vicki's world, dogs were far more special than people.

After saying good-bye to Vicki, we crossed over to Jabberwocky Bookshop, which was also at the Tannery. It was one of those rare shops some communities are lucky enough to have where you could see much of the city come and go. It was a true center of activity, a stimulating but comfortable place. After I browsed the latest books, we visited with Paul Abruzzi, the manager, and Laini Shillito, the bookkeeper.

We went to all those places and others around Newburyport because it was my way of putting together the stories for the next issue of the *Undertoad*. My competition, the *Daily News*, had been in business for more than a hundred years, and its reporters could sit at their desks and wait for news to come to them. But I wasn't that established, and I worked out of my apartment. So I took great efforts to go out and discover what was going on in our little corner of the world. The best way to do that was to see people and listen to what they had to say, and it always worked.

Wherever we went on our walks around downtown, Atticus was by my side and was greeted by everyone we visited. These people were our extended family, his aunts and uncles, and from the very first day they knew to treat him as I did—like an equal. There was no cooing baby talk, no high-pitched squeals. They talked to him as if he were an adult. Even in those first weeks, people said, "There's something different about him." And they meant it in the best way. They marveled at his almost-human demeanor, his self-assuredness and comfort, and they asked me how I got him to be that way. I gave Atticus much of the credit and joked that it was easy when the dog was smarter than the man. I also talked about things Paige was teaching me, and it always came back to her simple dictum to carry him wherever I went.

But there was another component to the way I raised Atticus that I kept to myself. I didn't want to go into it, because its roots were complicated. From that very first moment I held him in my arms, I treated him the way I wish I'd been treated when growing up. Rarely did I make a command. Instead I politely asked him to do something. I'd say,

"Would you have a seat, please," or "Please wait here for me." When he complied, I said, "Thank you." In short, I didn't treat him like a dog but like a friend. My Catholic upbringing simply referred to this as the Golden Rule: Treat others as you wish to be treated. And it worked wonders.

One of the reasons I treated Atticus this way went back to another bit of advice Paige Foster gave everyone who bought a puppy from her: "Whatever dysfunction you have in your life, that little dog will magnify it, so you best be ready." As with all of Paige's advice, I took it to heart and pledged to do my best by this little life she had entrusted to me. For that's exactly what she'd done. Paige took pride in matching up her "babies" with the right people, and she thought nothing of showing up at a delivery point to meet her Louisiana customers who came prepared to pay her cash and, after sizing them up, refuse to sell them the dog.

Because of Paige's advice, I not only paid attention to his every need, I also paid more attention to myself and decided it was a good time to begin improvements. If Newburyport gave me a hometown and Max gave me a home, it was Atticus who gave me a fresh start.

Fate had thrust Max into my life, and we changed on the fly and made do the best we could. In many ways he and I were alike: a bit neglected, a bit beaten up by life, and a bit worse for wear. But during the year and a half we were together, we bridged the gap between dog and man and formed a little family. For both of us it was life the way we'd always wanted it to be. My life had changed with Max when he reminded me what I was missing, and I liked it.

I was aware that it would change even more when Atticus arrived, because as a puppy he'd need constant attention. But I had no idea just how *much* it would change.

In the process of taking care of Atticus and creating a home, I started taking better care of myself. It began in little ways. We took progressively longer walks, and that helped me lose weight. I lost even more when I followed the South Beach Diet, and the more I lost, the better I felt and the farther Atticus and I walked.

But the most dramatic change occurred when we went away for a long weekend. In seven years in Newburyport, I'd never taken a vacation and I'd been out of town for only one weekend. It had been all Newburyport politics all the time. However, just a few weeks after Atticus arrived, I accepted a long-standing invitation from Gilbert and Gilda Tunney to use their second home, an old farmhouse in the Mad River Valley of Vermont.

The house sat on the side of a hill in the middle of nowhere. The closest neighbors were a herd of cows that grazed up against the fence abutting the sprawling backyard. This delighted tiny Atticus no end, and he sat respectfully at the fence and gazed at the large group of huge "dogs" with black and white markings not unlike his. The cows were just as curious about him and crowded against the fence to see the tiny "cow" with the floppy ears that looked more than a little funny. It wasn't long before they were gently touching noses through the fence. Thanks to those cows, and the trees and the rolling backyard filled with lush green grass, and chipmunks, squirrels, and butterflies, Atticus thought we were in heaven. I wasn't quite so certain, for I wasn't used to peace and quiet and having nothing to do. But after a couple of days of being anonymous and not checking e-mail or hearing the constant hum of downtown Newburyport or the ringing of my phone, I eventually relaxed. By the third day, my shoulders were no longer tense; I was sleeping through the night and waking up refreshed. On the fourth day, I took the greatest pleasure in lying blissfully on my back in the grass and taking inventory of the whitest clouds I'd ever seen as they sailed across a deep blue sea of sky. When it came time to return to Newburyport, I put it off for as long as I could.

Atticus and I returned to that old farmhouse several times over the next couple of years. When it was being used by Gilbert and Gilda or one of their friends, we stayed in Stowe, Vermont, twenty miles away, at an inn that catered to dogs and their owners.

To the casual reader, the *Undertoad* hadn't changed in the least bit. It was still hard-hitting and controversial. But it *was* changing, if only in the slightest way. My "Letter Home" to my father now appeared in every issue of the paper, and I wrote about our journeys to Vermont, or losing weight, or being able to walk up State Street without losing my breath. Of course there was always something in those letters about Atticus as well, for it seemed he was the catalyst of all that change.

That column served an important purpose for my paper—and for me. Not only was it a different, more relaxed and intimate style of writing, it also lightened the mood. Before I'd started printing my letters to my father, the paper was unbalanced, filled with the politics of politics, and I felt guilty about all the dirt I was uncovering. But the column also served another purpose. My father, who still lived in Medway, some eighty miles away, had never been to Newburyport, and since he wasn't comfortable driving that far, even as a passenger, he would never see it. So I described the city to him, and my readers loved the way I portrayed it and how I wrote to my father. I never talked about our troubled past but rather focused on the positive things he'd done in my life.

The trips Atticus and I took to the gentle mountains of Vermont refreshed me and added new life to my columns. They allowed me to take stock of my life and return to write about the heroes and scoundrels of Newburyport and then escape again. It also gave us a place where no one knew us, a place where I could literally put my feet up and relax. There was no need to constantly check the rearview mirror of my car to see if we were being followed. There were no slashed tires and no angry readers complaining about what I wrote.

I so loved that farmhouse in Waitsfield that I did the unheard-of and invited David and Eddie, two of my brothers, up for a weekend. It was the first time in twenty years when at least three siblings had spent a night in one place together. Such things just weren't done in the Ryan family. We weren't a close group. We were but survivors of the same ship-wreck, and there was little interaction among us. We got together for a few hours each Thanksgiving and Christmas, but other than that we rarely talked or sent e-mails, and this often drove me crazy. I could stand on a street corner in Newburyport, meet a stranger, and know more about him in ten minutes than I'd found out about any of my brothers and sisters in forty years.

The naturalist John Muir might as well have been talking about my family when he wrote, "Most people are on the world, not in it—have no conscious sympathy or relationship to anything about them—undiffused, separate, and rigidly alone like marbles of polished stone, touching but separate." That was us: touching but separate.

I once asked David how that came to be. "Why do I feel like I'm the only one who smiles and laughs and has a good time? What happened to everyone?"

David thought for a moment and shrugged. In his parched, matter-of-fact tone, he said, "I think Dad beat it out of us."

But being different from them didn't mean I wanted to be distant from them. To the contrary, I'd always hoped we would all be happy one day, that we could have the family we never had. That's why I invited David and Eddie for the weekend. I knew they liked the mountains of New Hampshire, and I figured they'd enjoy the tranquillity of Vermont as well. I was actually surprised when they accepted my invitation.

It was important to me to try to take another stab at being close with them, but I also wanted to thank them for taking care of our father. Out of the nine of us, they were the only two who had stayed behind in Medway, and they looked in on my father every day as he aged.

David was the responsible one. He would mop the floor, clean the toilet, fix things that were broken, regrout the tile around the tub, and do minor plumbing. He did my father's taxes and helped him with his checkbook. I found this wildly ironic, since while my father often looked at the whole lot of us as if we were thieves trying to cheat him out of something, he trusted David least of all. And yet when my father's mind started to go and he couldn't keep track of his finances, it was always David who straightened everything out.

During David's visits the two of them had little to speak about. But then again, David had picked up my father's stoic approach to all things family. After they offered each other a bit of fractured small talk, grunts, and nods of the head, David would go home to his wife for more of the same.

Eddie was not gifted like David when it came to fixing things, but he was there for my father in other ways. He made sure Dad was taking all his medicines and kept his numerous doctors' appointments organized. He worked in special education, and while he felt uncomfortable interacting with other adults, he was extremely gifted with troubled children. Some colleagues referred to him with reverence as a "child whisperer." I think that's why he got along with my father better than any of the rest of us did. He had the patience of Job and treated my father with the same kindness he extended to the children he worked with.

I wasn't sure what I expected when Eddie and David joined Atticus and me at the Vermont farmhouse. I suppose part of me was longing for the closeness I'd always hungered for, but the years had taught me better.

It turned out to be the right thing to do. We walked, talked, and laughed. Although when I say we talked, I mean we made small talk, but to me even that was a victory of sorts. There was no talk of relationships or love or of dreams achieved or deferred. It was mostly talking about what we always talked about—family. We retold many of the same old tales. I think our favorite time of each day was sitting out on the back deck in silence watching the sun drop behind the western hills. It was not the same uncomfortable silence we often shared as a family, but rather a silence blessed by nature, one that perhaps said, *This is as good as it gets for us.*

Although there were no groundbreaking conversations, I enjoyed that weekend more than any other time I'd spent with family. We went out to eat, explored the area, and drove the auto road up the highest mountain in Vermont—Mount Mansfield. When the road ended, the four of us got out and walked to the top.

It was a postcard-pretty day, and we lounged on the summit rocks and looked down at the pastoral countryside, and once again we were silent. But we were also content.

Something happened that day up there on the mountaintop. None of us mentioned it, but there was a newfound closeness, and we made plans to come back. When we did, there were even more of us. Seven of Jack and Isabel Ryan's children gathered for a weekend in Stowe, following up our first family reunion in more than fifteen years back in Medway. It was a sight I thought I'd never see.

It was those two visits to Vermont and our trip up Mount Mansfield that led David to invite Eddie, Atticus, me, and our brother Jeff to join him on a hike up Mount Garfield in New Hampshire.

David had decided to climb all the White Mountains of New Hampshire that were over four thousand feet high. There are forty-eight of them, and he was doing two or three a year. Once he'd climbed them all, he would be eligible to become a member of the Appalachian Mountain Club's Four Thousand Footer Club and he'd receive a patch and a scroll. I'd never heard of the club but accepted the invitation in the spirit of sharing another weekend with my brothers.

By this time Atticus was two and a half years old, and I had lost seventy-five pounds. I was still big, but nowhere near as large as I'd been. We had never climbed a mountain, and I knew there was a big difference between driving up the auto road on Mount Mansfield, then walking the short distance to the summit, and doing a ten-mile hike up a four-thousand-footer. It wasn't that I doubted whether or not Atticus or I could do it; I just wasn't sure we'd be able to keep up with my three brothers, who had all hiked through the years.

In a way, that trip to New Hampshire was to be a homecoming for me. The White Mountains were part of my past, and we considered them to be our father's mountains. He took us on many vacations, but we spent most of our time up in the Whites. He loved it there, and it is the only place I can remember him being happy and peaceful. They brought out the best in him, which made them special to us as well. We'd camped by the streams in the shadowy valleys at the foot of the great mountains so often that we came to know their lore and their history.

They were America's first great peaks. Long before the Rockies were discovered by Europeans, Americans knew about the magnificence of the White Mountains. They were the home to the Abenaki Indians, who looked upon the region as a sacred place and believed that the mountain-tops were the home of the great spirits, especially the mountain they called Agiocochook. When settlers came upon the Whites, they built roads and homesteads, which grew into villages, and they began climbing the peaks.

The 1800s became known as the century of the White Mountain painters, when approximately four hundred renowned artists came to New Hampshire to capture the grandeur and share it with the world. At the same time, writers such as Nathaniel Hawthorne, Henry David Thoreau, Herman Melville, and Ralph Waldo Emerson visited and wrote about their experiences and furthered many of the existing legends. What people saw in the paintings and read in the books caused them to flock to the mountains from New York, Philadelphia, and Boston. Railroads were built to accommodate the travelers. So were grand hotels. The golden age of White Mountain tourism had begun, and it led P. T. Barnum to refer to the Whites as "the second-greatest show on earth."

Toward the end of the 1800s, lumber barons saw the mountains as a way to make money, and they set about clear-cutting much of the land. They laid train tracks into every remote nook and cranny, and before long, sparks flew, fires started, and much of the once-pristine forest turned into a wasteland. But thanks in part to the love affair people had with the White Mountains, the Weeks Act was passed in Washington in the early 1900s. The trend of the government selling off forests was reversed in the name of the environment, and the land was returned to the people. Trees began to grow again, and the splendor of the mountains returned, but by this time the heyday had ended, because people were looking to the much higher Rocky Mountains for beautiful landscapes, and the advent of the automobile meant that tourists no longer had to go just where the trains took them. That put an end to all but a few of the grand hotels that had sprung up in the area.

By the time my father started taking us to the mountains, the glory days of the place had long passed, but not the brilliance. Whenever we were there, it felt as though the land had never been touched, and we could imagine what the first explorers must have felt like.

We returned often and got to know the three great notches that ran north to south. In the east was Pinkham, in the middle was Crawford, and in the west was Franconia. We stayed in Franconia Notch. We set up our trailer deep in the folds of the notch, often near a stream at one of the area's campgrounds. By day we explored the woods, going on small hikes. As evening descended, we'd sit around the campfire, and the mountains seemed to spring to life in the darkness. It was a magical time for us, made even more so by the transformation in my father. I don't have many great memories of my early years, but those I do have bring me back to the White Mountains.

When my father and I went to war with each other, I left behind the mountains of my childhood, just as I left him behind. But my brothers didn't. They still often came north, as they'd always done. And now I was being invited to return. It took all of one night in a small cabin along the Pemigewasset River at the southern end of Franconia Notch for me to remember the magic of long ago. As soon as the sun set and the moon appeared, I could feel the mountains come to life, just as they had when I was young. It was September, and the days were warm and the nights were cool, and we slept well. Early the next morning, David, Eddie, Jeff, Atticus, and I left the safety of our cars behind and marched single file into the thick, dark woods. The brisk, chilly morning gave way to a humid and hot day, and the air turned still and oppressive. For the next three hours, we stumbled, staggered, and swore our way up the back of the mountain. There were no views, but there were plenty of other things to keep us occupied: mosquitoes, hearts pounding like never before, back pain that felt as if someone was punching me in the kidneys, and the occasional leg cramp. Our clothes were soaked with sweat and stained with dried salt. From time to time, we'd hold on to a tree for balance or to catch our breath. We gulped water and Gatorade as if we were dying of thirst. We were a pitiful group, looking like four middle-aged and out-of-shape men who didn't belong in the woods. And because we were four men who were not used to being together, there wasn't much said.

Every now and then, someone would ask, "How much longer to the top?"

David, who had read the guidebook, would typically give the answer and reveal to us that we were barely halfway up the mountain, or two-thirds of the way, or that we still had a mile to go.

We stopped often and drank and stood breathless. Occasionally someone would joke about how sore he was, or about old age or the lack of views through the trees. And yet while the dearth of conversation might have seemed strange to another group of brothers, it was not unlike those sunsets on the deck back in Vermont: *This is as good as it gets for us.* I mean that not as a bad thing but as a good thing. For as the youngest and the one who saw his family disappear before his eyes and always longed to share something—anything—with them, those breathless gasps, occasional swears, and uncomfortable jokes were like gold to me. It didn't matter that we all looked and felt like hell; we were together for a change.

Atticus, on the other hand, looked great. It was as if he were made for the mountains. Unlike other dogs, who run back and forth and do three times the mileage of their human companions or go crashing into the woods on either side of the trail in search of wildlife, Atticus walked purposefully, staying on the trail, and kept a slow but steady pace. He seemed part mountain goat as he hopped from rock to rock with ease. Occasionally we'd come to a steep section of trail and I'd ready myself to help him, but when I looked up, he'd somehow managed to do it himself.

Most noticeable was how he kept a constant eye on me. This was new territory for the two of us, but all was well with his world so long as we were together. From the very first day we met, he believed it was his job to look after me, and he took it seriously—whether we were in city hall or on top of a mountain.

When at last we reached a sign that said we only had two-tenths of a mile to go, we took a break and then sputtered up a steep, craggy chute. There was more sweating, swearing, and gasping for breath. During that torturous last pitch, I thought for sure I was going to die of a heart attack. The trail thankfully leveled out, and I staggered to an opening in the brush and put my hands on my knees to rest. When I caught my breath and was able to look up, I saw Atticus sitting with his back to me, staring off into the distance. I followed his gaze and was immediately rendered speechless by the stunning serrated edge of the mountains of Franconia Ridge. They looked so close that I felt I could reach right out and touch them. My aches and pains, thirst and exhaustion evaporated, and my life changed in an instant. I'd never realized that such places existed in this world, other than in movies, never mind just two hours away from the pretty redbrick downtown of Newburyport. When we came to the mountains as children, we were but windshield tourists. We went where the road took us, and to the various tourist attractions. We'd never seen anything as wild as the view we had off the edge of Garfield.

Another hiker once wrote something that sums up the experience of that day. But he was writing about *poetry*, not mountains. That hiker was Robert Frost, and he lived in and explored the White Mountains. He wrote, "Permanence in poetry as in love is perceived instantly. It has not to await the test of time. The proof of a poem is not that we have never forgotten it, but that we knew at sight we never could forget it."

I knew the moment I looked from Atticus to the surrounding mountains that I'd never forget that day. My life had changed.

Throughout the cold, dark months of the autumn and winter, I often returned to Mount Garfield. But it was always in a daydream or when I was sleeping. Two things stayed with me about that day. The first was how I saw Atticus sitting calmly casting his eyes out to take in the view. "He's like a little Buddha," said a woman who arrived on the summit just after we did. The second was how I knew we wouldn't be going back to Vermont. We'd graduated to a new place.

During our next visit to see John Allison and DeeDee McCarty at John Farley Clothiers, I couldn't wait to tell them about our hike up Garfield, and they were thrilled for Atticus and me. They were even more excited when I told them that when the snow melted in the spring he and I would return and begin climbing the four-thousand-footers. As fate would have it, DeeDee had already hiked eleven of the mountains and had a plan to finish the entire list within the next two years. She invited us to join her, and I happily accepted. A few weeks later, DeeDee introduced me to a book by Steve Smith and Mike Dickerman, *The 4000-Footers of the White Mountains,* a guidebook that covered the various routes up each of the forty-eight. Like Atticus, it would become my constant companion, and I found myself thumbing through its pages repeatedly.

I'd never heard of most of the mountains listed in the book, and thinking back to that September day on Garfield, I couldn't help but wonder about the exotic places we'd see in the coming months. At night, when I was sitting in a meeting at city hall, instead of watching the evening unfold, I often had my nose buried in the Smith and Dickerman book. It became dog-eared, and my yellow highlighter stained its pages, and I wrote notes in the margins in blue ink. I wondered how the two of us would possibly make it up those mountains. There were those that reached high above tree line to the alpine zone and others that were located deep in the wilderness, requiring an eighteen-mile round-trip. There would be streams to cross, rock slides to scale, ledges to maneuver, and weather to contend with.

It would not be easy for a little dog who didn't like getting wet and a man who so feared heights I got dizzy standing on a stepladder to change a lightbulb. However, none of that mattered to me. It was a curious thing. We were being called to the mountains, and I had no doubt we'd somehow find a way to climb them all.

When the snows finally melted in late May, we started our quest in earnest. DeeDee, Atticus, and I climbed Mount Hale, our first four-thousand-footer of the year. I didn't realize it at the time, but Hale was a good peak to begin on. It was considered easy. The route to the top was just over two miles, and the elevation gain was two thousand feet. According to the Smith and Dickerman book and the Appalachian Mountain Club's *AMC White Mountain Guide,* which was also edited by Steve Smith, an elevation gain of a thousand feet per mile is considered a steep climb, and we were climbing two thousand feet in two miles. By the time we'd made it up and down the mountain, my body felt it, but I was so enthralled at having climbed our first peak of the year that I couldn't wait for the next one.

The following weekend was Memorial Day, and Atticus and I went north and hiked for three days, climbing peaks DeeDee had already done so that we could catch up to her. On the first day, we climbed Mount Tecumseh. Like Hale, it was considered one of the easier peaks. On the second day, we climbed Cannon Mountain, another short hike. Our final hike of the weekend took us to the summits of Osceola and East Osceola.

When I returned to Newburyport, I couldn't contain my enthusiasm, nor could I wait to tell DeeDee what we'd done. The plan had always been for Atticus and me to catch up to DeeDee and then hike the rest of the forty-eight with her over the next two summers. But instead of just catch up, we passed right by and kept going. I just couldn't help myself. (We did end up hiking with her a few more times and also with my brothers three more times as well. However, after those first three weeks, it was mostly just Atticus and me.)

Something was happening to the two of us in the mountains, and we were about to see the world in an entirely different way.

4

A Gift

We all have a bit of Adam and Eve in us. Sooner or later we come to a point in our youth when we lose our innocence and it feels like we've been kicked out of the Garden. Whether we admit it or not, all of us want to make our way back home to that time again. But innocence lost is difficult to find. Nevertheless, we look for it. We long for it, dream of it, and are haunted by it. Occasionally we glimpse it again, perhaps in the laughter of a child, the first snowfall of the holiday season, or when we hold a little puppy in our arms. And then in a flash it vanishes and we miss it all the more. But I'd like to think that if we can get our lives *just* right and become who we were always supposed to be—if we become the people we dreamed of being when we were young and pure and innocent, then and only then do we find our way home again. I don't think many make it. There are just too many distractions and obstacles. Yet I've come to believe that the worst we can do is to give up looking for it.

When I was a boy and my father's temper took over or sadness filled the house and I needed to escape, I disappeared into the woods at the end of our little street. There were only three houses on Neelon Lane, and the last was a bedraggled farmhouse owned by an ancient couple we almost never saw. Beyond their house lay a forgotten, overgrown field marked with the occasional tree that had sprouted up from neglect and the remnants of stone walls. The land sloped gently downhill until it came to a forest that at first was inviting but quickly became thick and ominous as it led down toward the Charles River.

I never went there alone. I was too frightened of the place to do that, so I went with my brothers or my friends. Even in the middle of the day, it could feel like night. It was primeval, mysterious, and magical. It was the stuff of fairy tales. Legend had it that Indians once lived there, and on occasion we'd hear of someone finding an arrowhead at the stony river's edge. My imagination told me those Indians were still there lurking just out of sight, watching our every move. Or maybe there was something else watching us, something almost unnatural, for it seemed as if the trees themselves were capable of movement and the shadows had eyes.

When Atticus and I threw ourselves into hiking the four-thousand-footers that summer, that's the place I returned to in my mind. It was that same childhood walk into the wild, and it was vastly different from the life I'd built in Newburyport—from the coffeehouses, the city-hall meetings, the constant exchange of information, and the never-ending drama. I felt refreshed by the anonymity I rediscovered in the mountains, the quiet forests, the songs of rivers and streams, how Atticus and I could step off the road and be swallowed whole into an enchanted realm. As we trekked wordlessly through sun-dappled woods, it was as if we were walking through a world of elves and hobbits, wood nymphs and fairies. Life felt less complicated, cleaner, and more hopeful in the woods.

The basic process of climbing a mountain was therapeutic, almost cathartic. There was the simple act of walking into the woods and away from the world. Then there was the climb itself, where the body worked: muscles flexed and released, lungs rose and fell, the heart beat. It was as if the complications in my life were breaking down and the only thing I cared about was the next place I'd put my foot or finding something to hold to pull myself up. After all that work to get to the summit came the views from the top. The failed Catholic in me saw it as a spiritual journey, much like the ones any holy man had made in leaving behind society.

Christ, Buddha, Muhammad—they all did it, and they came back with clarity. For me the climb was my confession, working out the troubles of my past. Sitting on top was communion. On each hike I allowed myself to be pulled apart and then put back together again.

Each weekend Atticus and I went north and rented a little cabin in Lincoln for a couple of nights. We hiked by day, sat by the fireplace in the evening, and fell asleep to the rush of the Pemigewasset River at night. Peak by peak we made our way through the list, and the experiences were so rich I can feel them to this day. I was changing from a man who knew everything that happened in Newburyport but seemingly little about himself to someone who heard his own breath and heartbeat for the first time. Each trip to the mountains was a stepping-stone, a journey among journeys. Atticus and I climbed mountain after mountain, becoming better, stronger, and more adept. All the while I was reclaiming a bit of innocence.

The climbing never got easy. It was always difficult to walk those many miles and climb thousands of feet in elevation, but I grew to enjoy the tests. And it often resembled exactly what had happened that time on Garfield. There was work to be done on the way up. I struggled, stopped often to rest, and gulped water and air. The better I felt, the more I pushed it, and I was tired all over again. And the whole time, Atticus waited for me.

No matter how much my confidence grew, my fear of heights stayed with me, and I hugged trees or rocks while moving along an exposed area of the mountain. My legs would quake when I came to the edge of a cliff and looked down, and I always feared that the hand of God would reach right up and pull me over, sending me plummeting to my death. Once while climbing the steep slide up the side of Owl's Head, I stopped and sat down to rest. What a mistake it was. I sat there for minutes, afraid of standing up lest I tumble off the mountain. I had to lie back on my pack and slowly roll onto my belly so I was facing the mountain and not the open air. Once in position, I got on all fours and could stand up again. And oh, how I hated walking down that slide or any steep trail that was exposed. I could envision nothing else but falling off the side of the mountain. But it didn't stop me. Sure, there were times when I thought, *What the hell am I doing up here?* as I wrestled with my fear, but we always continued.

Atticus, who hated getting wet, started the summer by refusing to even cross footbridges over brooks and streams. He'd wait for me and arch his back so I could slip my hand under his belly, and I'd ferry him across. He would drink from the streams but never wanted to walk through them. Yet even the stubbornness of a terrier surrendered to our quest to hike each of the forty-eight. He started crossing those bridges on his own, and if a stream wasn't too deep, he'd hop from rock to rock to get across it. On the rare occasion he slipped and fell in, he shook off the water and continued on his way as if nothing had happened.

The water crossings were about the only challenge Atticus had. Everything else came easy to him. He was a forest spirit who had come home. It's as though he knew the place and understood it. One day while he walked his customary twenty yards ahead of me, he stopped and sat in the middle of the trail just as it turned off into a stand of trees. I thought it was curious, and when I caught up to him, I realized he was watching a moose tenderly pulling leaves off a tree for her lunch. Slowly I sat down next to him, and we watched the gentle giant eat for several minutes. She knew we were there and glanced in our direction every now and again, but she wasn't threatened by us. I wasn't sure whether I should be more amazed by the sight of the moose or that Atticus seemed to respect her and didn't give chase or bark. He was simply intent on watching her. She ran away only when four hikers came from the opposite direction.

A week after that, at the beginning of a hike, Atticus left the trail and walked into the woods to go to the bathroom. I followed him through the brush as he sniffed and circled trying to find just the right place to go. When he found it, I decided to join him. I was wearing a new pair of hiking shorts, and it wasn't until that moment that I realized they didn't have a zipper. I pulled them down around my ankles. What a sight we must have been: a little dog squatting to poop and a grown man with his pants around his ankles so he could pee. Within seconds we both heard the snap of a twig and looked up to see a large bear staring at us not thirty feet away. We both froze as the bear sniffed the air in our direction. He then stood up on his hind legs and sniffed the air some more. If eyes could talk, both Atticus's and mine would have been saying the same thing as we glanced at each other: *Don't freakin' move!*

In an instant the newspaperman in me took over, and I could just imagine how my competition, the *Daily News*, would report my untimely death. I was sure the story would have a sordid lead saying something about the fact that I was found dead in the woods with my pants down around my ankles.

The bear was obviously not impressed, nor was he threatened by us, and he dropped back to all fours and slowly ambled away. It was almost comical that as he disappeared into the trees, Atticus and I went back to what we were doing as if nothing had happened before we returned to the trail.

Throughout all those miles hiked and mountains climbed, something else funny happened that summer. Our roles reversed. I'd always seen to it that we were as equal as possible, but Newburyport was my territory, and the rules of civilization are made for people, not dogs. So Atticus always had to take my lead, even though he had more freedom than any other dog I'd ever known. But in the woods he was in his element and I wasn't. It was foreign territory to me, while he was right at home and constantly led the way. On occasion he'd stop ahead of me, a little guide into the natural world, as I took a break. He stayed a constant ten to twenty yards in front even when we stopped, unless I tripped and fell or took off my backpack. If either of those things happened, he'd come trotting back. Taking off my backpack meant we were going to drink and eat, and we shared both in blissful silence. Often the only noise was the wind in the trees and the birdsong showering down on us from above.

When it came to climbing, Atticus was all business. He always knew that after we took a break on the way up a mountain and I stood to put my pack on, we continued on up. As far as he was concerned, we kept going up until there was no more up. It was uncanny how he seemed to know this. When we got to the top, we shared a ritual. I'd pick him up as I had when he was a puppy, and he'd sit in the crook of my arm, and together we looked out at the views. Whenever we did this, the only thing I heard from him was a contented sigh. At that moment I always said "Thank you," but I was never sure who I was thanking. It was something that slipped out when I picked him up on top of Mount Hale and continued to slip out with each summit reached. After we took in the view, we shared something to eat and drink, and he'd then go off a little ways and sit and gaze. He didn't lie down. He sat, and the only thing he moved was his head. The "Little Buddha" was meditating. I once timed him, and he stopped only when I interrupted him, after forty-five minutes.

In the mountains Atticus became more of what he'd always been, and I became less—less frantic, less stressed, less worried, and less harried. I felt comfortable letting him lead, and he seemed to know what I needed. He always chose the best route, if ever there was a question, and my only job was to follow. Most important, though, what made us happiest was being together in a place where we could be equals and there were no rules to adhere to.

And yet there was something about being in his presence on a mountaintop that made me not want to interfere with him. It was where he was most independent.

Paige Foster was right long ago when she said he was different. Indeed he was. I often wondered what he was looking at or what he was thinking. But all that mattered was that he was happy, and so was I.

As for Paige, we didn't talk as much as we did during the first year, but I sent her an occasional e-mail. That summer I sent her several photos of Atticus sitting on a summit checking out the view. In the past her responses had been so full of mirth and joy that I could almost hear the giggles through her written words. But that summer her responses were different. An editor of a newspaper learns to read things, even things that aren't there. That's what it was like when Paige responded to us. There was something mysterious in what she wasn't saying that was hidden between the lines, and I could sense that even she was surprised by what Atticus was doing.

In the beginning we hiked many of the easier mountains, but as summer drew on, we tackled the higher peaks, and while it was always work getting to the top, they weren't as difficult as I'd once imagined. Mount Washington, the highest peak in the northeastern United States at 6,288 feet, was of great concern to me, because its weather could be dangerous, no matter the time of year. However, the day we climbed it, our biggest challenge was getting a picture taken at the summit, thanks to the long line of sandal-wearing tourists who had driven up the auto road or ridden the cog railroad to the top. That was our first unpleasant experience on a mountaintop. It was the first time I'd felt that the outside world had caught up with us. The other time was when we stood atop Mount Liberty, a stunning peak on Franconia Ridge with astounding views in every direction. It was crowded, but at least each person there had hiked up. Yet a quick count tallied eleven people on cell phones! We quickly left the summit and went on to hike Mount Flume, its neighbor. When we returned on the way back to the car, it was less crowded, so we sat for a while.

There were days when we never saw another soul, and I liked those best. And there were days when we'd run into a few people along the way. And of course there were days like we had on Washington and Liberty when it was so crowded we might as well have been sitting in Newburyport's Market Square.

When we encountered people, they nearly always mentioned how small Atticus was. They'd ask, "Did he climb the whole way himself?"

"Yes," I'd answer, thinking it a silly question.

"You don't have to help him at all?"

"No, other than a stream crossing now and then and maybe an occasional boost."

"Wow! I've heard of Labs and retrievers, but never a miniature schnauzer climbing the Whites. Can I take his picture?"

Throughout that summer, word of a little black-and-white dog climbing the forty-eight started to spread, and people regularly stopped to take his picture or ask, "Is that Atticus?"

There was something else that happened that summer: I grew closer to my father. We had been getting along well, mostly because I was happy and didn't expect much out of him. I no longer sought those *Father Knows Best* moments that never came, and I understood he usually hated talking for long on the phone. I accepted what he could give and decided not to expect anything more. (In response to an e-mail in which Paige asked questions about Newburyport, my friends, and family, I gave her a short family history, and she said, "Well, that's too bad about your family, Tom. I always try to remember that people can't give what they don't have." And then she ended up on upbeat note: "At least you've got Atticus! Now, he's *real* family.") But since Atticus and I were in the mountains every weekend, a place he'd come to love through our family vacations, my father and I had more to talk about than ever.

My father once dreamed of walking the 2,100 miles of the Appalachian Trail from Georgia to Maine. Unfortunately, it went the way of many of his dreams, and when he finally had enough freedom to carry them out, he was too old. When we were kids, we hiked during our vacations to the White Mountains, but never a four-thousand-footer. We took the train to the top of Mount Washington or drove the auto road, and we'd gone to the top of Cannon Mountain and Wildcat Mountain during the summer, riding off-season ski gondolas. That's when my father was different. He looked peaceful and content as he gazed out and contemplated the various mountaintops. There was silence, not an uncomfortable silence but rather an understood one. There in the mountains, even his youngest son could feel like an equal to him as we shared the same sense of awe.

And here it was, three decades after those shared moments of silent intimacy, and I was climbing Jack Ryan's mountains. I'd call him each weekend from our little cabin in Lincoln and share the day's adventures with him. Those were the first conversations I can remember having with him when he didn't rush off the phone. We'd start out talking about the mountains, move on to the Red Sox, and actually linger, neither one of us wanting to hang up.

It was after my third or fourth hike that I decided I'd wanted to give my father a gift.

Steve Smith, the coauthor of the Smith and Dickerman book, became a friend to us that summer, and we relied on him for hiking advice and took comfort in knowing he was a member of the local search-and-rescue team. He also owns and operates the Mountain Wanderer Book and Map Store in Lincoln, not far from where we rented a cabin each weekend. Along with a marvelous collection of hiking books, he sells other items as well. One of the most popular is a T-shirt listing the names of each of the four-thousand-footers. The first time I saw it, I wanted to get one for my father but decided I had to "earn" it for him first.

Eleven weeks after we hiked Mount Hale with DeeDee, Atticus and I set out at six in the morning on a twenty-three-mile hike, the longest we did that summer. We were climbing our last three peaks: Bondcliff, Bond, and West Bond. Moving through the quiet wilderness, I couldn't help but think of all the mountains I'd gotten to know throughout the summer. For forty-four years, I'd seen most of them from roads and wanted to know their mysteries, the lessons they'd teach, their challenges and spectacular views. For forty-four years, I'd even wondered about their names. In some ways these larger-than-life giants of my childhood were strangers to me, but they'd always haunted me, always called to me. And so as we moved up Bondcliff, with Atticus in the lead as always, I couldn't help but think about our journey that summer and the experiences we shared along the way.

For eleven weeks I relished our escapes from downtown Newburyport. I had gone from writing about what was wrong with the world to seeing what was right with it in "the great fresh, unblighted, unredeemed wilderness," to borrow a phrase from John Muir.

I discovered I liked being alone, that when I encountered other hikers on the trail and went with them for part of the way or hiked with my brothers or DeeDee, the trip was more of an external experience for me. When I was alone with Atticus, it became more internal. And being alone, I learned that the tests were not just physical but also mental. It can be difficult to be alone with your thoughts without distraction for hours on end. And yet the deeper we went into the woods, the better I got to know myself.

Each mountain was also an emotional experience. One more gift to my father, who at age eighty-five had a hard time getting excited about much—especially since the Red Sox had finally won the World Series in his lifetime. There were nights in the middle of that summer when I had mythic dreams about him joining Atticus and me on a hike. But it wasn't the father I knew, the one who was jaded and worn down by life. Instead he was my age and we shared the forest together.

While I was walking all those miles, I could feel him with me. The dreamer in him would have loved our journey.

As I lifted Atticus up a little scramble onto Bondcliff and we looked off the edge of the cliff hundreds of feet down into the valley, I could not help but feel so many emotions churning together. We'd come face-to-face with the culmination of a goal, and I wasn't sure how I felt about it. In some ways I didn't want it to end.

Then came the trudge to Mount Bond. (I say "trudge" because on our previous hike I'd torn a tendon in my foot, and each step felt like I was walking on a nail.)

There were several people on the summit of Bond, so Atticus and I didn't stay for long before we were off to West Bond and number forty-eight.

A friend of mine who is not into mountains or nature or the simple blissful feeling that comes from the wind in your face once asked me, "What's the big deal? You get to a mountaintop and you see the same view you did from the last mountaintop. I don't get it."

I didn't have the appropriate words to answer her at the time, but once atop West Bond, while I was looking out on so many of the forty-eight we'd encountered throughout the summer, I had my answer: "How many times can you look upon the face of God?"

We'd come a long way from the days when I weighed three hundred pounds and was out of breath carrying a little puppy the block up State Street from Fowles News to my apartment. But there we were, standing on top of West Bond, and I was thankful that we had 11.3 miles left to go before getting back to our car. There are times when a man needs 11.3 miles to get his thoughts and feelings in order. This was one of them.

Like all good journeys, this one had left me with memories to catalog and thanks to express. As I limped along, I was grateful to my brothers for getting me into hiking, thankful to DeeDee for helping me take the next step, happy that Steve Smith had become a friend who welcomed Atticus and me into his store after each hike, and, of course, I was grateful for Atticus. He never complained, and he even overcame his fear of bridges and eventually his fear of stream crossings, and he always walked with a spring in his step, even on the longest and the hottest of hikes. I could not imagine a more faithful hiking partner.

The next day Atticus and I stopped at the Mountain Wanderer and bought my father that blue T-shirt. We then drove two and a half hours down to Medway. It was hot, and he was sitting in the air-conditioning without a shirt on. It was the first time I'd seen him bare-chested in his old age, and I realized how fragile his life had become. I showed him pictures, and we talked of mountains and our fantastic summer.

Earlier in the summer, I'd given him a wall map of the White Mountains, and each time we climbed another peak, I put a sticker on it. Sitting in his living room now, I felt proud when I looked up at the map with all those stickers over the forty-eight peaks, which to me were forty-eight gifts to him. At times like that, if you are lucky enough to have a parent live so long, you find that the roles have reversed—the father becomes the child and lives through the son. I was more aware of it then than at any other time in my life.

My father has never been emotional or expressive, unless angry, and when I gave him his T-shirt, he thanked me but quickly put it aside. I knew better than to expect anything. I said good-bye and left.

Just before I drove off, I realized I'd forgotten to take my photos with me, and when I went back into the house, there he was, standing up and proudly wearing his new T-shirt with the forty-eight peaks listed on the back, admiring himself in the mirror.

And just like that the journey was over.

5

"People Die Up There in the Winter"

Atticus and I proved that if an overweight, middle-aged fellow with a fear of heights and a twenty-pound miniature schnauzer could hike the four-thousand-footers, nearly anyone could. And many had. The Appalachian Mountain Club (AMC) formed the Four Thousand Footer Club in 1957, and by the time Atticus and I stood atop West Bond, more than eight thousand humans and eighty-three dogs had completed "The List" and earned membership.

And yet it was clear we were different from most. First off, it's rare to do them all so quickly. Most take years. Second, we just didn't look the part. One of us was much bigger than the average hiker; the other was much smaller. Not that there really is an "average hiker." But it was clear from pretty much anyone's point of view that we didn't look like a pair capable of hiking the forty-eight, never mind doing them so quickly. This was not a big deal to either Atticus or to me, but it obviously was to some others.

We often ran into hikers who looked upon us dubiously. We encountered one such fellow on the next-to-the-last week of that first summer. We were setting out to climb Mount Jefferson, the third-highest peak, by way of a short but challenging trail. As we entered the woods, he approached us and abruptly said, "You can't take that dog up there!"

"Excuse me?"

"You can't take that dog up the mountain. He's too small."

Atticus sat down next to me and gazed up at us.

I smiled. "He'll be fine."

The man looked at Atticus, then at me, and spoke as if trying to be patient with a child who just didn't get it. "You're new to hiking, aren't you?"

"Yeah, we started a couple of months ago."

"That's what I thought," he said. "I've been hiking for several years. . . . I'm almost done with the forty-eight. . . . Your dog really is too small to hike up here."

I smiled again but didn't say anything.

"Has he hiked a four-thousand-footer yet?"

I paused, looked down at Atticus, then into the man's eyes and continued to smile gently as I spoke. "This will be our forty-second four-thousand-footer in the past ten weeks."

The fellow didn't say another word. He blushed, nodded his head a couple of times as if he were trying to swallow something, and walked away.

If Atticus could have, I believe he would have given me a high five. But instead he bounded down the trail ahead of me. Two hours later we were sitting on the summit of Mount Jefferson sharing peanut-butter crackers and enjoying the view.

As much as I disagreed with such unfair assessments of my little friend based on his looks alone, I agreed with those who said that while Atticus had done a great job in the summer, neither he nor I should hike in winter. I'd always laugh and tell them not to worry, because it was the furthest thing from my mind.

It's the furthest thing from *most* hikers' minds. AMC statistics back that up. While more than 8,000 people had hiked all forty-eight, fewer than 350 had done them all in the calendar winter and applied for their "winter" patch and scroll. Add to that second list one dog who had hiked them all in winter. He was a 160-pound Newfoundland, a breed made more for winter hiking than summer. His name was Brutus, and he's the only dog ever to receive a patch for the winter forty-eight, and he'll be the only dog who ever will. After Brutus completed them, another dog and his owner took a tumble down an icy rock slide on the way up the Wildcats one winter day, and the Four Thousand Footer Committee voted that it was too dangerous for dogs to hike in the winter. They refused to be party to any hiker who brought his or her dog on hikes during the most dangerous season in the White Mountains.

When we learned of this and were advised not to hike that winter, I didn't need convincing or the typical refrain that came with the advice: "People die up there in the winter."

Actually, people die up there in all seasons and from all kinds of causes. But it was clear even to a novice like me that the margin for error in winter is far worse. One mistake and you can be stuck miles away from civilization in subzero temperatures fighting hypothermia—praying that a search-and-rescue crew finds you before death does.

As summer waned and autumn came, we hardly hiked anymore. My foot was still aching, and no matter how much I rested, it wouldn't heal. I decided we'd just wait for the spring thaw before hiking again.

Alas, the mountains had something entirely different in mind for us. I blame my dreams for what was to follow. Nearly every night I could feel the mysterious pull of the mountains. Many mornings I'd awaken to the fleeting fog of a dream where Atticus and I were standing on some snowy peak. I resisted those dreams and convinced myself that we belonged in Newburyport for the winter, eating hot soup and drinking cocoa, not freezing in the mountains. Besides, I didn't know anything about winter hiking . . . *and* the gear cost too much . . . *and,* most important, Atticus wasn't made for the cold weather or the deep snow.

And yet there was a nagging sense that we were being called back to the mountains. They called and called.

In late November, defying all logic, I surrendered and started the expensive exercise of shopping for winter gear. I wasn't sure where to begin, so I paid close attention to the two popular hiking Web sites that focused on the White Mountains, Views from the Top and Rocks on Top. Experienced hikers gathered on these sites and shared information about equipment, trail conditions, and techniques. I also picked up yet another Steve Smith book, *Snowshoe Hikes in the White Mountains*. Steve had a chapter on what every beginner needed to know about taking the first steps in winter hiking.

There was much to get: snowshoes, crampons, trekking poles, ski goggles, hats, gloves, socks, boots, water bottles, headlamps, layers and layers of clothing, and a bigger winter backpack to carry all that extra gear. It got to the point that every time I walked into an Eastern Mountain Sports store, the salespeople knew they were going to meet their sales quota for the day. Whenever one of them asked me what my plans for all that gear were, I told them Atticus and I hoped to replicate what we had done in the summer—hike each of the forty-eight in one winter. They'd give me a look as if they'd never be seeing me again and reminded me, "People die up there." But that didn't stop them from selling me more gear than I could possibly need. Add ignorance and fear together, and I probably bought twice as much equipment and clothing as I needed. They could have sold me anything and I would happily have paid for it. That's how much I didn't know.

I had it easy compared to Atticus, however. He'd always been a nudist by nature. He hated his leash and collar or anything that restricted him whatsoever. But if we were heading to the White Mountains in December, I had to find him a bodysuit that would keep him warm and dry, and he was going to have to wear his Muttluks on a regular basis. (Muttluks are ingenious fleece-lined dog boots. He often wore them in Newburyport during the winter months to keep the sidewalk salt from burning the pads of his paws.) I got lucky and found a bodysuit just a block down State Street in Pawsitively Best Friends. It was made by K9 Top Coat, and Atticus hated it at first sight.

The first time I put the suit on him, we were in the store, and immediately he looked like he'd been to a taxidermist. He stood stiff as a freshly stuffed dog. He wouldn't move his head. He wouldn't even move

Oh, the things people will say. What's a man to do when confronted by such a comment? I did what any self-respecting, quick-witted Irishman would—I smiled and said, "Well, thank you."

To which she said, "I was talking about the dog."

"Alas, that's always the case."

Eventually I solved the problem of Atticus's bodysuit rigor mortis, but it took a few days of dressing him in the suit and leaving him that way in the middle of our living room like some strange coffee table. I finally won the negotiations when I put him in the suit and drove my dead, stuffed dog to Moseley Pines, where Atticus loved to run free and chase after squirrels. I carried him into the woods about fifty yards, his legs as stiff as ever, then put him down. Nothing. Then I called out, "Look, squirrel!" And just like that Atticus was off and running. It was only after he treed the furry little creature that he realized he'd been found out in his effort to convince me that the suit was made of lead.

The look in his eyes at that moment was priceless. It said, quite simply, *Oh, shit!*

That old refrain from Paige Foster came back to me: *Y'all will work it out.* We had, once again. Not that Atticus was very happy about it. And not that he would admit to it, but there would come times that winter when he was happy to have that suit to keep him warm.

The AMC rules for winter hiking are simple. You do what we did in the warm-weather months, but you can't start your first hike until the winter solstice, and you have to be off the trail when winter ends. That gave us ninety days to hike the forty-eight.

Hikers on the two Web sites warned me that winter hiking was different. They continuously told me of the dangers, of how many of my hikes would either begin or end in the dark because of shorter daylight, and they warned me to carry more than one headlamp just in case one of them went out. "You don't want to be stuck on a mountain at night with temperatures below zero and no way to see!"

his eyes. And he stood like this for a couple of minutes in the
the store. Nothing I could do would get him to budge.

I knelt next to him and gave him the tiniest of nudges, hopi
would throw off his balance and cause him to move a leg for su
Nothing. I did it again. Nothing. I did it again, a little firmer. Still
ing. I did it a little firmer yet, and this time, instead of moving his leg
keep his balance, he toppled over onto his side—a dead, stuffed
with stiff legs. The cause of death was humiliation; rigor mortis w
immediate.

I rolled him gently over onto his back, and he looked like a table
turned upside down.

Okay, so I got the hint, but he still needed a bodysuit if we were
going to hike in the winter.

I picked him up and set him on his feet and tried to coax him with
words . . . then treats. I walked out of the store knowing he would follow
me, but for the first time ever he didn't follow me somewhere. Nope,
there was no budging him. His inner mini schnauzer had emerged, and
he was determined to let his stubbornness win out.

In the midst of all this drama, three middle-aged women, in town for
the day to visit the different boutiques, came charging into the store.
They were in the zone—deep in their shopping trance—and didn't
really care who or what was in their way as they barged through the tiny
shop. To make sure they didn't step on Atticus, I picked him up, sat him
in the crook of my arm, and stood off to the side. Every now and then,
one of the women would call out to the other two to look at this or that,
and they'd all scurry together to examine some newfound precious thing
they just had to have.

Then one of them stumbled upon my friend, looking like he was wearing an X-rated Aquaman suit, sitting stiff-legged in my arm, with only his
head, paws, and privates revealed for the entire world to see. She called out
to the others, "Oh, my God! Look at how cute this little dog is in his suit!"

They flocked around us. The loudest and boldest of the three took
one look and said, "Look at how big his penis is!"

I may have been ambitious, but I was also nervous, so I made sure to buy three headlamps, extra bulbs, and extra batteries.

They also warned me how trails could look different in the winter, how the paint blazes that marked them could be masked by snow and ice, and how if the snow was deep enough, it could even hide signs that were four or five feet high. And they told me how many of the same mountains we hiked in the summer would be even more taxing because the access roads to them were closed for the winter and it added mileage to some.

It didn't take me long to realize that what they said was true. Hiking in winter was completely different, and I discovered it on the first day. My intention was to start right at the solstice—1:35 in the afternoon, the exact start of winter and the shortest day of the year—but it took nearly an hour to figure out how to put on the layers of clothing and all my gear. By the time I finished, I was sweating as if I'd already climbed the damn mountain. My last act of preparation was to hoist the large pack onto my shoulders, and when I did, I nearly fell over from its weight. Laboring under all those clothes and the larger pack, I stumbled into the woods looking like the Michelin Man.

I chose Mount Tecumseh for our first winter peak, because it is the shortest at only 4,003 feet and from the road to the summit is only two and a half miles.

The first third of the trail crosses two streams and meanders through open woods and climbs gently. The middle part of the hike climbs steeply after it crosses a third stream. My pre-hike workout of getting dressed had me struggling the moment we entered the woods, but after that third stream crossing I really began to labor. I was not used to climbing in snow, even though it wasn't all that deep. I was still nursing the sore foot that had kept me off the trails for several months, so I was out of shape compared to how I'd felt in the summer.

It was somewhere in the middle of plodding that long, unforgiving ascent that I got my second wind, and I started looking around instead of down at my feet.

My God, it was beautiful!

I could see why there were some who loved the winter season. I had to stop from time to time to gaze with wonder at the trees and their thick icing. I felt like a child again, like I'd stumbled upon a place I never knew existed before, and almost felt guilty for being there, as if it were too good to be true. The pleasure was immense, almost sinful, and when I came upon a hiker who was heading down the trail—the only person Atticus and I encountered that day—he told me there was no one up top. It was suddenly an exciting prospect to be left alone with Atticus on our first winter mountain.

There is a point in climbing when you get quiet and are enveloped by the solitude. The hike turns into a walking meditation and becomes Zen-like. You stop trying so hard, and your stride falls into place with your heart and lungs. Your mind follows suit.

I had reached that point, and my mind blissfully wandered from here to there. Eventually I was transported back to the innocence and wonder of when I was a small boy curled up on the floor with Spot, the family beagle, surrounded by my entire family and watching *Rudolph, the Red-Nosed Reindeer* on TV. For that's what the trees on Tecumseh reminded me of—those thickly frosted trees in the show.

We were making good time, and winter hiking seemed like a breeze. When we came upon a spur trail just below the summit, I saw that no one had broken the path through the snow. I decided to walk that quarter-of-a-mile stretch to the only good viewpoint on the mountain, even though it meant we'd have to double back. The snow was deeper than I expected, and I had to stop repeatedly. When I was bent over gasping for breath, Atticus, impatient with my plodding, pushed ahead of me through snow up to his chest. By the time we made it to a rustic bench at the lookout, there were three sets of prints: Atticus's, mine, and those of a snowshoe hare.

Our little detour had exhausted me, and I could feel the cold creeping into my bones. I started daydreaming about the comforts of being at home: sitting in my big leather chair, book in my hands, Atticus on my lap, and a steaming cup of cocoa by my side. But that was interrupted when my scalp suddenly felt like it was on fire. I reached up and ran my fingers over my head, and I was stunned to feel icicles dangling from my hair. I checked the thermometer hanging from my backpack—the temperature had plummeted to eight degrees.

Where had the sun gone with its warmth?

It was as if someone had flipped a switch and our comfortable but tiring hike had suddenly changed its temperament. Day was giving way to night. After a brief rest stop, we returned the way we came, this time with my headlamp on. I'd never hiked at night before, and I could feel the darkness engulf us, bringing more cold with it. The setting had gone from cartoon cheery to haunting. My headlamp chased the darkness as best it could, but it made me feel like we were walking into a tunnel. The thin beam highlighted whatever was in front of us but left everything just outside it hidden in blackness. It was eerie and sad, and I found myself falling into a deep malaise where all the warmth in the world had been drained away, and I thought, *This must be what death is like—brittle, unyielding, frozen.*

Once back on the main trail again, I followed Atticus for the final short climb over rock and root on the western edge of the mountain. The higher we climbed, the more ghostlike it felt and the heavier I sank into the night, spiraling deeper into memories that wouldn't let go of me— the kind that haunt your subconscious, that surface ever so rarely in your dreams and wake you up in a sweat with a breathless gasp.

Each step emptied more hope and cheer from me. The thought of turning back was strong, but we were so close to the summit and something was drawing us inexorably up that mountain. The headlamp began to play tricks on my mind. It cast shadows and turned the sharp tree branches into hundreds of bony hands reaching out at me. Occasionally one would snag my jacket or my backpack and I'd whirl around to see who was there. Whenever I turned to look, the light brought the branches to life. Again I thought of the comforts of home as we walked farther away from it into that mournful, melancholy dream.

When we reached the summit, I didn't recognize it. It looked different from how it had in the summer. It was crowded, not with people but with evergreens. Coated in snow and ice, they looked huge and harsh, even ominous, not lush and green like the warm and endearing trees that had brought a smile to my face just an hour earlier. They were ghastly and sent a shiver running through my core. Despair grew. How strange to feel so empty and hopeless. I'm typically an upbeat person, usually smiling and laughing, and on a mountaintop I feel more peaceful than anywhere else. But then and there I felt an unbearable sadness.

I had the sensation that we were not alone, but no one else was there. The summit seemed haunted, the trees wraithlike, as if they were capable of harm. They stood above me like giant angels—not the sweet cherubs of greeting cards but fierce angels wearing armor, the ones that went to war for God, that wreak havoc, destruction, and hopelessness.

Without warning, my headlamp went out. Panic-stricken, I fiddled with it nervously, but it wouldn't turn on. I dropped to my knees and opened my backpack, searching frantically for my second headlamp. It was while my hands were plunging into the pack that I looked up at those trees once more. In the darkness, with me kneeling under a starless sky, they loomed even larger. I could barely breathe. The emptiness within was unbearable, and the sadness poured out of me. I gave in to it and stopped searching for my other lamp and just knelt there paralyzed by my horror. I have no idea how long I stayed like that, but Atticus eventually pushed his way into my arms. He was not looking at me, he was looking up at the trees, and there we stayed, man and dog, those trees glowering over us.

They sent me tumbling deeper into thoughts attached to soulful memories. I had felt that same way before. It was several decades ago on that very same week before Christmas. I was seven years old, and just after supper my father had summoned us. This usually meant we were about to be punished and were to line up and "assume the position" to receive "the belt," so we went with trepidation. Being the youngest, I took up the rear, but my father pulled me to the front of the group. He had something to tell us.

My mother had been in the hospital. Since my birth she had suffered from multiple sclerosis and was confined to a wheelchair. A month earlier, while some of my brothers and sisters were driving her to the grocery store to get the Thanksgiving turkey, there'd been an accident and she'd suffered an injury. Just before she was released from the hospital, she dropped a burning cigarette in her bed, and the flames had engulfed her. By the time they got to her, she was covered in third-degree burns. She died of complications from those burns six days before Christmas.

I was there again, seven again, there with my family again, while I was on my knees looking up at those trees. My despair was not so much for me or my siblings or the mother I never knew, but for my father. When my mother died, much of whatever was left of him had died, too.

My father never recovered. He would never be whole again, not for his children, not for himself. He was too busy trying to save his own life to save us.

It took me years to understand that my father, while ill equipped to handle what fate had delivered to him, nevertheless did the best he could. And as I crouched on my knees that night at the foot of those trees, my heart was filled with compassion for the man who had suffered for so long.

While kneeling, I thought about his recent decision not to hold the family Christmas in our childhood home. It was his latest act of surrender. He said he was too tired and didn't want to be bothered by having the family over. Since he'd made the announcement, I'd not given it much thought, but in the end that didn't matter a lot. The trees and the night and the mountain had conspired to make me feel more than I was willing to feel.

After I'd spent a long while on my knees, wrapped in my sad memories, those evergreens were no longer glowering. They were still there, of course, just as large and stately, but suddenly they were beautiful. It was as if they'd delivered their message and finished what they'd set out to do. In those tranquil moments, I continued to hold Atticus, and I contemplated what had just transpired. Both of us were still looking up at those angels.

Since I was already on my knees, I decided to say a few prayers. I prayed for my brothers and sisters, and I prayed for my mother, but more than anything I prayed for Jack Ryan.

Eventually my headlamp flickered to life again. I pulled some sausages out of my backpack to share with Atticus and kept looking until I found my other headlamps. To be safe I put them in the pocket of my coat before we made our way down. But I had a feeling I wouldn't be needing them.

The night wasn't as dark anymore. A few stars appeared and elbowed the clouds out of the way. My thermometer now read eighteen degrees. The trip down the mountain in the dark felt different. It was comfortable and lighter, and we finished without further incident.

Later, while driving home, I understood a bit more of what experienced hikers had warned me about—that winter hiking is entirely different from summer, and strange things can happen—especially at night. You have to be prepared for anything.

I also thought about the Abenaki Indians who didn't climb to the top of the great peaks because they believed that's where the great spirits lived.

It wasn't until we arrived back in Newburyport that night and Atticus and I slipped into bed that it hit me that we'd climbed our first winter peak. I couldn't really account for what had transpired up there, but it was so extraordinary I wanted more of it. As I fell asleep, I wondered what else our winter in the Whites would teach us.

Atticus's Muttluks and bodysuit proved to be essential for us at various times during the winter. We encountered colder temperatures and deeper snow than either of us had ever known. I learned to keep the suit in my pack until he started to get uncomfortable, and then I'd put it on him and he'd welcome its snug fit and warm fleece lining.

However, our most valuable piece of equipment was not something I'd bought. It was something we already had: common sense. We wouldn't push it, and we'd take only what the mountains gave us. On the best of days, when the temperature was moderate, the skies clear, and the forecast favorable, we'd climb one of the higher, more exposed peaks. Unfortunately, those days were few and far between. On days when things weren't as nice but still safe enough to hike, we'd climb where we would be protected by the trees and there wasn't as much exposure. On the worst of days, we simply wouldn't hike at all. There would be many such days.

As much as people worried about me, the way I saw it, I had an advantage over most. There were many days where I might have hiked if I were on my own, but I wouldn't expose Atticus to storms, high winds, frigid temperatures, or trails that were icy or too deep with new snow to make our way through. By refusing to subject Atticus to less-than-favorable conditions, I kept myself safe.

I was told by those who argued that dogs don't belong on the trails in winter that dogs don't know the difference between a bad day and a good one and that they'll go wherever their owners go. But I never had that problem with Atticus. Atticus always had a say, just as he always had in our life together, and if he felt he didn't want to go on a hike, he was never forced to.

There were two occasions that winter when he decided we weren't going. On the first we'd driven the two hours up from Newburyport, and when we arrived at the trailhead, the wind was wicked and the wind chill far below zero. Snow swirled in mini tornadoes, and when Atticus hopped out of the car, he turned right back around and hopped back in. He had spoken.

On the second such occasion, the weather was much better. It was a perfect day for hiking. But it was our third day in a row, and he was tired. When we parked at the trailhead and I was getting geared up, he stayed curled in a ball in the front seat of the car. I called to him, but all he did was twitch his white eyebrows as if to say, *Wake me when you get back.* I took off my gear, put it back in the car, and we drove home. It was a partnership, and if one of us didn't feel up to it, we weren't going to hike.

Another advantage was that Atticus had the innate ability to know things that other dogs might not. He knew when a frozen stream wasn't safe to cross even if it looked like it was, and he knew when it was safe, even if it didn't look like it. The same was true for some of the icy slides we encountered. On some he would walk confidently, leading me across. On others he'd stay back and let me go first, or he would wait for me to pick him up and carry him a short distance. His ability to read the conditions of the trails and to know his own limits was a great advantage for us, for we were challenged by an entirely different set of mountains and there was less margin for error. They were the same mountains we'd climbed in spring and summer; they just didn't look it, and they definitely didn't feel like it.

At its best, winter in the Whites was a wonderland. It was a walk through a crystalline forest under azure skies, and as we thrust our way through the last of the snow-covered conifers toward each summit, it was like stumbling into C. S. Lewis's magical wardrobe and pushing through the rows of clothes, knowing that there was something thrilling beyond it all. Stepping out of the trees and onto an open ridge or peak was like exiting the back of the wardrobe and entering our own special Narnia. It was a world apart, a world that belonged only to the two of us.

Winter at its worst meant that the woods were barren down low, the colors of the forest gone, replaced by a flat, desaturated monochrome. There was no sweet and sultry summer scent, no birdsong, and hardly any wildlife. It was as lonely and forlorn a place as I'd ever known. The wind cried out like a banshee or a dragon beating its thunderous wings as it circled above the treetops, and the cold would reach deep into my bones.

We mostly had the trails to ourselves, and I came to understand an entirely new level of isolation and how that brutal and silent world could play tricks on my mind and make me long to be back in Newburyport, surrounded by friendly faces.

Throughout that winter we experienced all there was to experience. There were frightening moments and glorious moments, moments of success and of failure. There were even comical moments. My favorite was when we climbed Mount Washington, one of the deadliest mountains in the world. It has taken more than one hundred lives and, until recently, claimed the highest wind ever measured on earth—231 miles per hour. The average winter wind speed is 45 miles per hour; the average temperature is five degrees. As the *AMC White Mountain Guide* states, these are conditions you expect to find in Antarctica, not New Hampshire.

When planning for the winter, I wondered if we'd have an opportunity to get Atticus safely to the summit of Washington. However, after two months of waiting, we got a shockingly rare five-hour weather window where there was to be no wind. Four hours after starting our climb, Atticus and I sat on top of the windless summit by ourselves. The temperature was a "balmy" thirty degrees, but it felt so mild that I wore only a fleece top instead of a jacket and I didn't bother putting on a hat or gloves.

After a while a group of eight men appeared on the horizon, led by a professional guide they had paid big money to get them there. All the men were fit young professionals. Their gear was top-notch and brand-new. Each carried an ice ax, climbing ropes, each wore a winter parka made for Mount Everest, snow goggles, and they all had other assorted expensive pieces of equipment strapped to or dangling from their backpacks. They'd come to challenge the great Washington, with its high winds and frigid temperatures. They'd come to spit in the eye of death and to return to their offices the following Monday to brag about it.

But instead of death, they came upon something that horrified them even more: a little dog and a fat guy sitting and eating a peanut butter and jelly sandwich below the summit sign as if they were having a picnic on Boston Common in the middle of summer.

When they were within speaking distance, they stopped in unison, their goggles fogging up with each heavy breath. It was so warm they were sweating profusely under their heavy coats with their hoods up and their balaclavas on. Neither Atticus nor I moved. I nodded hello.

Atticus calmly appraised them, enjoying another bite of my sandwich.

There was a priceless moment of stunned silence. Finally one of them broke it by speaking for all of them. Tripping over his disbelief, he asked, "How . . . how did you get up here?"

I took another bite of sandwich and tore off a corner for Atticus. I made them wait while I finished chewing. "We walked."

"You walked?" They looked with disbelief at my simple backpack. They looked at the little dog. They looked at me. "You . . . you and that little dog . . . you just walked up?"

I nodded and gave him a friendly smile.

As we said good-bye and walked away, I wasn't so sure they'd be sharing this story with their coworkers and friends, but I knew I would. It was the kind of response we would get quite often, a look of disbelief that this little dog was actually climbing in winter.

It was an amazing season, and we did well, but we didn't finish all forty-eight peaks. We fell two challenging hikes shy. But still, the two unlikeliest newcomers to the winter-hiking scene had caught people's attention without even trying. And once again our shared experiences brought us even closer. In some ways Atticus and I were creating our own little universe, one where we knew no matter what the world had in store for us, we'd handle it just fine so long as we faced it together.

I wrote my father a letter toward the end of the winter. I told him that one of my favorite childhood memories was of standing with him and my brothers Stephen, Jeff, and David on the cool pool of lawn in front of Lafayette Place campground in the creeping shade of a summer eve, looking up at the monstrous spine of Franconia Ridge. It was one of those childhood memories I looked back on often and remembered how safe and secure I felt. It was a moment when I first realized just how beautiful the world was.

On the night I wrote him that letter, Atticus and I were sitting on the floor of our rented cabin, snuggled up together in front of the fireplace. He was snoring blissfully, having earned his sleep with a tough hike. Earlier that day we were on top of that same monstrous spine, more than five thousand feet above sea level. The temperature was in the teens, driven even lower by the wind. It was noon, but if I had not had a watch on my altimeter, I wouldn't have known, for it was dark and dreary and Atticus and I were all alone. We'd come out of the trees and were fully exposed as we headed toward Mount Lincoln and beyond to Mount Lafayette. Gusts of wind toyed with us and pelted us with snow and ice, and I had to put my goggles and balaclava on to protect my face and keep from being blinded. The elements were such that there was not much to be seen as we walked along two miles of unprotected ridge. On a sunny day, there aren't many more beautiful places to be. But on a day like we had, when the weather changed for the worse, it was desolate-looking, a wasteland along a narrow, rocky path.

As discomfort grew, I kept thinking about the same simple pleasures that called to me throughout those cold months: a cup of cocoa, a hot bath, a good book, a thick sweater, some sunshine. It was a habit I'd fallen into. But reality came at us gust after gust, and I questioned my ability, as I'd done before throughout that winter. This was one of those moments I had come across where we were all alone up high, no sign of human life about, and I felt as weak as anyone ever has. I reached for strength I didn't seem to possess and found myself thinking about Guy Waterman, a local writer and climber of great acclaim, who chose that very ridge to lie down on to end his life. While I was not saddled with the depression he fought, I thought about how such weather can strip a man of hope and his good sense and make him feel lonely and empty. I thought about how easy it would be to just sit down and stop moving through the wind and gloom, but to sit would have made it harder to get up again. And yet the mists made me tired and wreaked havoc with my motivation, and I had to force myself to move onward.

I was exhausted, and my body was dragging. It was one of those times I found it most difficult to be alone up there, but I suppose that's one of the reasons I'd undertaken this winter-long adventure. I had decided to challenge myself and make myself stronger, to come face-to-face with who I was in those worst of elements and in an environment

I've always feared, with the hope I'd emerge a bit different from when I went into it.

Not for the first or last time that day, I looked ahead at the shrouded path and could see very little. On either side, not too far away, the ridge dropped off into a mist, and that was it. There was nothing but a gray abyss. My fear of heights heckled me. I told myself that with a few wrong moves across the ice I would be sorry. So I was deliberate with each step in my crampons, waiting to hear the bite of metal in ice before taking my next step. And while feeling all alone, the view of the landscape varying from fifty feet to a few hundred depending on the gusts and clouds, I was in need of inspiration and regretting my decision to take on the mountains in winter.

Where's the sun when you need it? I asked that question of myself a lot on stormy days up there.

But just as I asked, all I had to do was let my gaze travel through the mist some fifty feet ahead toward the cairn suddenly revealed by a receding cloud, and there in front of me was my inspiration—a twenty-pound dog.

Little Atticus had taken the lead, strong gusts be damned, and was ducking his head and floppy ears into each gust, marching forward with a sideways catch—like John Wayne.

At that moment I'd never felt more love for him or more pride in him. He was my ineluctable hero, there, as always, to lift my spirits and astonish me and even at times make me laugh. He wasn't supposed to be made for those kinds of conditions, and yet there he was, not only up there but leading the way—leading me to safety. He marched on inexorably toward the two peaks. How could I not follow? How could I not be lifted by his persistence?

I watched in admiration as he walked forward with strength and confidence, his small body unbowed by the storm or the great mountains. That little dog, who was supposedly made more for sitting on a lap or in a bicycle basket or a car seat next to an open window, reminded me again and again throughout that winter that limitations are something we put on ourselves.

A couple of days after that hike, I went out and paid three hundred dollars for a digital camera to replace one that I had dropped on another trail and watched slide off an icy cliff. When I'd bought that first camera at the beginning of the winter, it was for the purpose of taking video to show my father the mountains he would never stand atop. But I had another reason now. I wanted to capture images of Atticus for all time, so that someday when I'm old and gray I can look back on the videos and say, "I once knew the most amazing dog. . . ."

Paige and I were no longer having lengthy phone conversations. There was nothing wrong, just that she was living her life and I was living mine. I'd also felt a little guilty about how often we'd talked during Atticus's first year, for we could talk the day away. Minutes turned into hours whenever we were on the phone together. I reminded myself that she had many people who bought puppies from her and I didn't want to monopolize her time. But that doesn't mean I didn't keep her posted. I e-mailed updates of our winter hikes and sent pictures of the little dog she'd bred standing in his Muttluks on snow-covered mountaintops. Her responses were always breathless and filled with exclamation points. There was a sing-songy, breezy, and upbeat feeling to her words as she thanked me repeatedly for filling her in. I could almost hear her southern accent as she typed, "Keep making memories . . . and send them by the wagonload!"

She was astounded by what Atticus had done in the summer by hiking all forty-eight. But that paled in comparison to her amazement at what we'd done in the winter. We'd come up short by not getting to all the mountains, but not in Paige's eyes. "I told you I always thought he was different, but not even I expected him to do something like this!" she wrote. "I wonder what he has planned for us in the future!"

I didn't know it at the time, but that first summer and winter would get us ready for what was to come next: an adventure that dwarfed anything we'd done up to that point. It would change everything.

6

For the Kids

For many years I was self-appointed inspector of snow-storms and rain-storms, and did my duty faithfully, though I never received one cent for it.

—HENRY DAVID THOREAU

That was me, the Henry David Thoreau of Newburyport. I was the "self-appointed inspector of snow-storms and rain-storms," I "did my duty faithfully," and while I received payment for it, it wasn't much. But that was my choice.

I loved running the *Undertoad*, loved writing about the political storms and breaking stories, shifting the way the city saw itself, and chronicling a community full of characters. Every two weeks there were new stories to tell, a cast of heroes and villains—some new, some returning from prior issues, and on occasion some of them even reversing roles—and the continuing developing story of a city that was going through the change of gentrification.

However, better than any of that was how I'd become a part of a community. Every two weeks people invited me into their homes when they bought my paper, and I heard from many of them. Sure, the department head who was accused of lying, the zoning board of appeals member who supported a developer he did business with, and the mayor who was caught red-handed trying to secretly rush through a road that would financially benefit one of her handlers but hurt the rest of the city—they all hated me. But those who had lived in Newburyport for years and saw things like this happening again and again were thrilled to finally have someone bringing it all to light. These grateful readers far outnumbered the angry ones. Had it not been for their kindness and backing, I couldn't possibly have lasted so long. Since I had no staff, they were my support system.

I came to town a stranger, started the *Undertoad* a year later, and immediately commenced cultivating friendships with a colorful cast of characters. When I first published my letters to my father, it allowed people to see a more intimate view of the man who was revealing the intimacies of Newburyport, and that drew them even closer. They felt like they knew me. To some extent they did. They even felt like they knew my father. It's one of the reasons people reached out to me when Max died and then welcomed Atticus to town.

There weren't many days when I wasn't meeting with someone for breakfast, someone else for lunch, and having coffee or tea with yet another person in between. My dance card was always full. These were not just readers who had stories to share; they were also becoming friends. My critics would blanch at this thought, but I made the rounds connecting with people so often that I almost felt like the old parish priest. There wasn't much that went on that I didn't know about. It wasn't just politics either. If someone was sick, or had a baby, or if someone's kid had graduated from college or gotten the lead part in the high-school play, I knew about it. It felt great to have a home and to be included in the fabric of the city and of the lives of those who lived there.

One of my favorites was Vicki Pearson. Whenever we stopped to see her at the Tannery, I was impressed by the vast array of her duties in handling much of David Hall's business matters. David not only ran the Tannery, that wonderful complex of unique shops, he also owned a multitude of rental properties around town, and it was Vicki's job to stay on top of all those renters. She appeared to do it without much effort. But more impressive than her ability as a businesswoman was her heart of gold. I don't think there was anyone who didn't like Vicki, and that was a true rarity in little Newburyport. She was married, had a son from a previous marriage, had many friends, and she adopted me as one of them. She loved the *Undertoad* and subscribed to it from the very beginning. But best of all, she loved dogs, came to like me as a person and not just as an editor when I took Max in, and then fell for Atticus in a big way. It's why she'd insisted we eat at the Purple Onion, where Atticus could join us.

One day I received a call from her son telling me that Vicki was in Anna Jaques, Newburyport's hospital, and wanted to see me. I'd known she was sick. I just didn't realize how bad it was.

When I entered her hospital room, she looked nothing like the Vicki I'd grown to appreciate and love. Her skin was loose, hanging on her bones, and her eyes protruded from their sockets. She looked tired, frail, and broken. Then she spoke, and the old Vicki was back again, wasting no time in giving me my orders.

"I need some help," she said. "I'm planning my funeral." She said it with a little laugh, as if she were planning her own fiftieth birthday party, which she'd done the previous year.

It wasn't long before she had me laughing, too. We laughed the way we always had. Lots of quips and jokes about her short future—and then came the "no-nonsense" Vicki.

"I'm dying."

I swallowed hard.

"You know what the good thing about dying is, Tom? You can make people promise you things and they can't say no to you."

She then made several requests and had me promise that I would fulfill them. Among them was her repeated insistence that she wanted my help in planning her funeral. I was touched by her choreographing her exit so that she wouldn't stress her husband or son. Even in the end,

Vicki didn't want to burden them, and she acted with strength, courage, and grace. And yet none of it seemed real. She was too full of life to be dying.

Bright and early the next day Atticus and I were with Vicki, me in the chair next to the bed and him on the bed. Atticus was there for nearly every visit, and even as she started to slip away more and more, a combination of the morphine and the cancer making its way up her spine, she'd slowly open her eyes and say, "Hi, Atticus," whenever we'd arrive.

"What about me?" I asked.

"Yeah, you, too."

A former neighbor of Vicki's shared a story with me. Once the neighbor's dog had gotten out of its yard, and Vicki had found it wandering the street and taken it in. She liked her neighbor but was reluctant to return the dog because she felt it deserved better.

I think Atticus and dogs in general were close to Vicki because they can sense things many of us miss. In return, it was clear that Vicki saw the best in all dogs.

Toward the end, when Vicki was too weak to speak, I read to her. One day I shared the passage about animals from Walt Whitman's "Song of Myself" from *Leaves of Grass*.

> *I think I could turn and live with animals, they are so placid and self-*
> *contain'd,*
> *I stand and look at them long and long.*
> *They do not sweat and whine about their condition,*
> *They do not lie awake in the dark and weep for their sins,*
> *They do not make me sick discussing their duty to God,*
> *Not one is dissatisfied, not one is demented with the mania of owning*
> *things,*
> *Not one kneels to another, nor to his kind that lived thousands of years*
> *ago,*
> *Not one is respectable or unhappy over the whole earth.*

So they show their relations to me and I accept them,
They bring me tokens of myself, they evince them plainly in their
* possession.*

Her eyes stayed closed, but she gave the slightest smile and moved her hand slowly over Atti's head as he rested against her side.

What made Vicki so precious was that while she was impressed by nature and flowers and dogs and pretty much everything that is natural, she wasn't impressed by people who were impressed with themselves. That was another rarity in Newburyport, which took itself very seriously. That's why it was such an interesting marriage when she sat on the board of directors of the chamber of commerce. As with most such boards, there were plenty of people who were indeed impressed with themselves. Yet Vicki couldn't care less about status or position and was more aware of who and what she was, and who and what other people were, than anyone I'd ever known. And while she didn't like phonies and would have laughed at some of the folks who turned up at her funeral because it was considered the "right thing to do," she let others live life as they pleased, unless they crossed her.

She retired when she turned fifty to spend more time tending to her garden and her two favorite flowers—her grandchildren, one of whom she took to Disney World in Florida with her newfound freedom. It was then that she decided to run for the school committee, and she based her campaign on a very simple premise: for the kids. At one of our lunches, she confessed that there were many reasons she was running for office, but she gave me credit for motivating her to run because of things I'd written in the *Undertoad*.

"Every two weeks I read the *'Toad*, and I'd think, the kids deserve better, and so I decided to stop saying it and do something about it."

Being a member of the school board was a thankless position. In the hierarchy of elected offices, it was the lowest of the three. First and foremost was the mayor, then came the eleven city councilors, and finally the six members of the school committee. All these positions except the mayor's were handled by ordinary citizens who had day jobs, and the hours these elected officials gave were incredible. With school funding cut year after year, it was frustrating to be a member of the school board and have to deal with angry parents. You had to believe in what you were doing, and you really had to love kids. Vicki scored high on each of those points.

She won easily, but soon after the election her chest pains started. She thought she might be having heart problems, so they ran a few tests and gave her medication. Then came numbness in her limbs. By Thanksgiving Day, three weeks after the election, she couldn't shower without help from a friend. She couldn't stand. She was told it was only a reaction to the medication. Additional tests showed a large tumor on her back, and before anyone knew what had happened, this vibrant woman who'd participated in a three-day, sixty-mile walk to fight cancer just a year earlier was paralyzed from the waist down. She underwent surgery, but she would never walk again.

On Inauguration Day she sat by herself in a wheelchair in front of the stage. The rest of the school committee sat up on the stage with the members of the city council and the mayor. The two other new members of the committee did join her on the floor when the three were sworn in, but they later returned to their seats, leaving her seated alone, looking withered and exhausted.

Everyone thought she'd be fine. Not having the use of her legs wouldn't hinder Vicki Pearson. But it was soon discovered that the tumor along her spine was getting worse, and all hope was gone.

In a letter home to my father I wrote, "Vicki was aware enough to realize Atticus and I had stayed in Vermont for an extra day. We talked a lot that night we got back. It was after visiting hours, but we didn't pay any attention to those. That was the last good conversation we had. There were plans for an interview, but she has drifted too far away. While she seems so distant and tired of fighting for life, when I see her I no longer see the loose skin or the dry lips. I do not see her brittle hair or hear the morphine pump or smell the residue of urine from her catheter bag. I don't see legs that won't move. What I see is the Vicki I have known since moving to Newburyport. I see her in the faces of the nurses who attend to her, have been inspired by her, and have grown because of her. I see the Vicki no tumor can take from me or the city or anyone else. Long after she stops breathing, after her body is cold and decaying, after we have cried to the point where we cannot cry anymore, she will still be here—a wonderful spirit lasting with those who were touched by her for as long as they remember her."

During those days in her hospital room, Vicki shared with me the story of her life, what she called "the unedited version."

"It's important that you know it, Tom."

"Why is that?"

She licked her lips, closed her eyes and thought, then opened them again. "I don't know. . . . I think it has something to do with the *'Toad*. After all these years of reading it, I feel that you're the only person I've ever met who tells it like it is. I guess I just wanted to tell it like it is to you.

"Besides," she added, getting ready to drop a bombshell on me, "you and Atti are going to be standing up in front of the church giving my eulogy."

"What?"

"You heard me."

"I heard you, but I'm not doing it. Let your husband or your son or one of your friends do it."

"You guys are my friends, too—you and Atti. I can't think of anything I'd rather do than have my friend, the editor of the *Undertoad*, and my nephew, Atti, telling the story of my life at the church."

I continued to resist, but she trotted out her joke again: "You know what the best thing about dying is, Tom?"

"Yeah, I have to do what you ask."

But in the end I didn't do what my friend requested. I wasn't allowed to. When she died, nothing was in writing, and those close to her—I'm not sure who, exactly—changed her plans. I suppose someone thought it was more fitting that Vicki be eulogized by one of the local bank presidents instead of the controversial editor of the *Undertoad*.

Out of respect for Vicki, I didn't go to her funeral. She would have loved that. After all, it was no longer her funeral. Instead Atticus and I walked on the beach at Plum Island that day. I never struggled with my decision to skip it, but I struggled to figure out just how I could pay tribute to her. It would take a while, but I finally got it. I'd remember Vicki by doing something "for the kids."

Each year WEEI, a sports radio station in Boston, stops talking sports for a couple of days and devotes that time to raising money for the Jimmy Fund and the Dana-Farber Cancer Institute. It is an inspirational forty-eight hours of radio as sports stars play bit parts to the real stars—kids with cancer.

Growing up in New England and being a fan of the Red Sox, I was well aware of the Jimmy Fund. Since the days of Ted Williams, Red Sox players have visited children fighting for their lives at Dana-Farber Cancer Institute. WEEI, which broadcasts the Red Sox games, understood that relationship, and it was a natural fit for them to run the radiothon.

Atticus and I were driving north to the mountains on a Friday afternoon as I listened. The stories I heard were remarkable. Cancer and kids—it's such a horrifying combination. Yet paying attention to those kids and the battles they fought inspired me. Many of the children interviewed had an unbelievable outlook on life.

We were somewhere around Plymouth on I-93, right where the mountains first start to rise, when WEEI's reception started to break up. That was frustrating, because I wanted to continue listening to these astonishing stories. I found myself wanting to help in some small way, and right about that time, I looked out as dusk was falling on the mountains. I had my answer.

After thinking about it for a few days, I called the Jimmy Fund and told them I wanted to raise money for them. The woman I spoke with was pleasant but a little confused when I told her I wanted to raise money by hiking with my dog. By the time I explained it to her, she liked the idea and thought it was one of the more unusual fund-raising efforts she'd ever heard of.

The idea of hiking in the mountains in Vicki's memory was a perfect fit, since one of her most memorable experiences was her three-day walk for cancer, where she pushed her limits. I decided that Atticus and I would push our limits, too, by doing something I'd never dreamed of—hiking each of the forty-eight four-thousand-foot mountains *twice* in the ninety days of winter . . . "for the kids."

7

The Greatest Quest

Icalled our fund-raising endeavor the "Winter Quest for a Cure" and announced it in the *Undertoad* and on the two hiking Web sites Views from the Top and Rocks on Top. We would attempt to hike all forty-eight four-thousand-footers twice in winter of 2006–2007—ninety-six peaks in ninety days. It had been done before, but only once.

Cath Goodwin is the most prolific winter hiker in the White Mountains. During the spring, summer, and fall, she runs a landscaping business. But when winter starts, the mountains are her business. In 1994–1995, Cath, along with two of her friends, Steve Martin and Cindy DiSanto, became the first to climb all forty-eight in one winter. She would go on to replicate that feat several more times, and in the winter of 2004–2005 she became the only known person to do two rounds in a single winter.

I knew that Atticus and I were facing a great challenge. Not only would it be a physical test for both of us, but due to Atticus's diminutive size, we'd be limited by the number of days we could hike. We'd have to take advantage of the better weather days for our hikes above tree line. While most hikers would think that hiking Mount Washington by itself on a winter day was quite an accomplishment, we planned to hike Washington and then continue on to Monroe, Eisenhower, and Pierce. While others would be content with hiking Lafayette and Lincoln above tree line, we'd add Flume and Liberty, two additional peaks along Franconia Ridge. Whenever we could, we'd string peaks together and force as many into a day as possible. There would even be days when we'd do more than one hike.

In preparation we made several longer hikes throughout the summer to build up our endurance. These would go from eighteen to twenty-four miles, and on one August day we even set out to do the challenging Pemi Loop. It's thirty-three and a half miles and crosses ten major summits in the Pemigewasset Wilderness. We started the hike at one in the morning, saw sunrise on Mount Liberty, our second peak of the day, and were moving well—until the eleven-mile mark, when I felt light-headed and feverish. I called friends on my cell phone and stopped our hike short, walking the four miles down to the road, where they were waiting to drive us back to our motel room. I slept for nearly twenty-four hours. I chalked it up to the first stages of the flu.

Over the next four months, that mysterious illness would come and go. The symptoms became worse and showed up more often as time wore on. There were debilitating headaches, blurred vision, stiff and swollen joints, and at times my hands felt like they were turning into arthritic claws; I was increasingly fatigued, and there were mornings when I'd get out of bed at 7:00 A.M. only to be back in it three hours later. There were days I could still hike, but not a lot of them, and when the symptoms arose on a couple of hikes, I pushed through the discomfort, eventually feeling okay. But in the following days, I paid the price with increased fatigue. I started to think that once again I was going to fail in my attempt to pay tribute to Vicki Pearson.

With December growing closer, it was clear I wasn't getting better. I was actually getting worse. And all the endurance Atticus and I had built up throughout the summer was gone. I suspected Lyme disease and had my blood tested. The test came back negative. But that's the thing about Lyme; it doesn't always show up in blood tests. With time running out, I found a doctor who specialized in treating people with Lyme disease based on symptoms and not blood-test results. He was my last hope.

He put me on a couple of medications and several vitamins and supplements. I began taking them just two weeks before winter started, crossed my fingers, and took a leap of faith that I would be okay.

I organized my life so that we could stay in the mountains throughout most of the winter. There would be days I'd have to return to write the *Undertoad*, but I also let my readers know I was shutting the paper down for the first month of the winter. A few local businesses made donations to help pay for our lodging, and Muttluks contributed six sets of dog boots for Atticus to wear. Dawn and Jeff Price, owners of Newburyport's the Natural Dog, donated three months' worth of their best food and treats for Atticus.

I created a blog to record our adventures, raise money for the Jimmy Fund and the Dana-Farber Cancer Institute, and let readers track our progress. Our fund-raising strategy was simple: People dedicated a peak in the name of someone they knew who was fighting cancer, had beaten it, or had died from it, and they sent in checks made out to the Jimmy Fund.

When the first day of winter arrived, Atticus and I were up north and ready to go, even if we weren't in great shape. I hoped the Lyme disease would cooperate and the medication would do its part. I also hoped we'd have enough money to pay for our entire winter.

Cath Goodwin heard about our quest on a hiking Web site and invited us to join a group of people she'd put together for a winter-solstice hike up Cannon Mountain. We accepted, and at the start of calendar winter, 7:22 P.M. on December 21, we were off and hiking.

It was dark and frigid, but everyone there was a winter enthusiast and in good spirits. I would like to report that Atticus and I did fine on that first short, steep climb of about two miles, but I'd only be telling half the truth. Atticus did fine, but I was exhausted. I couldn't keep up with the others, and on more than one occasion I fell breathlessly to my knees to rest. Nevertheless we made the summit, celebrated in the biting wind, and then headed down.

One of the joys of hiking Cannon at night is that we used the ski trails. This is not allowed during the day when people are skiing, but at night it was just us and the grooming machines. On the way down along the open slopes, we looked out at the lights twinkling throughout the valley below and the brilliant stars above, and I thought of my beloved Thoreau, who said, "Heaven is under our feet as well as over our heads." I knew we'd be seeing breathtaking beauty throughout the winter, and I looked at that first night under God's firmament and above mankind's as a perfect start for a journey that would have us walking between those two worlds for the next three months.

The following morning we met with another group of people for a ten-mile hike to Mount Carrigain. It was the same story: I couldn't keep up on the climb. I didn't know if it was the Lyme disease, my lack of conditioning, or a combination of the two, but Atticus stayed with me, as always, to make sure I was all right. Once we reached the summit and met up with the others, I felt better, and the downhill was easy.

On the third day, it rained. I'd never been so happy about a rainy day in the mountains before, and we took advantage of it by staying under the covers and sleeping most of the day away. We woke up on the morning of Christmas Eve and joined Cath Goodwin and Steve Martin for the short hike up Mount Tecumseh, and I felt better. After we finished, we wished them a Merry Christmas, said our good-byes, and drove back to our rented cabin. We ate lunch, I changed my clothes, and we got back into the car for the drive north to Mount Waumbek.

This was our first hike of what would be many where it was just Atticus and me, and when we arrived at the trailhead, I was so tired I didn't want to get out of the car. Atticus seemed happy to stay curled up in a ball on top of his fleece blanket as well. That was one of the problems we'd have hiking alone—there would be times throughout the winter when we wouldn't be motivated to go. Hiking with others would help, but it's something I didn't want to do all that often. Neither of the hikes, Tecumseh or Waumbek, is considered difficult. The elevation gain is not all that much, and the round trip to Tecumseh is only five miles, while the round-trip up Waumbek is about seven. But put them together on the same day and it was more than I was ready for—mentally or physically. After wrestling with myself and thinking about our goals for the winter, I eventually got out of the car.

It was a dismal afternoon, melancholy and gray, and I forced myself to walk. My pack was heavy, as were my legs. For the first of many times that winter, my mind played tricks on me, and I thought about how everyone I knew was gathering with family and friends to celebrate the holiday, and here we were alone in the barren, frozen woods the afternoon before Christmas. I walked along listlessly and sweated, swore, and prayed my way up the lower portion of the mountain. The enormity of our challenge was finally hitting me.

What could I possibly have been thinking? I don't belong in those mountains, and neither does Atticus.

But as soon as the thought entered my mind, I looked up at the little dog in front of me and saw him bouncing along. He looked so out of place, with his floppy ears, thin legs, and tiny bum swaying back and forth, that I laughed out loud. Atticus stopped and turned back with a stern look on his face to let me know that there was work to do. In his own way, he was going to pull me up that mountain.

Waumbek is a misunderstood place. Hikers often consider it one of their least favorite mountains because of its lack of views. But I've always felt differently about it. The worst of the elevation gain seems to come in the beginning, and as the trail climbs, the trees become thicker and wilder, the forest more tangled and mysterious. A mile before the summit of Waumbek, the trail crosses the top of Mount Starr King (3,907 feet), named after Thomas Starr King, the first writer to fall head over heels in love with the White Mountains. He was a poor man's Ralph Waldo Emerson, an American Unitarian minister who wrote romantically about nature. His book of purple prose, *The White Hills: Their Legends, Landscape, and Poetry*, written in 1859, drew tourists in flocks to the White Mountains.

The trail from Starr King to Waumbek is a hauntingly beautiful stretch.

Tree bark is draped with "old man's beard," a plant that gives trees an ancient feel, much like the South's Spanish moss. Covered in frost, it lends a ghostly appearance. The saddle between the two summits sits where the wind slices through and creates an eerie cry, and in its wake it has left a wreckage of dead trees. And yet among those that have toppled over, life springs from below where saplings now have room to grow. This is the part of Waumbek that captivates me. I'm forever enchanted by this mile-long passage that shows both the beginning and end of life in one scene.

On our climb that Christmas Eve day, it was a bleak-looking place, with mist drifting slowly through the saddle between the two peaks. Winds whispered and moaned, and the trees groaned. I pulled the zipper on my jacket all the way up to keep the cold and loneliness at bay. When we finally reached the summit, the wind fell silent and the clouds on the western horizon lifted just enough to let the sinking sun cast a golden light through the evergreens, and the mood of the forest was transformed. It was as if the mountain was welcoming us now that we'd passed the test of walking through our fatigue and was inviting us to sit down and relax. We did just that. I sat on a toppled tree, and Atticus sat on my lap. We shared chicken sausages and cheese. It wasn't quite the feast that friends back home were enjoying at their festive gatherings, but it was enough for us, and it filled our hungry bellies.

I looked at Atti's innocent face and took in our unlikely holiday sur-roundings. It was definitely not something out of Martha Stewart's world, and yet it seemed to me that we were right where we were supposed to be. Our adventure had started, and I could only imagine what lay before us.

I raised a small bottle of eggnog to my little friend and marked that very different Christmas Eve with a toast: "We're not in Kansas anymore, Toto." Indeed we weren't.

It was just the beginning of our quest, but it was already a very differ-ent life for the two of us. The Lyme disease had receded enough to allow us those two hikes. It then allowed us to hike to North and South Kins-man on Christmas Day, before sending me to bed for two days.

It wouldn't be long before Lyme disease was the least of our worries.

8

The Little Giant

We led a simple life, and our temporary living quarters reflected it. It was a tiny, one-room cabin in Lincoln at the southern end of Franconia Notch, with a fireplace, a bed, a chair, a table, a dresser, a television (rarely on), a microwave, a small refrigerator, and my laptop. The cabin was cluttered with hiking gear, food, Gatorade bottles, vitamins, and supplements. And books. For company I'd brought along some friends: Ralph Waldo Emerson, Henry David Thoreau, John Muir, Thomas Merton, Alfred Lord Tennyson, and Joseph Campbell. As is true with all friends, they were great company, but as can happen with those who spend much time around one another in close quarters, there can also be disagreements. In fact, I had an argument with Thoreau one day, although I'm certain he didn't hear me swear at him because I was face-down in the snow in the middle of the Pemigewasset Wilderness, eleven miles from the nearest road.

The point of contention was something he'd written: "A howling wilderness does not howl; it is the imagination of the traveler that does the howling."

In his defense, Thoreau was right for the first eight days of winter. For the most part, there was nothing to fear. Winter had been kind to us.

December hadn't felt all that wintry. There was little snow, more rain, and some ice, and apart from one bone-chilling day, the temperature was mild.

My Lyme disease was a bit moodier and had sent me to bed for a couple of days after Christmas. After that, I felt stronger than I had since the winter began, and we hiked the three peaks of the Willey Range (Tom, Field, and Willey) through six inches of fresh snow. The following day we climbed Garfield and stood atop the summit under crystal-clear skies at ten below zero with the wind stinging our faces. That was twenty-three miles in two days, clearly the best we'd done to that point. I was feeling healthier. It was a good thing, because I'd need all my strength for our third straight day of hiking.

In the winter some hikes are longer because the Forest Service closes various access roads. A traverse across Zealand Mountain and the three Bonds stretches from nineteen to twenty-three miles because of it. And because of the marathon distance and the exposure during the middle four miles of the hike, which is mostly above tree line, and the fact that there are no bailout options, it was the most audacious hike we'd under-take that winter. The only way off the Bonds, once you reached them, was to either turn around or go forward. It's for that reason that we saved them for a good day—one in which it wasn't storming and the wind was moderate at worst. That and the stunning views.

The day after hiking Garfield, it looked like just that kind of day. Not a perfect one, but good enough so that we could walk twenty-three miles south across the Pemigewasset Wilderness from Route 302 up north to a second car parked off the Kancamagus Highway in the south. That second car belonged to Tom Jones, a Newburyport friend.

Some would consider Tom a bad choice for a partner on a marathon hike. You see, he had very limited experience in the mountains. He'd hiked only a handful of times, and each of those was with Atticus and me. He had joined us three times during our first winter and twice dur-ing the second summer. But Tom had qualities that were more important to me than hiking experience. He was exceedingly loyal, humble, in great shape, and tough as nails, and, most important, as a friend to both

Atticus and me, he understood that every hike was centered on making sure Atticus was safe and comfortable. Little did we know upon entering the woods at five o'clock that morning that keeping him safe and comfortable would be more difficult than we could ever have imagined.

The forecast called for temperatures around thirty degrees, with a 30 to 50 percent chance of snow showers. The higher-summits forecast called for winds between thirty and fifty miles per hour, with the stronger gusts coming after sunset. But the higher-summits forecast originates from the observatory atop Mount Washington, and that is fifteen hundred feet higher than the Bonds, so it figured to be far less windy for us. By the time the winds picked up, I expected us to be finished with our hike.

We walked the first six miles, which have only the slightest elevation gain, in relative silence through the darkness. As we started our first and most difficult climb of the day, toward Zeacliff, we thought little of the small snowflakes drifting harmlessly down from the dark gray sky.

The higher we climbed, the more the snow fell. Still, it wasn't anything we hadn't been through before. It was easy going. When we reached the top of Zeacliff, the snow was falling more steadily and was a bit deeper. By this point Atticus instinctively got behind me to let me break the trail out for him. When we reached the summit of Zealand Mountain, the temperature had plummeted, and we shivered when we stopped to eat and drink, so I put Atticus's Muttluks and bodysuit on him.

One summit down, three to go.

The climb from Zealand toward Guyot, a neighbor of West Bond, is protected by trees until you get to the top. Our only problem was the footing, as it was on new snow that hadn't attached to the rocks yet—that and the temperature, which continued to drop. Just before gaining the top of the hill, we stopped again and geared up for the wind we were sure to find coming out of the northwest. We knew it would be right in our faces as we crested the first of Guyot's two bald knobs, but when we reached the highest point and stood naked to the elements, we weren't ready for what met us.

Like a giant wild beast come to life, the wind roared and flung snow at us. Tom and I yelled to each other, but our words were drowned out. We moved closer and yelled into each other's ears. I looked around to check on Atticus, but the little dog—who never had a problem turning back—pushed by me and marched into the storm. I wasn't sure whether we should go on or not, but he made the decision for us. Soon he was swimming forward, up to his neck, but he kept going. I told him to wait, and we walked in front of him, using our snowshoes to beat down the trail, but as soon as we'd take a step, the wind would fill it in again. Snow drifted knee- and hip-deep, and the powerful wind brought it to life. We struggled with each step and were rocked by gust after gust. There were moments when we couldn't move forward.

There was no time to think; we could only act. I looked to the woods off in the distance that lay between Guyot and West Bond and decided that our best bet was to make it there and then regroup.

Once we turned toward the south, the gales rushed at us from the side, and we had to twist our heads to keep our eyes from being stung by sideways-flying ice and snow. We were pushed off the trail and used our trekking poles to keep ourselves upright.

Atticus struggled but kept moving forward. Ice clung to his face, and at one point I dropped to my knees, held him close, and brushed the ice away from his eyes.

With deafening winds swirling about us and snow and ice pelting us, another dog would have wanted me to keep holding him, sheltering him from the elements. But when I turned away from Atticus for just a second, he pushed onward.

When we reached the trees, it was like escaping a battlefield by sitting in a bunker. We could hear the war raging above the trees, but we couldn't stay there. We had to keep moving to keep Atticus warm. We all shivered as we huddled together and saw that the deep snow had sucked off three of Atticus's Muttluks. There was no sense looking for them, they were gone. I took out an extra set and put them on him, and I fed him some ground beef. Tom and I put on new gloves, since ours were freezing into place, and changed hats for the same reason. We chugged down smoothies. (It's something I picked up from Cath Goodwin. On cold days it was the best way for me to "eat" so we didn't have to stop and risk Atticus's getting cold.)

Then it was time to see what West Bond had in store for us. Mercifully, we were given a reprieve. The half-mile-long spur path to the summit was protected by trees, so the wind couldn't reach us. To give our backs a break, we hung our packs from branches at the start of the path. It turned out to be an easy climb, and there was little wind on the summit. It was cold, but nothing at all compared to what we'd just survived. But by the time we returned to our packs, the shoulder straps were nearly frozen solid. We had to bend them back and forth to loosen them up before we could slide our arms through them.

The climb to Bond was a slow slog through ever-deepening snow. I had Atticus get into third position behind us, and we broke out the trail for him, but this time the wind was not filling it in. I figured that the summit of West Bond, behind our backs, was protecting us by breaking the wind. It was an uneventful grind, and we made pretty good time. On top we stopped and took photos of each other.

Three mountains down, one to go.

It was calmer than I expected, and I hoped the storm had finally abated and we'd be safe for our last mile across the exposed ridge to Bondcliff. After Bondcliff we would drop down into the trees and have a long but protected walk to the car.

But it was as if the storm had a mind of its own and was stalking us. We'd been lulled by the last mile and a half, and when we stepped onto the long, sloping trail and out of the protection of the trees, all hell broke loose. I signaled for Atticus to stay behind me, and in turning I was nearly blown over. Tom and I yelled back and forth to each other, but no matter what we said, it didn't matter. There was only the constant roar of the beast.

The snow was deeper, up to my waist at times, sometimes just to my knees. It was also slippery, and the teeth of our snowshoes had nothing to bite into, so Tom and I slipped and fell more than once as we descended into the col. I led, and on one steep downhill I caught my leg between two rocks, fell forward, and heard a loud snap. I slid downhill and lay facedown. Excruciating pain shot through my thigh.

I feared the worst and didn't dare move. We were eleven miles from the nearest road. The blizzard raged, and when I raised my head, I could barely see ten yards in front of me. I tried to stay calm, even though my leg was throbbing, and take inventory of my body, wondering if my femur had snapped.

Time stood still. Ice formed on my eyebrows and lashes. My cheeks burned red. I knew I couldn't stay there, but I didn't dare move at first. The wilderness had come to life. It howled, it roared!

Funny what you think about on the day you might die, for this was one of those times I'd read about and feared, when the weather turns and you're too far away and they don't find you until it's too late. That's when I thought about what Thoreau had said: "A howling wilderness does not howl; it is the imagination of the traveler that does the howling."

All I could think at that time was, *Fuck you, Henry. What do you know?*

I then thought about Atticus and Tom. I had to do something. When I tried to use the trekking pole to roll over, I realized it was broken. It dawned on me that that was the snap I'd heard, and not my leg. This was great news in one way, bad in another: I needed both poles for balance to fight through the storm, especially not knowing how seriously my leg was hurt.

I looked for Atticus. He was struggling through snowdrifts deeper than he was tall. Under his frozen mask, he was nearly unrecognizable when he finally reached me. He checked to see if I was okay by pushing his nose against my cheek. I sat up, and he climbed onto my lap and licked my face, believing that he could fix whatever I'd hurt. His body trembled, and I held him tight. It was then I realized that both my jacket and the fleece layers beneath it were freezing into place.

We had to keep moving.

I looked at Tom, who was on his knees frantically digging through the snow trying to find the bottom of my trekking pole, and I yelled, "Forget it, Tom! It's gone!" I could see the look of shock on his face. Poor bastard. He'd wanted to join us in the worst way, but neither of us had expected this.

As I looked at Atticus and Tom, something happened to me. Something took over. I swallowed my fear and stood with my one trekking pole and tested my leg. I was in pain but okay. Tom tells me my face changed then, became something he'd never seen before. It was like I was going to war and nothing was going to beat us.

We started walking toward Bondcliff again, and the storm was at its worst, as if sensing a kill. It tossed us about like three vessels in a roiling sea, but the only way out was through, and so we pressed on. The climb up Bondcliff was slow and agonizing. I led the way, followed by Tom and then Atticus. We took longer strides to try to make it out of the storm sooner but realized it wasn't working for Atticus, so we changed to baby steps to beat down the path for him.

The trail was invisible, and we pushed from cairn to cairn. At times I couldn't see the next one, and I did my best to remember where the trail went from our two previous hikes over the Bonds. We walked sideways, with our backs turned toward the beast, and cheered on the smallest member of our group.

Until the day I die, I will remember the sight of Atticus pushing through those drifts, sometimes pushing ahead of us before we could break trail for him. He surely wasn't the biggest dog, but on that day I have no doubt his heart was as big as any creature's on earth.

A couple of days later, I would receive an e-mail from Tom. He wrote, "I know you hear this all the time, but I am just so impressed with Atticus's conduct on the mountain. He had to be dragging, but you wouldn't know it, he just kept on coming, like a game prizefighter. I love thinking about how tough he is."

While we trudged forward, the clouds parted for a brief moment to give us a glimpse of yet another tough climb ahead, and I turned back to encourage Atticus, but the wind reached out and grabbed my voice in midair. And while the gust stole my words, it could not stop me from moving, nor could the whipping snow, but the sight of that little dog did just that. Watching him marching along, sometimes swimming forward, sometimes lunging against neck-deep drifts, I was amazed. The fury of the wind was silenced. The snow stood still in midflight. I could not move; I could only look on in admiration, awe, and above all else . . . love.

We regrouped one last time and then pushed toward the summit of Bondcliff. We had just as hard a time finding the cairns as we had during the previous couple of hours, and the wind reached new heights as if realizing it had to "get us" right then or lose us forever. Each step was labored, but eventually I touched the largest cairn at the summit. I turned toward the storm, and it nearly knocked me over. I let out my own howl, as fierce as any we had heard that day. I howled again and again until Tom and Atticus stood there with me.

We had only to walk another couple of hundred yards and drop down into the trees and we'd be safe. As soon as we did, the wind fell silent . . . as though someone had flipped a switch. An eerie calm presided over the mountains, as if the storm had existed only to test us. Night soon fell, and the clouds parted, and the moon and stars came out, and the forest was bright enough that we didn't need our headlamps. The three and a half miles that remained of the Bondcliff Trail were tedious, with a lot of ankle and knee twisting from navigating the soft powder over uneven rocks. Through that and the remaining six miles of the night, we walked on in single file: two men and a little dog. We moved through the night in silence, our minds and bodies numb. No words were needed. None could match what we had experienced that day—the day of our longest journey.

I'd told Steve Smith, whose store was just a few miles down the road from where we parked Tom's car, that we expected our trip to take no longer than eleven, maybe twelve hours. I told him to worry about us only if he didn't hear from me by nine o'clock that night. Finally, nearly sixteen hours after we started, we arrived at the car with our clothes literally frozen in place. It was just before nine.

I was right about Tom Jones. He was chosen for reasons that made sense only to us, and he proved to be invaluable. He was there that day to encourage Atticus through the tougher parts, give him a boost where it was needed, and take turns holding him during our breaks to keep him warm.

In the following days, I wrote about our trek across the Pemigewasset Wilderness on the hiking Web sites, and word of our epic trek spread throughout the hiking community. Other hikers we knew tried to get to the same mountains over the next couple of days but didn't make it, and they wondered how we had.

While Atticus and I spent a few days resting, the legend of the little dog in the mountains continued to grow. I received several e-mails from other hikers, and even more donations came in. One woman wrote, "I can hardly wait to meet you and the Little Giant someday!"

The Little Giant. I liked it.

The Little Giant acted as if nothing had changed. But I knew it had. We were both different, both entering a different place in our lives. Adventure will do that to you. We were growing, and we were growing together.

9

Stars to Light the Way

Something died in the blizzard on the Bonds that day—something within us.

In surviving, we'd passed an initiation and in the process had crossed over the threshold to our great adventure. There was no turning back. I felt different: stronger, calmer, and more confident. I no longer wondered whether or not we belonged in the mountains during the most dangerous season. It was clear we did.

But change, even change for the better, isn't always easy to take. As excited as I was about the adventures to come, I felt a touch of sadness, too. Newburyport had been a constant in my life. *It was my life*. It was the first place I knew to call home after years of gypsying around. My identity was tied to my journal, which was tied to the city. I not only wrote the *Undertoad*, I *was* the *'Toad*. But all that was slipping away from me. Newburyport and I were like lovers drifting apart.

I was no longer enamored of small-town politics. I wasn't looking forward to covering meetings in city hall, sitting down with the mayor, or revealing the questionable ethics of a greedy businessman. The petty squabbles, clashing egos, and tempests in all those teapots I made my living writing about were nothing compared to the tempest we'd survived. My priorities were shifting. It was as Walt Whitman wrote: "After you have exhausted what there is in business, politics, conviviality, love, and so on—have found that none of them finally satisfy, or permanently wear—what remains? Nature remains."

Nature remains.

As is usually the case, my heart knew it before my head figured it out. Perhaps I wasn't ready to let go, or maybe I was just afraid to. I held on to the security we knew back in our little city by the Merrimack River where everyone knew our names.

I reminded myself that our friends were in Newburyport, and we returned for a couple of days to touch base with them. It was good to see many of them and to get together for a meal or a cup of tea. One morning we met up with Tom Jones. He was nowhere near as invested in our quest as Atticus and I were, but there was something different in his eyes. I could see it, for the same glint was in my eyes. We sat together in a back booth at Fowles, as part of the three-member fraternity who'd survived the Bonds. Following breakfast, Tom was going off to his job and we were returning to the mountains. I sensed the yearning in his face and how badly he wanted to join us. Part of me wanted him to come with us. However, a bigger part knew that this journey belonged just to Atticus and me. Tom had been a welcome addition, but he was only a supporting actor in our story.

After breakfast we hugged good-bye, and Atticus and I drove the two hours to New Hampshire and hiked North and South Hancock. The sun was shining, the sky was delightfully blue, and there was no wind. We moved along the trails as easily as if there were wings on our feet. It was mild and comfortable, and it couldn't have been more different from the last time we'd hiked.

After the two Hancocks, we hiked Osceola and East Osceola the next day and Cabot the third. We were on pace to reach our goal, having climbed nineteen peaks in fifteen days.

It was only after those three days of hiking that I realized something else had died on the Bonds—my Lyme disease. Oh, I didn't think it was completely gone, but I no longer felt the constant nagging symptoms or the fatigue. It was just as well; we had much to accomplish, and the weather would not always be as favorable as it had been, so we needed to climb as many peaks as we could before the heavy snows of winter arrived.

My confidence was growing, and I decided to undertake one of the more daunting hikes on our list. After a day to rest, Atticus and I would drive east to Pinkham Notch and set out to traverse the three mountains of the Carter Range, drop down into and climb up out of Carter Notch, and then walk across the two four-thousand-footers on the Wildcat Range. Although not quite as long as the trip across the Bonds, it would be a more challenging hike, with far more elevation gain. And there would be a new test waiting for me. One I hadn't expected.

That's the thing about a great quest: You don't just pass a test and then go skipping happily off into the sunset. There are always more challenges to face. You get beyond Lyme disease and survive a blizzard in the wilderness, but something else lurks around the next corner.

Luckily for Atticus, I was the only one who was going to be challenged on the Carters and the 'Cats. It would be my test, not his, and it would come with the night.

We started our day with the help of a fellow who knew us from the hiking Web sites. I recognized Woody from his photo on Views from the Top. He was in a parking lot waiting to hike with friends, and I asked if he'd give us a car spot. He graciously followed us down to the base of Wildcat Mountain, where I dropped our car, and then gave us a lift back to the starting point. Atticus and I made our way up to Carter Ridge, and once there we climbed over Middle Carter, South Carter, and Carter Dome. That in itself is a full day, and during the previous winter it had exhausted us. But with daylight waning, we still had miles to go. We descended into the notch and climbed up the Wildcat Ridge Trail. Soon after we'd reached our fourth summit of the day, night descended on us.

I wouldn't say I was afraid of the dark. Not by any means. I slept without a night-light and could walk down any Newburyport street or stand on the beach at Plum Island late at night without a second thought, but you don't know darkness until you stand in the middle of a *forest* in the middle of the night, miles away from the closest soul. It gives an entirely new definition to the word "black." And while I'd hiked at night before, I usually did so when I had company, and the monsters that lurked in the dark recesses of my childhood stayed hidden. There was strength in numbers.

I pulled my headlamp out of my pack and was grateful to have two backups with me. But there's a problem with using a headlamp, especially when you're afraid of things that go bump in the night and are alone on a place like the Wildcat Ridge Trail, where the mountaintops are densely covered with evergreens tangled and mangled by the harsh winds. The headlamp casts its beam out into the night, but as soon as it catches a branch, it brings it to life. It reminded me of our first winter hike up Tecumseh, and it was just as frightening. The branches became clutching hands and swiping claws. And with thousands of those trees on the Wildcats, it felt like we were walking through a sea of the dead and they were reaching out to make us one of them.

It had been a long day, and in my weariness my imagination took over. I should have been happy having already checked four mountains off our list, but that dense, undulating stretch of trail toward that last peak of the day brought back my childhood fears. My throat grew tight; the slightest snag of a branch on my backpack had me spinning around expecting to come face-to-face with a witch or some unimaginably horrid creature. These were incredibly irrational imaginings for the editor and publisher of the *Undertoad*, who fearlessly took on the bullies every two weeks. But in that kind of fight I could see what faced us. In the mountains, in a forest, in the dark, there was nothing to see except shadows.

Oh, for some good companionship, warm conversation, silly jokes. It was the first time I wished we had someone with us. I tried to occupy myself with thoughts of days gone by, of women loved and women lost, of the simple yet joyous memories. I took inventory of the day and the winter, but I kept returning to wrestle with my loneliness.

I tried turning off my headlamp, but high clouds covered the hope of the stars and moon, and that only made things worse. When I turned it back on, Atticus was standing in front of me looking up as if wanting to know what was wrong. This was nothing to him, and the way his tiny pink tongue barely stuck out of his open mouth made it look like he was smiling.

"I'm okay, Little Bug," I told him. "Nothing to worry about." I said it hoping I would believe it.

He took off again, disappearing beyond the beam of my headlamp, swallowed up by the night. A minute later I saw him off in the distance, walking as calmly as if we were out for our nightly stroll along the Newburyport boardwalk.

No matter how much I tried to think of something to take my mind off the night and those clutching, hungry hands, I failed. They were everywhere, constantly swiping at me or grabbing at my hat or backpack.

I picked up the pace, but the faster I walked, the quicker those hands came at me: shadows darting, flailing, grasping, and closing in.

In the middle of a series of frightful gasps for breath, I closed my eyes against the night and spoke out loud. "Please, please . . . help me get through this." I wasn't sure who I was talking to.

That's when I saw Vicki. She was in her hospital bed, but she didn't look sick. Her hand gently stroked Atticus, who was lying next to her.

"I need some help," she said. "I'm planning my funeral." She said it with a little laugh, as if she were planning her own fiftieth birthday party, which is what she'd done the previous year.

Those days with Vicki in the hospital came back to me.

I thought of what she'd gone through, how life had ended just when it seemed as if it were beginning, and how she never complained about it. Death, like birth, was part of the package of life. She had come to peace with that. It was those of us who were left behind who struggled with it.

In contemplating my late friend, I remembered something Mark Twain had said that I'd used in a letter to my father about Vicki's last days: "Courage is resistance to fear, mastery of fear—not absence of fear." That was Vicki. I wanted it to be me as well.

I was suddenly ashamed of my childhood fears. With her in my heart, I walked on. My fear wasn't gone, but at least I was keeping it in its place.

I realized then that Atticus and I weren't really alone on that mountain. We had Vicki with us, and she'd brought reinforcements.

The main component of our fund-raising effort was accepting donations for the Jimmy Fund from people who dedicated specific mountains to loved ones who'd died of cancer, were fighting it, or had survived it. Whenever Atticus and I reached a summit, I'd say the name out loud, take a moment, and say a little prayer for that person, and then we'd move on.

In the midst of my despair on that blackest of nights, I thought of Vicki and all the peaks we'd climbed since the first night of winter. That got me through, and soon we were standing on top of our last peak of the day, our twenty-fourth of the winter.

Twenty-four mountains, twenty-four names.

There is *strength in numbers,* I thought again, and I said it out loud. "There *is* strength in numbers."

I picked up Atticus and held him as I do on every summit, and I spoke the name of the person the peak was dedicated to. I said a little prayer. We paused, and then I started from the beginning. I remembered each mountain and the particular person it was dedicated to. I said them aloud; I said them with the courage they all needed to fight cancer. I said them with love, the love they had for life and the love of those who supported them during their bleakest hours.

A few minutes later, Atticus and I stood high atop the ski trails on Wildcat Mountain. The skiers had been gone for hours and left the mountain for us. As we started our walk down I continued giving voice to those names. That became my mantra.

For the second time that winter, we were walking down a ski slope at night. Across Pinkham Notch, Mount Washington loomed in the darkness. The Abenaki called her Agiocochook, home of the Great Spirit. I could see her massive summit barely outlined and imagined her to be alive and breathing. A few minutes earlier I would have looked upon that incredible mass and felt frightened and vulnerable, being right out in the open as we were under her watchful gaze.

How strange we must have looked, these two unlikeliest of winter hikers, if Agiocochook were indeed watching us. We would have seemed as tiny as a couple of rabbits in comparison to the mountain we were on, and just as insignificant, but after an exhausting day we also would have looked stronger and bolder than she would have expected. She would have seen the Little Bug bouncing down the trail in the jaunty, carefree fashion that comes at the end of a hike, and for the first time in hours she would have seen that I was not walking in fear. Agiocochook would have heard those twenty-four names spoken again and again, almost like a song, and she would have been impressed to see me look right up at her and tip my frozen cap to her.

The journey across the Carters and the 'Cats was more than fifteen miles long, with six thousand feet of elevation gain—a truly rugged test. In the end, however, it didn't seem like that big a deal considering all those people we were walking for, the people who loved them, the battles fought, lost, and won, and what they'd been through. The night no longer seemed as dark, and it didn't scare me anymore. We had wonderful company with us as we marched toward our waiting car.

When I decided to undertake the cause of raising money for the Jimmy Fund and the Dana-Farber Cancer Institute that winter, I never realized the ramifications. I never realized we wouldn't be hiking alone anymore—that we would have company every step of the way, and there would be stars above us even on the darkest of nights.

10

The M. Is Important

It was never just Paige or my friends who looked at Atticus and realized there was something different about him. Strangers had always been drawn in by his looks but held captive by his personality even when he was only a small pup.

"What's his name?" they'd ask.

"Atticus. Atticus M. Finch," I'd reply.

There was often a gleam of recognition on their faces, and they'd say, "From *To Kill a Mockingbird*?"

People loved his name because they loved Harper Lee's main character, whether they'd read the book or watched Gregory Peck play the character in the movie. But there were also some who couldn't quite place the name, and their responses were interesting, even comical. I'd hear, "Hello, Attica," as if I'd named him after the prison, or "Hi, Abacus," as if I would name him after an adding machine. Some would remember it as a character from a book or a movie but get confused and say, "That was Russell Crowe in *Gladiator*, right?"

No matter what they heard or thought they heard, it fit. It was a name of distinction for a distinctive little dog. And yet as often as people responded to his name, they never asked about his middle initial. To me that was the most important part.

The M. was all-important. It was a life carried over, part gratitude, part tribute. The M., of course, was Max.

It was a reminder for me to do right by this little puppy, to raise him the right way. I'd see to it that he didn't have to go through what Max had: being passed from one person to the next like a hand-me-down piece of clothing. I always cringe when I see dogs being treated like they are a bracelet or a purse or some other object made to fit into someone's life. From the beginning it was important to me that Atticus was . . . well . . . *Atticus*. I wanted something more than just an accessory.

The M. helped. It wasn't that I wanted Atticus to be like Max; it was more as if I were looking for a little guidance from Max. Luckily, Atticus was different from the start, and I determined that my only job was to protect him, give him food, water, a place to stay, and a lot of love, then just get out of his way and let him be.

I sought guidance from Max in other ways, too. On our first day together, right after he arrived in Boston, I took eight-week-old Atticus down to Plum Island. We stood where the ocean met the land, and I kept him warm against the chill wind that spit snow at us.

Snow in late May? A fine introduction to New England for the tiny pup from Louisiana, but as it turned out, a fitting one for a dog who would learn to love the mountains in winter.

He was so tiny, so vulnerable. He weighed barely five pounds as we looked out at the vast ocean. And yet I think I was more nervous than he was. I wanted to do right by him, and that would be doing right by Max. After all, how do you thank someone for touching your life, even after that someone is gone? The best way I know is to take what he or she gave you and do your best with it.

That moment on the beach was a time for good-bye and hello. I took some of Max's ashes and threw them into the ocean. Then I took a bit more and gently rubbed them on Atticus: a small amount over his paws, forehead, spine, and heart, just enough to hope that Max would watch over him.

I was thinking of that day as Atticus led me up Mount Jackson through new snow and temperatures around ten below zero. Who would have thought way back then that that shivering little puppy would be climbing the winter Whites? Or that I would, for that matter?

I chose Jackson for a reason, as I chose every mountain. It was so brutally cold and windy that I wondered if Atticus would even get out of the car when we pulled in to Crawford Notch. But he did.

I wanted to get a peak in, but I didn't want to chance too much exposure. Jackson was perfect. It was only 2.6 miles from the car to the summit, and all but the last hundred yards or so was covered by trees and protected from the wind. We would be above tree line for only five minutes at most.

We made good time and passed several hikers on the way up. It was a Saturday, and it seemed as though everyone else had the same idea about Jackson as we did. Whenever we passed people, they'd be standing on the side of the trail trying to keep warm, but once they saw a little dog in Muttluks and bodysuit pass by, they turned their attention to him in amazement. A handful of hikers recognized him and wished us well, but for the most part, people were too cold to be all that sociable.

The fact that we were passing so many people showed how far we'd come in a month. And it wasn't until just below the summit that someone would pass us.

We stopped to put on my wind coat, thicker gloves, and face protection. I drank a smoothie and gave Atticus some treats. When he finished eating, he sat up in the crook of my elbow while I rubbed cream on his nose to keep it protected.

Two men approached from behind. They were fit and rugged and looked as if they'd climbed right out of a hiking catalog. They had quality gear and a seriousness of purpose in their eyes, and they moved with confidence.

Just before they pushed by, I nodded and yelled "Hello!" over the wind. The more rugged of the two, the one with the cleft chin, chiseled jaw, and thick mustache, stopped when he got a good look at Atticus and started to laugh. He spoke with a French-Canadian accent. "Your dog . . . he looks like he's in pajamas and slippers. He's ready for bed, I think."

His friend also laughed, and they said something in French to each other and then laughed even louder.

"What's so funny?" I asked.

The more rugged-looking one spoke again, "We both agree . . . your dog looks like he should be home on the couch eating bonbons." With that, they left us behind, and their laughter faded as they passed around the corner.

We saw them again only a few minutes later. They were standing where the stunted pine trees stop and the exposed rock begins, holding on to the trees with all their might as the wind lashed at their clothing and made it ripple and billow. They were yelling back and forth to each other, but I couldn't make out what they were saying. When I approached, they looked at me. Their eyes were wide. One of them shouted something to me. I couldn't tell which. By this time they both had on face protection. I put my hand against my ear to let them know I couldn't hear them.

"Too much wind! We're turning back!" As he said it, his eyes darted from mine to something below, and I saw his head move. He was watching Atticus push by them and advance toward the summit. Head down, legs bowed to lower his center of gravity, his size keeping him out of the worst of the wind. I hurried after him. Immediately the wind broke against my back like a great wave, and I was shoved forward. I fought to keep my balance and dropped my center of gravity just as he was doing.

Atticus ducked and weaved between rocks like he was avoiding sniper fire. He was determined to make it to the summit marker, a large stone cairn. Instinctively he sat behind it where the wind couldn't get to him. When I caught up, I held him in my lap. We huddled together just long enough to call out the name of the person to whom Jackson was dedicated, take inventory of ourselves, and for me to do something else

I'd done quietly on every other mountain. I removed my gloves, reached into my pocket, opened up a small plastic bag, and broke the wilderness rules of "leave no trace" by leaving something behind. It took only a second for me to empty the contents, but by the time I shoved the empty bag back into my pocket and put my gloves back on, my fingers burned red, stung by the cold.

I told Atticus, "Let's go home, Little Bug," and when we left the protection of the cairn, the wind slammed into me and stood me up. I wasn't able to take a step forward against the stronger gusts; I fought just to hold my ground. The wind tore at my clothes. Tears formed in my eyes, and the exposed flesh around them burned. I was struggling, but Atticus was fine. He ducked headfirst into the wind and moved like a little tank, wasting no time as he headed for the safety of the trees.

Thoreau wrote, "The savage in man is never quite eradicated." That's what I felt like in winds that registered somewhere between fifty and eighty miles per hour in subzero temperatures. The savage in me was unleashed, and for the second time that winter I let out a wild howl and thrust my arms up into the air. The wind shook me as if to shut me up, but I howled again.

Never in my life had I felt as invigorated or as wildly alive as I did at that moment.

We had been exposed for only a few minutes, but by the time we returned to the trees, tiny icicles had formed on my eyebrows and lashes. Another hiker who went up right behind us returned to the trees after his brief trip to the cairn, and his cheeks were frostbitten.

We regrouped. I warmed Atticus by holding him close, and he took care of me by licking the ice off my face. The wind roared above the treetops and circled again and again, but it couldn't get us anymore. We were safe.

We hurried down the mountain, thoughts of a hot lunch dancing in my head. For a change, Atticus fell in behind me at first. I stopped to make sure he was okay and saw him using his Muttluks to ski down the steeper parts of the trail. When he reached me, he passed by and then resorted to his regular casual trot, as if we were walking down State Street back in Newburyport.

We made it to the car just in time to see the two French Canadians speeding off. Something told me they wanted to get away before we returned. After all, what would they say about the little dog in the pajamas and slippers now? He'd reached the summit while they turned back.

There were so many reasons we hiked that winter. We hiked for "the kids" at the Jimmy Fund. We hiked for Vicki. We hiked for those who had mountains dedicated to them. And we hiked for the dog who'd paved the way for Atticus.

Dear Maxwell Garrison Gillis never knew the freedom Atticus had, saw as many beautiful sights, got to duck his head and charge into the wind on Jackson or behold the stark but beautiful loneliness of a mountaintop shrouded in snow and ice. Yet Max was with us on every hike, and it wasn't just in spirit. We had been on top of thirty-one peaks in thirty-one days, and a little bit of Max was sprinkled on each summit.

I wasn't sure why I hadn't thrown all his ashes into the ocean that day on the beach. Perhaps somewhere deep within, I knew there was a better place for Max. How I enjoyed knowing that whenever we'd return to any of the four-thousand-footers, Max would be waiting for us . . . along with all the other great spirits of the White Mountains.

11

"Our Faith Comes in Moments . . ."

Winter stretched on. Each day brought different tests for us, sometimes in the form of mileage or elevation gain—or both. Other days it would be the weather we had to contend with on a hike, or weather that didn't allow us to hike; those were the worst days of all. We were trying to cram ninety-six peaks into ninety days and stay safe while doing so. It was taxing both physically and mentally.

Each night we'd sit alone in front of the fireplace in our little cabin, expatriates from the world we were used to, isolated from friends who were far away and had a hard time relating to what we were doing. I'd write while Atticus slept next to me, curled into a little ball—more cat than dog—against my hip. I'd watch his body rise and fall with each breath, and I'd listen to his snores fill the cabin. No matter what we'd done that day, no matter how easy or rough a time we'd had of it, he slept as if he didn't have a care in the world.

Watching him like that, when we were alone, there were times I'd get choked up. It was humbling to see that little dog fearlessly lead me over ice and snow on mountains that most would never dare dream of climbing. And even I found it hard to believe that the little dog next to me so deep in slumber was actually doing all those amazing things. I considered myself lucky to have such a friend, but I was also lucky to have a front-row seat to witness something remarkable taking place.

As a boy who grew up enamored of the legends of the White Mountains, that winter I began to realize I was with a legend in the making.

I'd once read that the world's best marathoners keep their minds numb until they reach the twenty-mile mark. At that point they tune in for the last six miles of the race. That's the way I approached our winter: stay numb and get close enough to finish. That was my strategy by day as we busied ourselves making it up mountains. But when the sun went down and my mind grew as quiet as the night, I took time to register just what we were doing. That's when I would comprehend that we were creating the winter that would never end for us. It would live as long as my mind was healthy enough to hold on to it.

It's one of the reasons I enjoyed hiking alone with Atticus. I wanted to soak it all in without distraction so I would never forget it.

Whenever we hiked with others, the trip was filled with lively conversation and fun, but the wind, the trees, the streams, the mountain, and the entire magical sense of place took a backseat and became merely supporting characters. I wanted to hear what the mountain had to say, and when I talked with someone else, I didn't hear the wind, or the creaking of the trees, or the whispering mysteries of the hills that don't always get passed on by words, and I was left wanting.

That's what it was like when we joined eight others to get to the isolated summit of Owl's Head. In the summer it's an eighteen-mile round-trip. In winter it's closer to sixteen miles, because it's shortened by two bushwhacks that eliminate some of the stream crossings and sidestep the dangerous Owl's Head slide. We went with a fun-loving group, and there were plenty of jokes and laughter from beginning to end. And it's a good thing we joined them, or Atticus and I wouldn't have been able to reach the summit that day, for there was snow to break through and all those snowshoes to beat down the trail for Atticus. (In the previous winter, when it was only Atticus and me, it took us three hours to climb just the last mile up Owl's Head, so I was more than happy to have help.)

But our success in reaching the summit came at a cost. Because of all the people and the noise, instead of feeling as if we were hiking with a purpose and for a purpose, I felt as if we were in the middle of a roving cocktail party. By day's end I hadn't given Vicki or the cancer survivor Owl's Head was dedicated to as much thought as I normally would have, or even the mountain itself. It had simply become a checkmark on a list. I hated that.

The next morning we slept late. We were finally on the trail to North and South Hancock at twelve-thirty in the afternoon, and during the first two miles we encountered several people who were finishing for the day. Some suggested we turn back because it was too late to start out. One fellow posted the following on a hiking Web site: "Ran into Tom & Atticus getting a late start. I hope his headlamp battery holds out."

I knew there was a good chance we'd finish after dark, but I didn't care. We had a mountain to ourselves. It was refreshing to be alone again. Surrounded by the tranquillity of the forest, I didn't care if it took us all night.

The Hancocks were the first mountains we repeated that winter. We'd worked so hard the day before, and even though it was a ten-mile hike, it was perfect for us, because they are relatively easy to get to. (How funny to think that the man who used to lose his breath walking the block from the newsstand to his apartment thought that a ten-mile hike in January was relatively easy, but it was evidence of just how much our lives had changed.) Most of the route was flat. Then there was a notoriously steep half-mile section leading to the top of the northern peak. A stairway to heaven, if you will. In previous hikes on the Hancocks, I'd come to know that slow, painful climb as the place where I paid for my Ben & Jerry sins. I'd take twenty steps, stop, hang over my trekking poles, gasp for air, let the sweat run down my face, and swear off junk food forever. Another twenty steps and I'd repeat my penance. It was like saying the Rosary—but with a lot more cursing. Each time I'd stop and hang over my poles, I'd look up and see Atticus standing above me with a stern expression on his face—half wanting to make sure I was okay, half wanting to know what was taking so long.

That first climb of the day, of any day, was always the worst part. My body was not made for going uphill. I was too heavy. And yet it was often during those moments of oxygen debt, when I was forced to stop and just breathe, that I'd hear nothing but my own breath, the beating of my heart, and the forest. In winter, on a windless day, the forest is silent, and that minute of duress turns into a halcyon moment. That's when the world comes around. It's where clarity is found. It's times like that when I find my kinship with Thoreau and Emerson, Einstein and Wordsworth. It's when their words come to me like a prayer.

That's how I've always struggled up a mountain. It didn't matter whether it was Garfield on that first September hike or the Hancocks—I struggled on every climb. Aches, pains, and breathless panting begat epiphanies. Emerson wrote, "Our faith comes in moments; our vice is habitual." That most painful part of every trip was where I found my religion.

As for my religion, it was a free-form faith, meaning I picked and chose what worked for me. However, that didn't always work for other people.

A woman I knew in Newburyport—who used to be a good Catholic but became a good Congregationalist, until the church decided to become "open and affirming" to gays and lesbians, so she became a good Baptist—once asked, "In your 'Letters Home' to your dad, you mention God a lot, but you don't go to church."

"That's right."

"So what religion are you?"

"I don't have one."

"You have to have a religion if you believe in God. If you had to choose a religion, which one would it be?"

"I wouldn't choose. Who needs the middleman? I believe in God, isn't that enough?"

"But say God came to you and said, 'You have to choose a religion,' which one would you choose?"

"I don't think God would do that."

"But just say He did."

"Okay, if I had to classify myself as one thing, I'd say I was a pantheist."

The woman gave me a disgusted look and stalked away. A couple of days later I ran into her boyfriend, and he wanted to know why I'd been so rude to her.

"Huh?"

"When Susan asked you what religion you'd choose, you said you'd worship panties."

I had to explain that pantheism was a belief that God was in nature.

That's what the mountains were to me. They were my religion—the only one I wanted—and I found it in my struggles when I was literally forced by my exhaustion to stop moving and look at my surroundings. When your body is like that, so worn down that there's no distraction other than your own breath and heartbeat, you feel everything. You feel part of everything.

When I reached the summit of North Hancock, Atticus wasn't waiting for me. But I knew where he was. I pushed to the left through the snowy pines and saw him sitting on the ledge. It was a fine day, warm and calm, and he sat the way he did in the summer months, a little Buddha looking out at the Osceolas, watching the late-afternoon sun paint them a golden yellow. I regarded him for a while, not wanting to interrupt.

I watched that little dog sitting placidly on a mountaintop in winter, miles away from the life we'd come to know, as if it were the most natural thing in the world to be doing, and that's when it struck me: Our quest was about so much more than reaching ninety-six mountains or raising money for a good cause. It was about us and what we shared and saw together and what we were becoming. It was one of those moments when you realize that this is truly the time of your life.

Eventually Atticus turned his head and looked in my direction. Our eyes met, and I saw that gentle, invincible calm he enjoyed on mountaintops. I hadn't seen it the day before, or on any of the hikes we'd done with other people. It was something we shared when we weren't in a hurry and, more often than not, when it was just the two of us.

Atticus continued looking at me without moving a muscle until I walked over and sat next to him. He gently leaned in on me. We were no longer looking at each other but out at that breathtaking view. And time disappeared.

A couple of days before that, I was moved when I read something Thomas Merton had said in a talk he gave: "The deepest level of communication is not communication, but communion. It is wordless, it is beyond words, and it is beyond speech, and it is beyond concept. Not that we discover a new unity. We discover an older unity. . . . We are already one. But we imagine that we are not. And what we have to recover is our original unity. What we have to be is what we are."

When Atticus and I hiked, that's exactly what we shared. It was a communion between man and beast that didn't differentiate between either. More important, it was a communion between two friends.

Owl's Head had wrung us out and left us weary and parched. We were both tired when we started out that afternoon, but the woods and sitting together on the ledge renewed us.

After leaving the north peak, we reached South Hancock and headed for home. During the last few miles, we bounced along the trail in high spirits and enjoyed lighthearted interchanges. We were but a boy and a dog at play with each other. As the day was waning, I looked up to see the bruise-colored Osceolas as we left the forest. We made it out before sunset, even with the time spent summit sitting.

I believe that each mountain has lessons to teach, stories to tell, and on that simple Sunday afternoon I was reminded again of the good company I keep and of how grand it feels to be swallowed whole in the woods.

That day was the turning point of our winter. It had been just the two of us on most of our hikes, but from that moment on I'd be even more careful about keeping it that way. We'd hike with others on occasion, but they would be select company, for our days in the mountains really were the times of our lives.

12

Atticus in Disguise

Along with announcing our Winter Quest for a Cure in the *Undertoad* and on the two hiking Web sites, I had started a blog. I updated it daily and occasionally would post a trip report on the hiking sites. We had a small but loyal following of readers.

Yet with winter halfway over, our little journey took on a more public face.

When Atticus and I reached the aptly named Mount Isolation in wind chills registering thirty below zero during a fourteen-mile hike while everyone else was home watching the Super Bowl, my readers in New-buryport became more captivated than ever by the Little Giant. Our blog became a popular read, and that brought more donations for the Jimmy Fund.

New Hampshire newspapers also took notice of our fund-raising efforts, and we were featured in lengthy articles. Soon I was receiving e-mails and Atticus was receiving fan mail and care packages of various treats. Unfortunately, his celebrity status extended to the trails as well. I say "his" because I could blend in easily enough, but he couldn't. Most people in the mountains recognized me only because Atticus was with me, and there was no disguising his look. On weekends, when the trails were busier, hikers saw him and wanted to stop and talk. We received numerous invitations to join people on future hikes. A woman e-mailed and said, "I don't hike, but how about the three of us go out for coffee sometime. Love to get to know you. I'm single, by the way."

We'd come full circle. We left Newburyport behind that first summer, in part because I reveled in the anonymity of the woods. The mountains offered us privacy and peace and quiet. But the peace we'd just reclaimed on the Hancocks was being threatened. It's not that I was a misanthrope—anyone in Newburyport could attest to the fact that I was out and about and constantly in conversation with people. It's just that in the mountains we led a different life.

New Hampshire had become our sanctuary, a wonderful escape from a hectic existence. I wasn't sure how I felt about losing that.

On a hike to Mount Moriah, we had another late start and ran into five different groups of hikers on their way down the mountain. Four of the groups recognized Atticus and asked if they could have their photos taken with him. They were thrilled to meet him, but for Atticus, who'd grown up thinking that everyone knew his name, it was par for the course. He enjoyed saying hello but was just as happy to move beyond his admirers after he received a few pats, even if they were still fawning over him and wanted him to linger awhile longer. I was pleasant to them but was also happy to get going. The last group we encountered told us to be careful, because they didn't think there was anyone else behind them and we'd be all alone.

Be careful? I thought. *This is what we love the most!*

The prospect of solitude thrilled me.

About a mile from the summit, while walking in peaceful reverie along the spectacular ledges of the Carter-Moriah Trail, with views over the western hills of Maine, we soaked in the warmth of the day. We were feeling as strong and peaceful as we'd ever felt on a trip. I fell into a walking meditation of prayers, thoughts, and gratitude. It was so quiet, so still, so blissfully peaceful.

Suddenly, out of nowhere, a man coming in the opposite direction on the trail burst from the woods and startled both of us. We didn't see him, we heard him. He literally gasped when he saw Atticus, lifted up his hands in surprise, and said, "OH. MY. GOD! . . . It's him! It's really him!"

He stopped and stared, his mouth agape. I'm sure mine was, too.

Before I could say hello, he spoke again. "My friends are going to be *so* upset they decided not to come today! Ha! They will be *sooo* jealous!" He fumbled with his camera case and quickly yanked out his Nikon for a picture. I got the sense he was talking to himself more than to me, because he wasn't looking at me when he spoke. "We were talking about Atticus just last night at dinner!" he said, aiming the camera at Atticus.

I'm not sure what made me do it—perhaps it was because he was loud and obnoxious and had pierced the serenity with his shrieks—but I said, "What did you call him?"

Maybe I just longed to be private again.

"Atticus! I'd recognize him anywhere!" he said. And he chattered just like that: fast and loud, with every sentence ending in an exclamation point.

"I think you're mistaken," I said. "This is Sparky."

Panic came to his face, and he dropped his camera to his side. "But aren't you Tom of Tom and Atticus?"

"Nope. I'm Mike."

"Are you sure? He looks just like Atticus," he insisted, cocking his eyebrow with a bit of suspicion. "Aren't you guys hiking them all twice this winter or something crazy like that?"

"Sorry, you've got the wrong guys."

He was crestfallen. He dejectedly put his camera back into its case.

"What's the big deal about this Attica anyway?" I asked.

"It's Atti-*CUS*! He is famous—very famous!"

"What . . . did he rescue someone or something—kind of like Lassie when Timmy fell down the well?"

"No, but trust me, he's famous!"

"But what's he famous for?" I prodded.

"Lots of things!"

"Like what kinds of things?"

"Listen, it's hard to explain—he's just a remarkable dog! He does a lot of neat things!"

And with that, he gave me a look as if *we'd* interrupted *his* peaceful hike and left us behind without even a good-bye to Mike or Sparky.

I'm not sure what Atticus was thinking when I said, "Onward, by all means, Sparky."

When I told a couple of friends about the encounter, they were disappointed in me. They said I'd played a cruel joke on that hiker. I didn't really feel that way, but maybe they were right. Maybe I should have felt a bit guilty, but I wasn't ready to give up our privacy quite yet.

That trip to Moriah was one in a stretch where we hiked four days in a row. It was the first time we'd ever done that. We were peaking at the right time. I moved with ease and felt light and nimble. Atticus had a constant bounce in his step. Our spirits were bright. It was as if we couldn't get tired. Hikes took less time than they'd ever taken us, even in the summer months. My Lyme disease was but a memory. Life was good.

We'd climbed forty-nine mountains. In order to reach our goal we'd have to hike forty-seven peaks in thirty-nine days. We were well within reach.

Unfortunately for us, the snows of winter were about to arrive.

13

The Spell of Agiocochook

My father always had a difficult time being happy. He was witty and charming in public, with the cashiers at the local pharmacy or supermarket, or with the people at town hall, but alone it was a different story. He was hard on himself and critical of his children. He was good at many things, but intimacy wasn't one of them. What he and I had shared that first summer Atticus and I were in the mountains was as close as we would ever get. But when Atticus and I returned to hike them our first winter, my dad built a wall between us. He was back to being distant, to pushing me away, and to at times acting belittling.

I didn't understand it, but my friend Ed Metcalf did. He was from my father's generation and offered me the following perspective: "Your dad was thrilled when you hiked the mountains in summer because he could see himself doing them. Lots of people do them. But in winter you were going someplace he couldn't go. He couldn't see himself doing that. You were overshadowing him."

I knew Ed was right—I just didn't want him to be.

Toward the end of our first winter, when it was clear we weren't going to finish all forty-eight, I was disappointed and called my father to let him know.

"I didn't think you could do it," he'd said. The words were not tinged with emotion; they were flat and matter-of-fact, but some arrows don't need to be dipped in poison to kill.

There was only one way to love him, and that was through a buffer. That's why when I visited him in spring or summer, it was during a Red Sox game. Or during a Patriots game in football season. He felt comfortable conversing for half an hour before or after a game and was happy that one of his children had come for a visit—provided we didn't stick around too long when the game ended or talk too much during it.

Another buffer was the *Undertoad*. He enjoyed getting every issue, even though he often went to great lengths to point out the misspelled words and would count the ads to see how I was doing financially. He would never admit to it, but he was proud of me.

There was a time he'd wanted to be a newspaperman, and he went through his life as a frustrated writer. His eloquent letters to the editor, which were often the highlight of the local newspaper, were the closest he came to being published.

When Atticus and I began our Winter Quest for a Cure, my father and I hadn't talked for months. Our last conversation had taken place right around the time I let him know our goal of ninety-six peaks in ninety days. But I wrote to him, every two weeks. He liked getting letters. As he grew older, the only personal mail he received was from his daughter-in-law, Yvette, who wrote wonderful, flowing letters, and from me.

He was a voracious reader, often going through three or four library books a week. He loved the fast pace of mysteries, but when he was younger, he'd read the classics. With his typically heavy-handed approach, he'd tried to force *us* to read when we were young, but I was willful and fought it. There was something about words that lit a fire in me, but to read would have been giving in to him. You see, the son could be just as obstinate as the father. When I finally moved away from home, I allowed myself to enter the worlds of Emerson and Thoreau and Tennyson and Frost. Those names were familiar to me, for they were men my father admired, and he'd read their masterpieces.

Life is funny. I set out to be nothing like the man I both loved and disliked, but I ended up becoming a newspaperman, reading the same authors he admired, becoming a big political fish in a little pond, and even climbing his mountains. Somewhere in my efforts to get as far away from my father as possible, I had adopted his dreams as my own. I had become his son.

My letters home were our bridge. They kept us connected, even when we weren't talking. When the Valentine's Day nor'easter came and Atticus and I sought shelter back in Newburyport, I wrote to my dad about the mountain gods of New Hampshire. I suggested they were not unlike their counterparts from Greek mythology. They amused themselves by toying with mortals. And boy, how they toyed with Atticus and me.

First there was the Lyme disease to slow us down. Then, on our first trip above tree line, they conjured up a blizzard over the Bonds. We snuck by them on Jackson as they delivered frigid temperatures and winds strong enough to keep others away. And once we finally hit our stride and were moving through the wilderness as I had hoped we would when I'd first made our plans, they brought forth the biggest storm of the winter.

From the third floor of the Grand Army Building in Newburyport, we watched helplessly as winter ticked away. There was no sense going north; the snow was too deep for a little dog to get through. So we waited. And we waited. We ended up waiting eight days, and our quest was beginning to seem hopeless. I was not ready to concede. But the harsh truth was that there were only thirty-one days left, we still had forty-seven peaks to climb, and among them were all of the highest, most exposed, and most dangerous mountains. And we had to do them twice.

Time might not have been on our side, but I had faith, and I figured that had to be worth something. Besides, the gods had their benevolent side, too. Joseph Campbell, the mythologist, pointed this out: "I have found that you have only to take that one step toward the gods, and they will then take ten steps toward you. That step, the heroic first step of the journey, is out of, or over the edge of, your boundaries, and it often must be taken before you know that you will."

A leap of faith.

Our winter had been a series of leaps of faith, and we leaped once again by not giving up. I hoped the winds would die down for the first time that winter. Our faith was rewarded.

We began a remarkable stretch in which we hiked six of the next nine days—but they weren't just any hikes. They were over many of the most rugged mountains in the Whites. We did both Osceolas one day, then the four mountains of Franconia Ridge. We took the next day off to rest and the following day off because it was too cold and windy to bring Atticus out. On the next day we did the two Twins and Galehead. Then came the great Northern Presidentials: the second-, third-, and fifth-highest mountains (Adams, Jefferson, and Madison). After finishing the Bonds in December, we had only to reach those three to become the rare man and even rarer dog to climb all forty-eight in winter by combining them with what we'd done the previous winter.

It took two months, but we finally had the right weather. On top of Jefferson, I held Atticus above my head to celebrate the feat. Other dogs might have squirmed uncomfortably when lifted so high, but in typical Atticus fashion he took advantage of his seat on the crow's nest, slowly turning his head from one side to the other to take in the sweeping views. And, of course, each time we reached a summit and he sat up in my right arm, I thought of Paige: *Carry him wherever you go. . . .*"

It was a joyous moment. When we'd started out, the only dog that had ever done them all in winter was Brutus, the 160-pound Newfoundland. And now 20-pound Atticus had done the same thing.

The very next day, perhaps the nicest day of the entire winter, we were robbed of a hike above tree line when a New Hampshire television station set up an interview with us but canceled at the last minute. I didn't want to miss a day of hiking, but friends had convinced me that the exposure from the television piece would help with raising money for the Jimmy Fund. We were behind schedule, and we'd lost a perfect day above tree line. I hoped it wouldn't hurt us.

The following day the winds returned in earnest and it was cold again.

The Mount Washington Observatory called for winds between twenty and twenty-five miles per hour and temperatures in the single digits. That was good enough for us—barely—and we headed for the summit of Mount Washington, the home of Agiocochook, the Great Spirit.

It was a surreal, windswept day. We had climbed the highest peak in the Northeast, and the plan was to continue on to Monroe, Eisenhower, and Pierce in a fourteen-mile hike.

The clouds were different, even for up there at the top of New England, where weather is fierce. There was something ethereal about them. Some were like ghosts, rising like steam from the ravines below. Others were thick and white, flying rapidly by overhead, blocking out the sun for seconds or minutes at a time, but not all of the blue sky, and casting fast-moving shadows over the snow. Those clouds were an ideal fit for the day, for it had a different texture to it as well. It was charged with a palpable energy, both haunting and mysterious. It felt the way all beginnings and all endings do when they sneak up on you and the earth beneath your feet shifts and you tumble out of control, your life taking an unexpected and quite different course.

Atticus was ahead of me. With a wind chill of twenty below zero, he had his Muttluks and bodysuit on, and he ducked into the gusts as they came, his ears taking flight, his little body bold and steadfast. We were descending Washington's massive dome and headed for Monroe. The trail was packed down by the wind, and the snow was as hard as the rocks it hid. Atticus walked on top of it easily, his boots slapping with each step. My snowshoes grabbed hold, their teeth biting into the crust. The mountainside, a craggy mess of tumbled dark and unforgiving rocks in fairer seasons, was now mostly flat and washed white with an occasional black shard jutting up.

I followed Atticus, and he followed the cairns. They lined the trail like corpses of soldiers who had fallen in an ancient battle and were frozen in place for all time in a harsh and desolate landscape. They were there to show the way on the worst days, when the clouds hang heavily on the mountain and visibility drops to nothing. They wore coats of rime ice on the windward side and were naked on their leeward side. If it weren't for these markers, it would be difficult to know where the trail went, for the winds that scour the mountain obliterate all signs of coming and going.

I will never understand how Atticus knew to follow the cairns, but it's something he'd done from the start. He always seemed to know where the path went, no matter the season, no matter the mountain, even on a day like that on Washington when the trail was covered in snow and ice.

Those otherworldly clouds came and went, revealing and then stealing away views that left me breathless. At that elevation the whole world looked as if it were below us. I stopped often to snap photos, fumbling to take off my gloves so I could better handle the camera, then quickly put them back on before my hands stung and went numb. With each stop I could feel the cold catching up to me; the sweat running down my back beneath all those layers caused me to shiver. My head was covered by a balaclava, and sunglasses protected my eyes from the wind, but it wasn't enough to keep small icicles from forming on my eyelashes and eyebrows.

Coming off the top of the mountain, the path jogged to the right toward Jefferson, Adams, and Madison. The three peaks had been hidden by the clouds, but when the curtains parted, it was like encountering three giant beasts face-to-face, and I was stunned by their presence.

Atticus kept his head low, protecting his eyes from the wind as he swaggered on. I was a constant twenty yards behind, just as I'd been all winter. You'd think I would have grown used to it after more than sixty mountains, but I still watched in astonishment as my little friend marched along, undaunted, as if it were his duty to be up there getting me to where I needed to go.

This was a rare day in that we hadn't seen another hiker the entire time we were on Washington, and it made the trek all the more unearthly.

In front of us, the clouds lifted again, and the string of mountains came into focus, then were quickly veiled again.

We came to a segment of trail where it looked as if the mountain ended abruptly and there was a dangerous, unseen chasm to cross before getting from this world to the one that held those peaks we wanted to reach. It was one of those mountain moments when angles play tricks on the eyes, moments that often frightened me but never seemed to faze Atticus. While I hesitated, he showed faith—or maybe it was just his ability to know these mountains as if he'd lived in them his entire life—and he moved forward. In an instant he disappeared over the edge. I panicked and hurried forward, only to see that he had not fallen off the end of the world but had just descended a steep set of rocks and was now in sight again, moving nonchalantly.

As I walked in the mountains that winter with only Atticus and my thoughts for company, my mind often wandered. At that moment I thought about death. I wondered what it would be like—not the day, but the moment of death itself. Would I be walking toward the *light*? Would there be angels and music playing, or would it be too horrifying and devastating to bear?

I wondered.

I hoped it would be a day like that day, with stark, stunning beauty all around. The music of the wind, blue skies masked briefly by lively clouds in a hurry to get somewhere, the top of the world, a world at its end engulfed by sweet peacefulness, me enjoying an almost perverse pleasure in being separated from everything and everyone I'd ever known, the excitement of being someplace I never could have imagined in my dreams, the gentle thrill that this might be heaven.

That's what it was like on Washington. We had both died and found ourselves on another plane. There was no one in sight, no sign of life whatsoever. No buildings, no streets, cities, no sign of civilization. It was just two travelers, two faithful friends walking down the spine of a mountain range in a world where wind and clouds lived but nothing else did.

Watching Atticus in those conditions inspired me. He would often be the inspiration I needed during our winter treks, but never more so than on Washington. In snow and ice and wind, on a mountain that had killed so many, I drew strength watching him in an environment that would have unnerved me in the past. If he could be up there, as out of place as one could imagine, then I could, too. If he could trot forward, marching down this steep mountain, then why couldn't I?

At one point, moving steadily along, Atticus did a most unusual thing. He stopped and waited for me.

He had stopped and waited for me to go first on rare occasions throughout the winter, but usually it was when we came to a stream that was running wild and he knew he had to be carried over it, or if the stream looked frozen but wasn't, or because a downward section of mountain was icy and he wanted me to lead the way. Whenever he did that, he would step to the side and let me go first, all the while continuing to look forward, nervously flicking his tongue. But where he had stopped that day there was no running stream and the trail was not all that challenging. The wind was steady, but not so strong as to deter him. He showed no signs of anxiety. I got ready to move in front of him nevertheless. However, he didn't move to the side. Instead he turned and sat looking straight back at me. This was a most unusual sign in a winter where we had spent many days in wordless communion.

When I reached him, he stood up on his hind legs and placed his front paws on my thighs. He wanted to be picked up. As I did so, I cradled him in my arm, the way I always do, and I looked over at his face. He regarded me for a moment and then turned his gaze in the direction we were headed. We always did this on mountaintops, but it was out of the ordinary for it to be happening in the middle of a frosted wasteland.

There we stood, partway down the cone of Washington, still high above the other mountains we would climb as they came into view and then disappeared again behind gauzy, fast-flying clouds. I watched Atticus curiously while he stared off into the distance. He was calm and relaxed. After a moment my eyes followed his. For the first time that day, all the clouds shifted and completely lifted out of the way, revealing a vibrant blue sky that stretched over the mountains, which were now a brilliant white, glowing under the sun.

It was so stunningly astonishing, so striking, I was speechless. It was so beyond definition or description that my heart ached and tears welled up in my eyes. Man and dog, connected in adventure and solitude, stood together, gazing out at a world few had ever seen before.

Something changed when those clouds lifted. Not "out there," but inside us. Our lives would never be the same again. I'm not sure how, but I knew it. At that place, at that time, under the spell of Agiocochook, I understood that there would be no going back to what we used to know, not now that we had shared a winter's worth of success and hardship together. Not ever.

There are some things in life too powerful, too vivid, too life-altering to possibly leave them behind. They stay with you forever. They shape you from that moment on. We'd come to such a time and place. Atticus and I had reached it together, and the bond forged was truer than any I'd ever known. We had gathered a lifetime of experiences across all those mountains; there could be no returning to share them with others. No one would understand, no one *could* understand. This was our bond to share, our gift. But it was also a curse of sorts, *because* we would never be able to completely share it with anyone else.

We stood there together, two friends gazing out toward that sea of mountains, watching them fold one behind the other, until our eyes reached the horizon.

In retrospect, I now realize we were not just looking at the mountains, but toward all our unimagined tomorrows. We had arrived at unknown territory, and as frightening as it was, it somehow felt right, for we were there together.

When I put Atticus down, he started walking again as if nothing had happened, and I followed. I knew we were headed for the three mountains closest to us, but I had no idea where we were going after that. I'm not sure how, but it was as if he knew what was to come. It was a lot like that moment at the ledge earlier in the hike when he disappeared out of sight and I panicked and hurried to see what had become of him. He had faith when I didn't. Faith had never been my strong point, but he was determined to help me with that.

The only hikers we would see that day were a pair on the summit of Eisenhower who had come up from Crawford Notch. They were bundled under many layers, and one of them was clearly exhausted. The other stood at the summit and watched us coming from the opposite direction. His friend was breathing heavily and sat on the rocks. They looked at Atticus and me, and the one who wasn't out of breath yelled over the wind, "Where did you come from?"

I pointed to Washington. "We hit Washington first, then Monroe!"

"Where you headed?" he yelled.

"Pierce!"

Both of them kept staring at Atticus in his little bodysuit.

I asked if his friend was okay and was told it was his first hike.

"I'm impressed. Your first hike is a winter hike."

But he didn't look impressed with himself. He looked like he wanted to throw up.

The fellow who was standing spoke again, "That little dog climbed Washington?"

"Yep!"

"He's something!"

"Yeah, he is! When we reach Pierce, he'll have hiked each of the forty-eight this winter!"

Their eyes opened wide. The one who was sitting down and breathing heavily looked like he needed to lie down.

His friend said, "You've climbed forty-seven mountains this winter? That's amazing!"

"Actually," I said, "Pierce will be sixty-five this winter! We're hoping to do two rounds!"

The talkative one laughed and asked if he could take a picture of Atticus for his wife. His friend didn't say anything. I think he passed out when he heard how many mountains we'd been to.

———

We climbed North and South Kinsman the next day before heading back to Newburyport. It was the culmination of an incredible stretch, and with twenty days left we had only twenty-nine peaks to go. Since nearly all of them could be reached on hikes that would get us to several peaks in one day, for the first time that winter I felt that the improbable and nearly impossible was actually within our grasp. I knew we could make it.

But the mountain gods were feeling mischievous again. They were whipping up another big storm.

14

Five Astounding Days

Pinned back in Newburyport by several feet of fresh mountain snow, I felt helpless as the days ticked by. I found a bit of salvation during our twice-daily walks through Moseley Pines. On one of them, while sitting by the Merrimack River, I apologized to Vicki. I often talked to her that winter. I wished I'd been able to fulfill all her deathbed wishes. Unfortunately, some were out of my control. I was hoping my second attempt to honor her would turn out differently. However, the recent weather was a recurring reminder that we were at the mercy of the mountain gods.

After we'd missed seven days to the latest storm, our race was probably over. It would be nearly impossible for us to reach twenty-nine peaks in thirteen days. Nevertheless, I decided that Atticus and I would continue on. Early on a Friday morning, we returned north and climbed Mount Moosilauke, the tenth-highest peak. It is a large, bald spread of a mountain that sits off by itself to the southwest. It was a frigid and blustery day, but the sunny blue skies made it seem a little warmer. Once again we had a mountain to ourselves.

The winds pushed us around a bit, but it wasn't dangerous and not nearly enough to make me feel as drained as I was by the time we returned to the car. I was suddenly very tired. It was as if the Lyme disease were flaring up again.

Our original plan was to climb Cannon Mountain on a separate hike after Moosilauke, but I was exhausted, so Atticus and I were in bed at 4:00 P.M. We slept heavily and woke up before 3:00 the next morning, had a quick breakfast, drove over to Cannon, and started our hike. It was so cold that I gave half a thought to going back to bed, but I figured it was the "now or never" moment of our quest.

The sky was clear and black as ink; the stars shone bright. I tried to concentrate on them instead of on how tired I was as I put one foot in front of the other and used my trekking poles to help pull me up the ski trails. They were the most direct route to the summit but also the steepest, and I felt it. There were numerous stops to catch my breath, to swear at myself, at the mountain, at the night, and at the weather that had us behind schedule. As much as it hurt, though, my pain was once again rewarded when we stood on top of the observation deck above the summit. In the frozen predawn darkness, I held Atticus and we looked out just as we had that first night of winter at the lights below and the stars above. We were ending up in the very place I'd seen that first night, somewhere between heaven and earth. It was both enchanting and bittersweet.

With the icy wind swirling around us, I knew that when winter was over, we'd be starting a new chapter in our lives. I just couldn't figure out what the next step was. So I did what we did all winter long: I put one foot in front of the other and Atticus and I walked.

The trip down Cannon was easy, and when we finished, we returned to the cabin. I showered, we had a second breakfast, and we got back into the car and drove over to Mount Waumbek. By the time we arrived, the world had woken up and other hikers were already on the trail. It was a Saturday, the next-to-the-last one of winter, and those who were "collecting" winter peaks were out in full force.

Near the bottom of the mountain, we ran into a friendly couple with their dog. The man's name was Kevin, hers was Judy, and their dog's was

Emma. Kevin did the talking. He talked on and on, and it was clear how much they loved Emma. Eventually it was time for Atticus and me to press on, so we passed them and worked our way to the top.

The following day on the Mount Washington Observatory Web site's discussion board, Kevin wrote a post about meeting us along the trail:

> It turns out, in only their second full year of hiking, they
> are on their second time through the 4000 footers, THIS
> WINTER! After climbing Cannon Mountain at 3:30 Saturday
> morning, they drove to Waumbek and climbed it and then
> finished up the day by driving to Mount Cabot and summiting.
> Unbelievable. It took me 3 years to do what they're doing twice
> in 90 days!

It was the first time we'd hiked three separate times in a day, and my legs felt like lead. I had to push myself to get to the dinner we were invited to by Steve and Carol Smith and our mutual friends Ken and Ann Stampfer. When we finally made it back to the cabin that night, I collapsed without taking off my clothes, and neither one of us stirred until the alarm buzzed the next morning.

The first thing I did was gulp down as much water as I could. I was parched, and my legs were sore. Next I guzzled some flaxseed oil. I stretched my tired muscles and helped Atticus stretch his legs and hips as well. After making three trips in one day, we were off to do the sixteen miles to bag Owl's Head. It was a busy place on Saturday, and there was a well-trodden path to the top. This made it much easier than the first time we'd climbed it, and we flew through the long hike without a care in the world. We were both upbeat when we finished and felt fresher and stronger than we had at the beginning of the day.

The following morning Atticus and I returned to the Bonds. We were attempting the same traverse we'd done with Tom Jones back in December, but we were on our own and we added Mount Hale to it. Extra miles, extra elevation again. We had no choice; winter was winding down. It was another beautiful day, and I looked forward to seeing the views from the Bonds that second time around. However, we had an ominous beginning. On the climb up Hale, our first mountain of the day, I felt dizzy and sick to my stomach. I fell to my knees and vomited. I thought about turning back, but we were so close to the top that I willed myself to keep going. By the time I reached it, my head was spinning and I threw up again. We took some time to regroup, and I made the decision that instead of heading toward Zealand and the Bonds on the Lend-a-Hand Trail, we'd return by the same route we came and make our way back to the car.

It seemed to take forever to get back down the mountain, and at the trailhead I sat with my head between my knees. I was sick and despondent. We'd come so far, and we were so close. I wanted to go on, but I was feeling sicker than ever.

I was thinking about Vicki again and what she'd gone through at the end of her life, the pain she'd endured but never showed, and how she was more concerned for others than she was for herself. I stood up, put my pack on again, and started walking. But instead of walking back to the car, we headed instead toward the Bonds. If Vicki could handle what she'd gone through with such fortitude, then I could keep going.

Turning back on Hale and then choosing a different route added two miles to our already grueling day. And yet somewhere along the climb to Zeacliff I felt better, as though I'd not been sick at all.

We flew from Zeacliff over to Zealand, then up Guyot and over to West Bond. Between West Bond and Bond, we ran into two groups of hikers, and while I didn't know any of them, they all greeted us warmly and called Atticus by name. Another hiker posted about his two-day trip to the Bonds on one of the hiking Web sites and wrote, "We ran into Tom and Atticus. We are not worthy!"

No one had gone from Bond to Bondcliff that day, and there was some shallow snow to break through, but we did it without much effort. The second time that winter on Bondcliff was completely different from the first. The sun was bright, the winds nonexistent, and I hiked without a jacket or a hat or gloves. By the time we finished that afternoon, we'd covered twenty-seven miles in just over ten hours.

Our strength held up, and we hiked for a fifth consecutive day. Atticus and I took advantage of another fine day above tree line and traversed the four peaks of Franconia Ridge. When we finished, we were tired, but I was also elated. In five days we'd made seven trips, climbed fifteen mountains, and walked over eighty-seven miles. That's more than many hikers cover in an entire year. It was an inconceivable accomplishment for two of the White Mountains' most unlikely winter hikers.

We had peaked at just the right time, and amazingly we were once again within striking distance of our goal. With eight days left, there were only four hikes to go: Moriah, Isolation, the five Carters and the 'Cats, and a Presidential traverse covering eight peaks. I had no doubt we could do it; my only doubts concerned something out of my control—the weather.

Atticus and I returned to Newburyport, and I was more excited than I'd been all season. We were close to making history. But our race wasn't just against the clock: More snow was falling.

15

"Thank You, Friend"

Robert Frost wrote, "I have never started a poem yet whose end I knew. Writing a poem is discovering." I could say the same for our quest, or for that matter, any quest.

I knew from the beginning that hiking ninety-six peaks in ninety days was a long shot, and it would be an even longer shot because I would not endanger Atticus by bringing him above tree line except on the best of days.

Throughout the winter there were days I was sure we would finish and others when I thought it a lost cause. There were nights when I was frightened or lonely, days when I thought we had undertaken something far beyond our reach.

We ended December with fourteen peaks, January with another twenty-four, and February with an additional twenty-seven. Then came March, typically the most moderate of the winter months. But not this year. We entered the last eight days needing to finish four hikes to reach all ninety-six peaks, and I was confident about our chances. Unfortunately, it was snowing in the mountains again. We waited for the weather to let up, waited for a day when Atticus would be safe. Slowly, agonizingly, the days ticked by, one after another in which we couldn't hike.

I received e-mails from a couple of hikers who had followed our progress, suggesting I leave Atticus behind and do the last four hikes on my own, or force him into the weather with me; I considered neither. This was *our* journey, and we'd either succeed or fail together.

In the end we never got to the peaks we needed to finish. When we were ready to hike again, we were going to do the Carters and 'Cats, but I pulled the plug when I checked the higher-summits forecast and the extended forecast and realized that it would be too dangerous to do a traverse that would carry us over the eight peaks of the Presidential Range before winter ended. Our final tally was eighty-one mountains climbed.

We set out to hike ninety-six peaks, and we came up short. It didn't matter to me whether we finished with eighty-one or eighty-six or eighty-eight. It was not going to be ninety-six.

Having nothing more to do in the mountains, we returned to Newburyport, and the first day of spring found us walking the beach on Plum Island at low tide. It felt like the first day of spring should feel, and winter was already a world away.

Atticus was romping along the firm sand, ears flying like flags in the breeze. If I hadn't known better, I'd have thought he was preparing for liftoff, and I half expected to look up and see him soaring with the gulls at any minute. I'd not seen him that way in quite some time. Over the previous three months, his gait had been strong, but steady and slow. He picked his way along trails, through snow and ice and rock, always conserving energy for the long haul ahead. Always a constant twenty feet in front, unless the snow was deep and needed breaking—then he was inches behind my snowshoes. But on the beach he opened it up, put the pedal to the metal, and ran deliriously under the warm sun. He was oblivious to the waves lapping at the shore or the call of the gulls.

Off in the distance, he saw a cluster of dogs and people. The dogs were milling around, almost mindlessly, waiting for the humans to do something. But the people *were* doing something. They were attached to their cell phones and Starbucks cups and gabbing with one another. Their dogs were but an afterthought.

Atticus veered toward the group, arriving with several four-legged Tigger bounces as if to say, *We're back! We're back!* But the dogs just gave him a few halfhearted sniffs. Atticus took off sprinting down the beach, then pivoted quickly and raced back toward me. Just before reaching me, he spun playfully away and ran toward a small jetty revealed by low tide. He climbed up on top of the large, craggy rocks and leaped from one to another, working his way toward the line where sand and sea met. I followed, thinking of the climb up Madison, Adams, and Jefferson.

When he reached the last rock, he settled his furry bottom down and looked out toward the horizon.

Little Buddha was back.

I took a seat behind him and settled into my own reverie. I thought about the past week—the last week of winter. It seemed more like a dream than a memory. I followed Atticus's gaze toward the horizon, and that's when the dream came back. It came back as I hope it always will.

In his book *Hymns to an Unknown God*, Sam Keen wrote that first as a minister and then as a psychologist he saw that most people were yearning for something to surrender to. They wanted to be submerged in something greater than themselves.

For three months Atticus and I had done just that. We'd left behind the politicians and the personalities, put our regular lives on hold, and made the mountains our priority. We'd surrendered to the winter Whites in the name of adventure and in honor of a friend. We'd set out to give, but in the end we received.

When winter started, I'd had various goals: pay tribute to Vicki, raise money for the Jimmy Fund, get to ninety-six peaks in ninety days, and finish the peaks we didn't get to the previous winter. However, one goal stood out above the others. I wanted to keep Atticus safe, but I also wanted him to enjoy the adventure. I'm proud that no matter what happened, I never compromised his well-being. There were difficult times, but he handled them with aplomb.

What I learned along the way was something I already knew, but it became even clearer: Climbing mountains in winter is a wonderful and challenging game, for weather is a fickle mistress. There's no way of predicting the outcome. All you can do is watch and learn. I did that. I learned to take what the mountain gods and the weather gods gave us. I learned to be patient. I learned to trust Atticus more than ever; he knew his limits and told me what I needed to know as long as I paid attention to him. And I learned that we would be forever linked to the people we were hiking for, even the total strangers who had mountains dedicated to them.

We came out four hikes shy but with a stronger sense of strength, endurance, and confidence. We raised more for the fight against cancer than I'd initially thought we would. And I can tell you that when it was dark and cold and I was filled with doubt, fear, and loneliness, I was fortified by the company, love, and loyalty of an abundantly special little dog.

Sitting on those beach rocks, I looked at that curious little dog gazing out on the vast ocean, and any lingering frustrations at the outcome of winter vanished. Seeing him happy and safe meant more to me than those four hikes ever would.

Ninety-six mountains . . .

Eighty-one mountains . . .

To a man who just two years before had difficulty walking up the street—what was the difference?

I'm proud of what we accomplished, and I knew I wouldn't have done any of it had Atticus not been there with me. We never would have taken up hiking had he not thrived on Garfield that first September day with my brothers. I was looking for something we could do together. I had no idea at that time that I was bringing Atticus to a place he belonged even more than I did.

We sat in silence for several more minutes and listened the soft lapping of the water on the shore. When it was time to leave, I leaned forward and kissed Atticus on top of the forehead and said, "Thank you, friend." Normally he would have turned around when I talked to him, but he was intensely watching the horizon just as he'd done on Washington a couple of weeks earlier. It was as if he knew something was coming.

Little did I know we were about to face a challenge that would dwarf anything we'd faced during our entire winter.

Part II

Light over Dark

*It is by going down into the abyss
that we recover the treasures of life.*

*Where you stumble,
there lies your treasure.*

—JOSEPH CAMPBELL

16

A Heartrending Turn of Events

The secret of my success with the *Undertoad* was that when I came to town, I was completely captivated by the charming characters. It was as if I had discovered a community composed entirely of bit players from old black-and-white John Ford or Frank Capra movies. You know the kind. They were so genuine and gritty with their less-than-perfect looks, not like the supporting actors of today's films. I watched with delight and studied them and got to the point where I could often predict their next moves, even if they couldn't. It was as if I were watching a favorite movie for the fourth or fifth time. It wasn't a job; it was mostly a pleasure.

Of course I had my trusted sources, too, and they clued me in on stories and taught me the lay of the land. I was an eager student with two eyes, two ears, and one mouth, and learned to use them accordingly. However, it didn't take long to discover that in a city with a wide cast of supporting characters the star of the show was Newburyport herself.

She was beautiful, especially in the soft light of daybreak and sunset. She was mysterious, especially at night when secrets were forged and broken. She was seductive, and she evoked passions in her lovers: jealousy, rage, ownership. There were some who wanted to lock her up and keep her a secret, and others who wanted to let her breathe, to share her with the outside world. The lines of demarcation formed on the battlefield of gentrification fascinated me. But so did the age-old feuds between the natives and, in Newburyport's case, even entire sections of the city.

The city had been divided for a long time. Many old-timers held generations-long grudges because they lived in the once-bedraggled South End ("down-along" in local parlance) and were looked down on by those who lived in the North End ("up-along"), while both were looked down on by those who lived on stately High Street. Where they met was the downtown. If you lived up-along, you didn't go down-along, and vice versa, unless you were looking for trouble.

John Battis, a popular member of the city's Greek-American population because of his letters to the editor, his commonsense political opinions, and his ability to play a mean sax, often waxed poetic about the old days. "When I grew up," he said, "I knew there were certain parts of town I did not belong in and places I was not welcome. But it didn't matter. It was a simpler time, and I just understood that that's the way it was. I kind of liked it. Life was easy."

But John was different from most. He loved Newburyport more than anyone I met. And it wasn't just lip service. He'd taken a section of abandoned railroad that had devolved into a dumping ground, cleaned it up, planted flowers, and turned it into a little neighborhood park. Against his protests it was eventually given the name Battis Grove. I almost believe he wouldn't have gone to the effort if he'd known it would be named after him. Recognition was never his motivation.

John was always doing things people didn't know about. My favorite was a simple act of reverence. Each Memorial Day, geraniums magically appeared at the grave of Pulitzer Prize–winning novelist John P. Marquand. No one ever knew how the flowers ended up there, but I did. And it's not as if John had known Marquand. As a matter of fact, in old Newburyport, with its antiquated caste system, they probably wouldn't have crossed paths very often, and if they had, Marquand probably wouldn't have given him the time of day. For he was a gentleman, and John Battis was but a "lowly" Greek American.

Marquand was buried in Sawyer Hill Burial Ground. It was hidden and somewhat exclusive, and many townies didn't even know that it existed.

And yet John admired Marquand's writing, and as a fellow son of Newburyport he thought someone should remember the late writer.

But John's attitude, and his actions, stood in stark contrast to those of many of the old-timers who perpetuated the feuds of old Newburyport, with roots that ran deep enough to permeate many contemporary issues. To this day the best way to predict the mayor's race is to figure out which of the two candidates people dislike the least.

John once told me that Newburyport was the only place he knew of where they could have a parade to celebrate a local boy made good—perhaps an astronaut landing on the moon, or a great athlete, or a movie star—and on the day of the parade the route would be filled with people telling you that in fourth grade the honored hero once stole a candy bar. Cannibal City. At breakfast one morning, as he repeatedly tapped my arm with the back of his hand while leaning in closer than I would allow anyone else to get (which he had the habit of doing), he said, "You are the only one I know who could get away with writing the *Undertoad*. You don't have kids in school. You don't have a job in town. You don't have a wife. They can't get at you."

"They," it was understood, was how old Newburyport operated. It was the damning rumor mill, the backroom deal, the threat against the landlord who dared rent you an apartment. If you weren't for 'em, you were agin 'em. And if you were agin 'em, they'd do what they could do to stop you—which mostly turned out to be making your life miserable in as many ways as possible.

I learned local history from John Battis and an army of other townies, but I also learned a lot from the newcomers, the so-called carpetbaggers. From where I sat, I could see over both sides of the fence.

What I saw from my vantage point on the third floor of the Grand Army Building was that both natives and newcomers loved Newburyport and that on any given week a war of passions could break out about what to do with two dirt parking lots on the central waterfront, whether or not to accept grant money from the state that would make improvements but cheapen historic High Street, or whether or not to put bike lanes on city streets. Things that might not be a big deal in other places were divisive issues in Cannibal City.

New skirmishes sprang to life weekly—battle lines drawn, sides chosen, arguments made, aspersions cast. If a certain person stood on one side of the issue, I just knew that a certain other person would be on the other side, no matter what it was, simply because they didn't like each other. Tip O'Neill once said, "All politics is local." In Newburyport, all politics was personal.

It was a curious and passionate place, and I loved every bit of it. For a writer needs good stories to tell, and good stories need tension. I believe that Newburyport herself, the star of the show, loved it just as much. For as beguiling and outwardly beautiful as she was, she was also dysfunctional. What she wanted more than anything was to be fought over, because that showed her she was loved. And she was—both fought over and loved.

What she couldn't abide was an inattentive lover, and that's what I'd become.

Atticus and I returned home three months to the day after we had left. We had come back on occasion in the interim, but it was always a hasty trip to get out the latest issue of the *Undertoad* or to seek refuge from a storm. But it was clear we'd moved on with our lives, in spirit if not body. So when spring came and I returned home, I returned numb.

I was like a marathoner who suffered symptoms similar to postpartum depression. I had nurtured a dream, protected it, devoted all my energy to its care, and when it was over . . . when it was over, I was spent and empty. There was nothing else to chase after, no intensity of purpose, nothing more to surrender to.

Atticus and I had endured an exhausting, soul-satisfying quest, and we were returning to the mundane. We were back where we'd started, but it just didn't feel right any longer. I was depressed.

Newburyport did her best to win me back over. She was a jilted lover who would do anything to keep me around. She dangled the customary assortment of rascals, strange and incestuous bedfellows, usual suspects, good old political buffoonery, and the occasional hero in front of me. She tempted me with a mayor who was both inept and arrogant, industrialists who suffered delusions of grandeur, and a big-fish Boston billionaire developer who bought up nearly the entire downtown, held its future in his hands, and didn't care enough about Newburyport to actually come to town.

Oh, how Newburyport tried! She showed me all these characters, knowing I could never have resisted the temptation to harpoon and lampoon them in the past. She assured me a good living and plenty to write about, if only I'd stay.

But it was too late.

Mary Baker Eaton, the grande dame of Newburyport political bloggers, recognized it. In her Newburyport Blog, she wrote, "I remember watching Tom at a Newburyport City Council meeting after that experience was over, and thinking to myself, *The mountains have captured him. And they had.*"

But I wasn't the only lost soul. Atticus was having a hard time returning as well. After that first day on the beach, he was no longer himself. He moped about, often letting his head hang down. I chalked it up to his own form of depression and did whatever I could to cheer him up. We'd go for numerous walks each day and drop in on friends, and I made sure he got his favorite treats. But nothing helped.

Atticus stayed closer to me than ever. He developed the curious habit of touching his cool, wet nose to my bare leg. He did it in our apartment but did it even more out in public. When we walked down the sidewalk, he stayed by my side. He had no desire to lead the way as he used to. When we crossed the street, he stuck as close to me as possible. In a crowd his nose would find my leg more often. When I sat at my desk, he'd often ask to come up and would lie next to my computer as I wrote. He was reaching out, looking for reassurance.

I worried about him but recognized the symptoms because I was feeling pretty much the same way. I had returned to a city I'd once had the pulse of, but now I felt like a stranger. All I had, it seemed, was what he and I shared in the mountains.

However, it turned out that Atticus was suffering from something much worse than mere depression. One morning I tossed a cookie to him. It landed on his blanket. I watched, stunned that he didn't see it even though it was only three inches in front of him. I picked it up and tossed it again. He still didn't see it.

Something was wrong with his eyes, his beautiful, beautiful eyes.

I called John Grillo's office, and they saw us immediately.

John examined him and said, "Cataracts. He's got cataracts."

"But he's only five years old," I said. Immediately I thought of the hikes through the snow over the course of the past two winters. "Is it because of all the hiking through snow and the reflection of the sun?"

John Grillo had a sympathetic face—I knew it well from the last days of Max—and he assured me it wasn't from the snow. I wasn't sure I believed him. He pointed to sled dogs in the Iditarod race as an example and said there was no history of eye disease with them. He then referred us to Susan Hayward, a veterinary ophthalmologist.

Over the next twenty-four hours, Atticus's eyesight deteriorated rapidly. He bumped into furniture, tripped over curbs on the street, and had a hard time following me through a crowd.

The next night the phone rang. It was John Grillo. He told me there was something wrong with Atticus's blood and it took precedence over the cataracts. He had tested positive for hyperthyroidism.

"What does that mean?" By the tone of his voice, I knew it couldn't be good.

There was a pause on the line before John spoke again. He said that canine hyperthyroidism was very rare and then said something else, but I couldn't hear him. I mumbled a few things, regained some footing, and asked, "What causes it?"

Another pause. He sounded tired when he spoke again. "Hyperthyroidism in dogs is nearly always associated with thyroid cancer."

I asked John if he could do another test, and he said he would. That's all I remember before my world went black. More words were spoken, but they were a mere fog. Atticus was sitting on my lap with his head against my chest. I'm certain he heard my heart breaking.

A month before, he was leading me over mountains, and suddenly he was going blind, and it appeared that the little dog who raised thousands for the fight against cancer had it himself.

Word spread rapidly. The little dog who had mesmerized much of a city with his adventures in the mountains was sick.

One of Newburyport's own was hurting. So was the man who lived with him.

People reached out, and the answering machine filled up quickly and frequently, because I didn't want to talk with anyone. There were hundreds of e-mails to respond to. Everyone wanted to know what was wrong with their friend Atticus.

I was strong for Atticus but collapsed in every other area of my life. Instead of talking to people, I used the e-mail chain I'd started during the winter to give them updates.

Soon the hiking community heard the news, and they responded as well. More e-mails, more cards, more calls of assurance telling me they'd help however they could. Whatever the Little Giant needed, they'd be there for him.

As for Atticus, for the first time in his life he was lost. He wanted nothing but to be with me and to be held. We went to Moseley Pines and sat in our favorite grove two or three times a day, his nose constantly seeking out my leg. There were days I had to redirect him so that he wouldn't walk into a tree or get tangled in the bushes. For the first time since he'd arrived in Newburyport, the squirrels of Moseley Pines didn't have to worry about being chased.

The second blood test showed the same results.

Grillo's assistant called and told me that an ultrasound specialist was making a special trip to their office and bringing a portable machine. They would use it to look for the tumor, or tumors, they expected to find in Atticus.

That afternoon Atticus and I stopped at Jabberwocky Bookshop to visit our friend Paul Abruzzi, the manager. He'd always treated Atticus well, as had Sue Little, the owner, and the entire staff, and he suggested we might get some help from an unlikely source.

Every two years or so, a group of Tibetan monks spent a few days at Jabberwocky building a sand mandala. They were coming that week, and Paul suggested I bring Atticus by to see them. "He should meet Geshe Gendun."

I didn't know anything about Geshe Gendun, but I was game for anything that might help.

I liked Geshe Gendun the moment I saw him. He had a kind, round face, and he liked to smile. There was a genuine and gentle spirit to the man. I was curious about his life and learned he was my age, born in Tibet in 1961, that he had escaped to India in 1963 and had become a Buddhist monk when he was only eight years old. His Holiness the Dalai Lama had ordained him in 1981. And so it came to be that a little floppy-eared dog from Louisiana and a Tibetan monk sat facing each other.

Geshe Gendun sat in a chair, wearing his colorful robes. Atticus lay naked like a sphinx at his feet. Both were very serene. Geshe Gendun smiled warmly, and Atticus met his gaze through his cloudy eyes.

The monk spoke so softly I couldn't hear him. It was as if he were whispering a secret to Atticus, and the way Atticus looked up at him, it was as if he understood every word. Geshe Gendun slowly moved his hands in the air around Atticus's throat and his shoulders, then touched him gently. This went on for a couple of minutes, and then, as quickly as the union between the two of them had begun, they went their separate ways—Atticus back to me and Geshe Gendun back to supervising the building of the sand mandala. Not a word was spoken. As the monk left, he gave me the slightest nod of his head with a knowing look in his eye.

I won't pretend to have a clue what happened between Geshe

Gendun and Atticus, or if anything happened at all. The reporter in me told me to be suspicious of such things, but the man who had rediscovered the wonders of nature and had grown so close with a special little dog wouldn't discount anything. At worst I figured we could add one Tibetan monk to the number of people who were praying for Atticus— which seemed to be at least half the city by that time.

Twenty-four hours later, in a starkly different setting, my heart broke again to see a couple of John Grillo's vet techs holding Atticus down on a cold steel table. John and the specialist came into the room.

"Thank you for getting here so quickly," I said to the specialist. "I understand it's usually a longer wait."

"Yes," he said excitedly, "it is. But this is rare, and I wanted to see it."

As he spoke, he shaved strips of hair off Atticus's throat, chest, and belly. Everyone else in the room was quiet, perhaps a bit tense.

When the specialist turned the machine on and slid the probe along the shaved areas, everyone leaned in to see the tumors. The specialist was in his glory, and the rest of us watched. I suppose I was the only one who was truly nervous about what they'd find, and John Grillo and his techs were probably more curious than anything else, but I told myself they were also rooting against what they expected to see.

First the probe slid along Atticus's throat, then down to his chest, then his belly.

I was led to believe we'd see something pretty dramatic. But the specialist looked a bit confused, as if there were something wrong with the equipment. He adjusted some knobs. The excited smile faded slowly from his face. He tried a different angle, thought he saw something, then looked disappointed when it was nothing. He kept going over the shaved areas. He gave us a play-by-play. "Nothing there . . . No, nothing there either . . . Um, what do we have here? Oh, nothing. Nothing there either."

He continued to search and continued to find nothing. He actually looked disappointed and while I was thankful he'd squeezed us in as quickly as he had and was happy that he wasn't finding anything, the more disappointed he grew, the more I wanted to punch him. God, how I wanted to punch him.

Now, I suppose he was just doing his job, but I got the impression he needed to be reminded we weren't just dealing with tumors and machines, we were dealing with heart-and-soul and feelings. We were dealing with a little dog's life. We were dealing with my best friend.

When he finally gave up, he had the most perplexed expression on his face.

"Nothing, then?" I asked.

He found it hard to believe. "No, nothing. Huh, that's strange."

At that point I no longer wanted to hit him, I just wanted them all to let go of Atticus. And, of course, I was relieved that they didn't find any tumors. I took it as a victory, but John told me that even though they hadn't seen any tumors, Atticus still had hyperthyroidism. I asked him where I could bring him for the best care possible, and he suggested either Tufts Animal Hospital or Angell Animal Medical Center. I went with Angell, mostly because I liked the sound of it, and he gave me the name of a doctor there.

No matter what it cost, I was determined that Atticus would get the best possible treatment. What I had forgotten in my zeal to take care of him was that after our winter I was nearly broke. But I wasn't thinking about that. All I could think about at that moment was Geshe Gendun and Atticus sitting together. Einstein was right: "The most beautiful thing we can experience is the mysterious."

17

"I'm Not Leaving Him Alone"

When Atticus was very young, I was still sleeping on my couch. He was so tiny, and I didn't want to crush him if I rolled over in my sleep, so I placed him above my head on the pillow. This way I knew he was safe, but I would also be able to tell if he had to go to the bathroom in the middle of the night. His stirring would wake me up, and I'd rush him to the puppy pads on the kitchen floor. As he got a bit older and a bit more disciplined when he had to go the bathroom, if he stirred in the middle of the night, I'd run him down the two flights of stairs to the little patch of lawn across the street.

We'd slept together ever since. It wasn't long before I bought a real bed, and typically when we went to sleep, he'd be near me, but not always touching. By morning I'd awaken to find him snug up against me. But when he was going blind and was sick, he couldn't get close enough. He'd fold his back right up against my chest. He was afraid and needed reassurance.

On the day of our first visit with Susan Hayward, the veterinary ophthalmologist, I woke up to Atticus sitting above me with a horrifically sad face. I was still groggy, but there was something terribly wrong with him. I sat up and saw that his right eye was completely covered with a grotesque yellowish paste. It wasn't the "little sleepies" all dogs get from time to time. His eye was glued shut.

He gave me a look that said, *Please help me, Tom.*

I ran a washcloth under steaming-hot water and pressed it over his eye. A minute later I took it off and saw that the paste was still thick. I needed to try something else. I rewet the washcloth and gently scrubbed away the discharge. It took several minutes of cleaning before I could get his eyelid pried open.

That afternoon we met Susan Hayward for the first time. She was a busy, bookish woman with a bit of distance to her. She was nice enough, and she knew her stuff, but it was clear she didn't want us to get too close. Not physically, just in a human, warmhearted way.

While she examined Atticus, I told her a bit about our winter to give her his background, but she didn't seem to hear a word I was saying. She was proficient in the way she looked at Atticus's eyes and moved around the room.

Both eyes were bad and needed surgery, she said, but the right eye was worse. The cataract was fully mature, and, worse yet, it was infected. She called it uveitis. That's where the discharge came from. She wasn't sure if it was too late to save the right eye, and she was concerned about retinal detachment. She couldn't operate on it as it was and prescribed medication for me to apply in the hope that it would bring the swelling down. But there was a chance it wouldn't and we'd lose the eye.

She did an ultrasound on the right eye. The retina wasn't detached, but if it did detach, there would be no hope of saving the eye.

"How much can Atticus see right now?" I asked her.

She had me look at the fluorescent light on the ceiling with my eyes closed. I saw the glow and some shadows, but little else.

"That's what he sees with the right eye. The left eye is better, but not much," she said.

"How did it come on so quickly?" I asked. "Was it because of the snow and the hiking?"

Like John Grillo, she told me it had nothing to do with the snow. She explained that it just happens in some dogs, and although it may seem sudden, Atticus had most certainly been going blind for quite some time.

I told her we'd do the surgery but that I needed to find some money first. She said good-bye and scurried out of the room, leaving us with her vet tech, who explained what I needed to know. "He'll have to be at the hospital for three days and two nights. You can bring him in the night before the surgery, and he can go home the day after the surgery."

She asked me if I had any questions.

"Yeah, where will I be sleeping?"

The young woman laughed, then caught herself a few seconds later when she realized I wasn't joking.

"I'm not leaving him alone. We're never away from each other, and he needs me now more than ever."

"But we don't allow people to stay overnight," she said.

"I'm sure you can make an exception," I said with a smile. "I'm sure we all want what's best for Atticus."

She tried to explain the policies of the hospital, but I interrupted her.

"I'm not leaving him alone overnight."

After an awkward moment, she excused herself. Several minutes passed, and Dr. Hayward breezed back into the room and told me I could bring him in the day of the surgery, take him home that night, and bring him back first thing the next morning for a checkup.

Atticus and I were smack dab in the middle of a shit storm. We needed to rely on our strengths to survive it, and our greatest strength was that we had each other. I was not about to give up our only advantage. Luckily, Dr. Hayward seemed to understand that.

Walking out to the car, I thought better of Susan Hayward because of it.

Atticus had always loved riding in the car, but not in the head-out-the-window, tongue-flapping-in-the-wind, silly-looking way of some dogs. He was statelier than that. On occasion he'd stick his head out the passenger-side window, but typically he'd sit up and look out through the windshield, even though he was barely tall enough to reach it. But on the ride home from the ophthalmologist, he didn't sit up. He lay down, his head hung over the edge of the seat. It was a look of defeat and despondency.

I reached across and petted him softly. As I felt his little body and his soft hair under my hand, I couldn't get something that Susan Hayward had said out of my head. It was the part about how Atticus had most certainly been going blind for quite some time. The blindness hadn't come on suddenly.

Then how did he do it? How had he led me over those mountains?

I couldn't fathom how he did it, or why he did it, other than that he knew it was important to me and since day one he always saw it as his job to lead me and look out for me.

But still, he didn't just climb a mountain. He climbed eighty-one of them, in winter, through a blizzard, high winds, heavy snow, ice, subzero temperatures, and in darkness. Never once did he show a sign of hesitation or discomfort. Always, always, he was looking out for me. He'd stop and watch to make sure I was okay on the trail.

I thought about the Bonds, thought about the Northern Pressies, thought about Washington, Monroe, Eisenhower, and Pierce in one day. I thought about Franconia Ridge. How did he do it?

I had to pull the car over to the side of the road, because it wasn't just Atticus who couldn't see. I was suddenly blind myself, tears flooding my eyes, rolling down my cheeks. I picked Atticus up and hugged him and whispered, "Thank you, thank you . . . *thank you, Atticus.*"

18

The Friends of Atticus

What is the worth of a true friend? Are we willing to walk hundreds of miles and climb thousands of feet over rocky and dangerous mountains in winter for a friend who touched our life through her living and her dying? Are we willing to lead someone we love over that same distance, in that same season, while going blind? I know the answer to those questions, because I've both given and received.

And what is the worth of a couple of eyes? The painter, the photographer, the reader—they'd all argue that vision is priceless. There are some, though, who seem to go through life seeing nothing.

And what of a dog's eyes? I knew of many dogs who'd had cataracts whose owners thought four thousand dollars was too much to pay for surgery, especially since surgery, while usually successful, was not guaranteed to work. I knew some who'd paid for it and weren't happy with the results. I'd read stories about how dogs learn to live without their sight, how they adapt with their keen sense of smell, which some believe is more important than their eyesight. To Atticus, though, his eyes seemed more important than anything else. There was no question that he needed the surgery.

But what if the uveitis worsened and surgery wasn't an option and he lost that right eye? What if his left eye had the same trouble? And what if the ointment worked and the uveitis lessened and he was able to have the surgery but it didn't work?

I was sure he'd still climb the mountains, he'd find a way to follow the scent and feel the breeze on his face up high. But those eyes of his, they were different from any other dog's I'd ever heard of. He so loved sitting on a mountaintop and gazing outward. Surely no creature had ever made better use of a gift from God than Atticus had with his vision. And my dearest friend, the Little Buddha, was in danger of losing that gift.

I religiously applied the medicine Susan Hayward had prescribed and prayed that his right eye would get better enough to allow the surgery. But my patience was tried. It was like waiting for the snow to stop, waiting to be able to get back out to the mountains. There was nothing we could do, nothing except sit and wait and pray.

While we were waiting, I worried about money. How would I afford the surgery? Most of my money was gone, put into raising funds for the fight against cancer. My business was sagging because I had neglected it during our quest, and keeping the *Undertoad* afloat had been hard on my credit.

I wasn't sure what I was going to do.

I'd often worried about Atticus's medical bills as we walked the two blocks down to the post office, aware that there was inevitably yet another past-due notice in my mailbox for something, reminding me how broke I was. And yet we kept going to the mailbox every day; it was part of our ritual. It was good for business and good for Atticus. He had always enjoyed the walk because he met so many friends along the way.

Such a stroll should have taken no more than ten minutes in each direction. But the walk there and back would usually take at least an hour. People pulled over and wanted to talk; a city employee would tip me off to something happening at city hall; a businessman would have something to say about what was wrong with the city; I'd get comments, both pro and con, about the latest issue of the *Undertoad*. The street was my office. It's where I got much of my work done.

With Atticus no longer able to see, each day I led him along those two blocks, just as he had always led me. He'd sit outside on the steps waiting while I went in and got the mail, and people would walk by and greet him, people who knew him, people he knew. He was one of them. He was a Newburyporter.

There was a time when Atticus had been allowed to go inside the post office, but he paid the price for being my dog. He was banned simply because he belonged to the editor of the *Undertoad*. It was one of those things John Battis had told me about Newburyport. "They" couldn't get at me: I didn't have kids or a wife, I worked for myself, so "they" attacked where they could: slashed tires, disgusting rumors, anonymous death threats. Most silly of all, since "they" weren't having much success with any of that, "they" saw to it that Atticus was not allowed in certain places anymore.

I once received a phone call from a woman telling me she was from the postmaster general's office. My caller ID showed the call came from Virginia.

"Mr. Ryan, we can have you arrested if your dog goes into the post office anymore."

"Why?"

"Dogs aren't allowed in any U.S. post offices unless they are guide dogs."

"Then why do they give him dog biscuits when he goes inside?"

She tripped for a moment, then found her officious manner again. "Rules are rules, Mr. Ryan. Let this be a warning to you."

I asked her how someone at her office so far away was handling a complaint about a little post office in Newburyport, Massachusetts.

"We've had complaints."

"Who complained?"

"I'm not at liberty to tell."

"They" complained.

It was okay, it was part of the game played in Newburyport. I wrote what I wanted, and "they" came after me in ridiculous ways. It was par for the course. It was the price of admission.

Atticus didn't understand why he could no longer go in, and he definitely didn't understand the sign that appeared on the front door at city hall saying, YOUR DOG *MAY* BE ASKED TO LEAVE (translation: your dog *will* be asked to leave if his name is Atticus M. Finch), when yet another new mayor was elected.

But whenever he sat outside, he sat patiently, and people were happy to see him waiting for me without his leash on.

"Good morning, Atticus."

"It's a fine day, Atticus."

"How are you today, Atticus?"

When he went blind, though, the tone was different. It's like when you know that someone has cancer. You can't help but say, "How are you feeling?" and have it come out sounding a little different from the way it used to. It was no longer a cursory greeting. People really did want to know how he was feeling, and they spoke as if they expected him to understand what they were asking. They wanted him to know they cared.

One day while Atticus sat outside with his cloudy eyes, I came out with a couple envelopes, sat on the steps next to him, and opened them. One was addressed to Atticus. It was a handmade card. Inside, in a small child's writing, it said, "Dear Atticus, My mommy and daddy told me you weren't feeling well and you needed to go to the doctors so I'm sending money from my piggy bank."

It was from a four-year-old girl who had overheard her parents talking about Atticus, left the room, and come back with her bank saying she wanted to help. She'd taped a combination of coins inside the card. Sixty-eight cents total.

In the other envelope was a five-dollar bill from an elderly woman, a longtime subscriber to the *'Toad*. "As you know, Tom, I'm on a fixed income. I just wanted to help with Atti's medical bills. If I can afford it, I'll send more later."

The next day an envelope came with a hundred-dollar bill. It was anonymous but came with a typed quotation from *It's a Wonderful Life*. The typist had changed it a bit, "Atticus, remember, no man (or dog) is a failure who has friends. Thanks for the wings, A friend. P.S.: You gave us all wings when you took us along on your adventure this winter."

The letters came out of nowhere. If I wasn't on the verge of tears because of what Atticus was going through, I was close to crying because of those incredible gestures. And they were only the beginning.

In the ensuing days, more envelopes came, and they didn't stop coming. They came from all over New England, and they came from California, Oregon, Colorado, Georgia, Florida, and New York. They came from so many places I lost count. But most, of course, came from Newburyport.

Some were anonymous donations of cash. Others were checks. Most were small. Nearly every one of them included a note written to Atticus. All the notes wished him well, and some thanked him for touching their lives. One person wrote, "Thanks for restoring my faith that anything is possible. What you did in the mountains will never be forgotten."

The owners of a farmstand put up a milk bottle with Atticus's photo on it near their cash register, and over the next several weeks they had to empty the nickels, dimes, quarters, and bills often. That little milk bottle brought in hundreds of dollars toward Atticus's medical expenses.

Tom McFadden, my chiropractor, held a fund-raiser and told people that a portion of what they paid for every adjustment he did that day would go to Atticus. Linda, who owned Abe's Bagels, another place where Atticus was banned (because "they" had turned her in to the health inspector), sent along a sizable check. So did Pam at Pawsitively Best Friends, where Atticus had gotten his bodysuit. A local business sent a check for thirteen hundred dollars. A woman we didn't know from Cambridge, who had followed our blog and was moved by Atticus, sent two thousand dollars.

Paul Abruzzi at Jabberwocky launched the Friends of Atticus, along with Terry Berns, who was married to Tom Jones. A bank account was set up.

Kids sent in their allowances. Cancer survivors sent checks with notes of thanks. We received donations from members of the hiking community, including from Kevin, Judy, and Emma, whom we'd met on Waumbek.

In only three weeks, nine thousand dollars came in!

Money appeared indirectly as well. The *Undertoad*, which had been struggling due to my neglect, was filled with ads. Businesses paid to advertise because they wanted me to have money to afford whatever Atticus needed. Shops that already advertised upgraded their ad size. Full-page ads, typically rare, started appearing more regularly in the *'Toad*.

I don't think the money would have stopped coming in if I hadn't told people we had enough. If the medicine worked on Atticus's infected eye we'd go forward with the cataract surgery and the follow-up visits he'd need, and we'd soon be going to Angell Animal Medical Center to start our battle with hyperthyroidism.

If we needed more money, I told them I'd let them know. But judging by the number of friends Atticus had made in his lifetime, something told me I wouldn't need to.

19

Soul Work

I had a friend and mentor, Doug Cray, a retired newspaperman for the *New York Times* who had covered Kennedy and Johnson in the White House. Whenever turbulent times hit during my *Undertoad* years, he used to tell me, "Hold on to yourself, man."

It was sound advice, but there were times when that was easier said than done.

The community was there for Atticus and me, but I was still lost. The post-winter letdown left me ill equipped to deal with Atticus's health issues, and I was trying to catch up to a world that had spiraled out of control. I did my best to stay strong for Atticus, and I succeeded, but in every other aspect of my life I felt like I was trying to stand on only one leg in a raging storm.

I'd sit alone with Atticus, listening to the phone ringing and people leaving messages, but I couldn't bear to talk with most of them.

I had all I could do just to hold on to myself.

However, there was one person I sought out. The reporter in me wanted answers. I called Paige Foster. We hadn't spoken in two years, but I'd been keeping her abreast of our adventures by sending her photo updates of our winter quest. Occasionally I'd get a cheery e-mail back, but more often than not I heard nothing and figured she must hear from a lot of the people who'd bought puppies from her.

I wanted to know if Atticus's parents ever had cataracts or thyroid problems.

Now, let me tell you, talking with Paige on the phone was always a treat. Consider her a cross between the late earthy, rabble-rousing Texas columnist Molly Ivins and a Gypsy mystic. In spite of the circumstances, it was comforting to hear her voice again after so long.

She told me that as far as she knew, none of her dogs had ever had eye or thyroid problems, and she asked what the doctors were doing. When I filled her in, she said, "Y'all have something going for you no one else has. Y'all have each other. Don't ever forget it."

In her strong, saucy twang she continued, "Down here in Louisiana, I never thought I bred a mountain dog, but looking at all those pictures of Atti sitting on the summits, I realize that little boy belongs in the mountains. You need to get him back up there where he can do his soul work. Because that's exactly what he's doing when he's sitting there. Soul work."

"But, Paige, he's nearly completely blind. He can't see. And they think he has cancer—"

She cut me off. "I don't care what they say, you get him back up where he belongs. He needs those mountains, Tom."

Had anyone else suggested this, I would have dismissed her quickly, but I always thought of Paige, to put it bluntly, as "intuitive," and she seemed to understand things others didn't. Most people would have considered Paige's suggestion insane, and they would have considered me doubly so for following her advice, but deep down I knew she was right. Atticus needed the mountains more than ever. And that's where we were going, two days before his eye surgery.

I trusted Paige, but more important I trusted Atticus. He had earned that trust. He'd been on hikes when he didn't want to go any farther, so we turned back. It didn't happen very often. As a matter of fact, it hardly happened at all. But it was enough for him to know he had a say, and for me to know he could express it. He'd always let me know what he needed. My job was to listen to what he was saying.

As soon as we arrived at the trailhead, I knew we'd made the right decision. He might have looked like an elderly dog climbing gingerly out of the car, and not the five-year-old who had bounced out of it just weeks before, but it was clear he wanted to be there. He walked around the edge of the parking lot, following his nose, then found the trail. And we were off.

It would be like no other hike we'd ever been on.

Although it was spring, the forest was still sleeping. Nothing was green, and the underbrush, in various shades of gray and brown, was hard for Atticus to see. This made it difficult for him to know where the trail went, and he continuously stumbled to the side or bumped into rocks and trees. I could feel his frustration grow each time he got tangled in the brush and had to work to free himself. On one occasion he misjudged a little ledge he would have climbed nimbly in the past and stood help-lessly in front of it. I lifted him up.

Watching him struggle, there were several times I wanted him to stop and prayed he would, but he knew what he needed. From the very beginning, I had wanted Atticus to be whatever he wanted to be. To find his own way. And that's what he was doing.

In that forest my heart broke time and again watching the little dog who used to trot along without a worry. I felt he'd been betrayed by the very powers that put him on earth. It didn't seem fair that one so pure and true should be robbed of so much he loved when others took for granted what they had.

By the time we got through the forest and out onto the first ledge, he had collided with or tripped over so many rocks and sticks that I sug-gested we turn back. "Let's go home, Atti," I said hopefully, and started walking back the way we'd come. But he'd have none of it. Instead he sat and refused to move.

We were going on.

On the edge of that first ledge, we stood hundreds of feet above the shimmering Mad River. A hawk riding the wind called out to us. Atticus looked to where the noise had come from, but I'm sure he couldn't see it.

I picked him up, and we stood feeling the wind on our faces just as we'd done hundreds of times before. But things were different, oh, so different.

"How does it feel to be home, Atti?"

He let out a sigh and laid his head on my chest. Who would think so simple a gesture could have such a profound effect on a grown man? At that moment, if I could have, I would have given him my eyes. Considering all he'd given me, it seemed only right.

I wanted to give him something, something valuable. So I made a promise. I made a promise to Atticus and to God that if we came through it all, then I would sell the paper and we would move up to the mountains where we were happiest.

I asked him again if he wanted to go home, but when I set him down, he made his way toward the higher ledges. I wasn't surprised. We were on a mountain, and to Atticus that meant we went up until there was no more up—blindness be damned.

Neither Mount Welch nor Mount Dickey is a four-thousand-footer. They aren't even close, but they offer profound above-tree-line views throughout most of the hike. The loop is 4.4 miles, and after the ledges it's not all that taxing. I chose it for our hike because of the relative ease and because it was snow-free and would allow us to get above tree line. Besides, we'd been there before, plenty of times, and Atticus liked it. But this time around, it had to be frustrating for him, struggling to find his way on the open ledges, constantly having me correct him, or having to reach out with his nose to find my leg just to make sure I was still there. A couple of times, I boosted him up and he didn't hesitate. He'd move forward—just not as fast as he used to move.

There were times he had to follow me, times I was certain he was going to turn back, times I thought I couldn't go another step myself. And the more he struggled, the more I wanted to scream out for him to stop. Under my sunglasses, tears filled my eyes, and I cried until there were no more tears to shed. How could I not, seeing my friend striving with everything he had to get to a place he loved, doing something that used to be effortless but was now nearly impossible?

I believe he would have crawled up that mountain if he had to.

I have often stopped short when watching Atticus on the trails, seized by a moment of awe or wonder. There were times I've felt honored to be able to do that, as if I were watching something truly special and unique, for I have never felt as comfortable anywhere as he felt on a mountain. He was made for it as a bird is made to fly and a fish to swim. Even though so much had been robbed from him, he refused to think about anything else but getting to where he wanted to be. Or maybe it was where he needed to be.

When we finally reached the nub of rock on the summit of Dickey, he slowly pulled himself up to the very top. And then he sat.

He sat and cast his unseeing eyes to the wind and looked like a blind king sensing his kingdom below. From our vantage point, I could see several four-thousand-footers, and I imagined that somehow he knew they were there calling to him. Eventually I heard his sigh and saw the Little Buddha settle in.

And I'd been wrong—all my tears were not spent.

We sat there for more than an hour—I watched that little dog and he did his soul work. Paige had been right. There was something about that day that recharged Atticus, and me. He seemed more at peace after that and ready for the eye surgery. I was stronger and ready for the fight.

When the day of his cataract surgery came, my phone never stopped ringing. The answering machine filled up, and there were countless e-mails wanting to know how Atticus was doing. But I had nothing to tell them. I was waiting as helplessly as the rest of them.

When I did bring him home from the hospital that evening, there were cards and flowers and dog treats piled up outside the door to our apartment. A local restaurant dropped off Atticus's favorite—their meatballs. A friend left steak tips.

The first thing I did when we got inside was take that plastic cone off his neck. They'd put it on to keep him from scratching the stitches in his eyes, but I wasn't worried about that. He was always such a good dog. I simply told him, "Leave it be, Little Bug," and instead I'd ever so gently rub over his closed eyelids, and that would bring relief.

I laid Atticus across my lap and sent out a group e-mail telling everyone that the cataract surgery appeared to be successful, but we would have to wait to be certain. Susan Hayward said it could be months before we knew if his vision was going to be okay. She was still particularly concerned about his right eye.

He was heavily sedated, but it was beautiful out, and I wanted him to feel the breeze. I carried him downstairs, laid him on a thick blanket in the bicycle basket, and rode into the cool night.

When we pedaled up State Street and past Agave, the Mexican restaurant, I remembered a bike ride from the past. A woman sitting at one of Agave's outside tables saw Atticus in his basket atop the handlebars, noble and relaxed. She fell so utterly in love with him she asked me for his breeder's name. Soon after, she contacted Paige and bought a little male that looked similar to him. She called him Atticus.

During our most recent conversation I had asked Paige how "the other" Atticus was doing.

"Oh, that's right, you haven't heard."

I thought she was going to tell me that something bad had happened to the little guy, and I braced myself.

"There are now five Attici."

As Paige told it, various people who had met Atticus through the years had sought her out, gotten a dog that looked like him, and named it Atticus.

"You know, Tom, they saw what you and the little boy have together and they wanted the same thing. They figured they'd get a dog that looked like him and gave him the same name and then they'd have what you guys have. They're all good dogs with good owners, but none of them share what you two do.

From the very beginning, Atticus had a strong sense of self. He knew what he liked and didn't like. Here, just a few months old, he contemplates the purpose of his leash.

I have never gotten over my fear of heights; however, I just had to step out onto Bondcliff for this photo.

The "Little Buddha" can't get enough of summit sitting . . . no matter the season.

Look closely and you'll see Atticus heading toward the summit of Mount Monroe, the fourth-highest peak in the White Mountains.

Standing on top of Mount Jefferson under bright blue skies on a rare February day when it was warm enough to go without a hat, a coat, or gloves.

The most unlikely winter hiker sits atop deadly Mount Washington one March day.

"We sit together, the mountain and me, until only the mountain remains." —Li Po

This is the stormy-day look. It says it all:
"When can we get out and hike again?"

After a full day traversing Franconia Ridge,
we take in the view from Mount Flume.

Winter in the White Mountains can be enchanting, as is evident here on the way to Mount Field on the Willey Range.

Atticus and I don't believe much in limitations. Whatever people may say, for him, winter was just another season for hiking.

Atticus has always been happiest when outside,
particularly in the woods or on top of a mountain.

"I've always prided myself on matching up my babies with the right people, but I've never seen anything like the two of you."

We pedaled past Agave, through the night, along the cozy and shadowy tree-lined streets of the South End; by the old clam shack on Joppa Flats; along the waterfront and the boardwalk where the moon reflected on the Merrimack River; up Green Street by the police station and city hall; around Brown Square and the statue of William Lloyd Garrison, where I sat with Max the last night we were together; up to High Street and by the houses once belonging to sea captains.

I imagine that Atticus must have had the strangest dreams of flying, or maybe he thought he was on top of a mountain and was feeling the wind upon his face.

When I called Paige soon after and told her about the bicycle ride, she said she thought it was the perfect thing to do for a little dog with a big spirit.

Paige saved me during those troubling days. Atticus and I had many friends who would have done nearly anything for us, but I shared something different with Paige. I couldn't quite put my finger on it. Everyone else I knew had seen Atticus and me together, and while she never had, there was no question in my mind she knew us better than anyone did. We chatted often when we were going through the cataract and thyroid problems, and when we did, we talked as we had during Atticus's first year. Conversations lasted for hours. She asked me numerous questions about the mountains, my paper, Newburyport, our friends, and, of course, Atticus. But when I asked her questions, she gently deflected them. She was more interested in us, she told me.

I didn't know much about Paige. I knew she lived on a farm and raised puppies. I knew she was married, although she didn't talk about her husband all that much. And the reporter in me, always with my radar up, had the impression that there were things Paige wasn't telling me. It's not that it mattered, for I cherished our conversations anyway.

One day she asked, "Tell me, Tom, how does Atticus respond when you have a lady friend in your life?"

I admitted there hadn't been one in a couple of years. When he was young, I'd dated a couple of women, but the relationships never lasted very long, and I confessed that once we'd started going to the White Mountains, I almost didn't care about dating anymore. I was content.

"Don't get me wrong, Paige, I'd love to find the right person. I'm just not actively looking for her. Besides, it's going to take someone special to add more to what he and I already share."

There was a pause on her end of the phone, and then she said, "I'm sure Atticus will let you know when the right one comes along. Until then, love is love, Tom. God tells us we are supposed to have love in our life. He doesn't say it has to be between a man and a woman. Seems to me Atticus gave you the family you always wanted."

As always, Paige was right. It was all the more reason I worried about losing Atticus.

20

Bread Crumbs

Perhaps it was because Atticus had turned into the family I'd always wanted that even after all those years I never gave up hope that I could be close to my father, my brothers, and my sisters. I saw what it was like to have that special bond, and it made me believe I could have it with them one day.

I think the biggest tragedy of my father's life was that he never believed he was loved. He got glimpses of it now and again, but for the most part he couldn't see it and didn't believe it.

One glimpse came following a car accident that took place in May 2003. He had a diabetic seizure while driving and crashed into a telephone pole and a stone wall. He broke most of his ribs and was lucky to live. It would be a tough accident to go through for any man, never mind one a month shy of his eighty-third birthday.

In the months that followed, my brothers David and Eddie, the two of his nine children who still lived in Medway, checked in on him daily and on most days twice. I helped out, but being eighty miles away with a business to run, I couldn't be there as much. I drove down two or three times a week and spelled them whenever I could. My other brothers and sisters also helped out, but less often.

During my father's recovery, I arrived one day to find him sleeping. On the kitchen table was his ever-present yellow legal pad filled with his scrawl. He'd written that when the accident had occurred, he was angry with God for not taking his life. He couldn't figure out why he'd been left to live in such pain.

I could understand that. There was not much left to live for. His body was like an old car falling apart piece by piece. Heart, lungs, eyes, ears, mouth, diabetes, back—you name it, he had a problem with it.

But then he wrote that he believed God had spared his life so he could see how some of his sons had altered their lives to take care of him. He was humbled.

He didn't use the word "love"; no one in our family ever used it. But it was clear he felt loved.

My father never realized that he taught us many things in life, and it was only when he was heavy-handed or acting the part of the bully that we shut him out, just as he had shut us out. What he didn't see was that I learned from him in other ways. After I got away from him, I adopted many of the things he loved: writing, reading, classical music, politics, an appreciation of some of the greatest minds in history—men such as Thoreau and Emerson and their peers—and, of course, the White Mountains.

Without knowing it, he'd dropped these bread crumbs along the way, and I'd picked them up. When Atticus was recovering from his cataract surgery, I picked up yet another.

Multiple sclerosis drove my mother to a wheelchair, but my father was intent on having her experience as much of life as possible, and he refused to accept the limitations dictating where she could go. He brought her everywhere, which wasn't the norm back in the sixties. All of his children noticed that, and we carried it with us forever.

I wanted Atticus to understand the same thing: No matter what happened with his eyes or his thyroid, we were going to do our best to ignore limitations. That's why we wasted no time in getting back to living the life we'd grown used to. Only ten days after surgery, Atticus and I returned to the mountains.

He squinted a lot and needed drops put in his eyes, but he could see again. He was back to bouncing lightheartedly along trails, scampering up rocks much bigger than he, and drinking in the views. He was back to being the Little Buddha.

He had fun climbing mountains and spent a good portion of each hike waiting for me. We had lovely weather in which to enjoy the views. On Saturday we hiked Mount Pemigewasset in the morning and Welch-Dickey, the same mountains we'd climbed right before his surgery, in the afternoon. On Sunday we walked along the ridge of the Squam Range overlooking Squam Lake.

Pemigewasset and Welch-Dickey are big-bang-for-your-buck peaks. I didn't want to push him too hard so soon after surgery, but I wanted him to be on mountains where he could enjoy the views from the top with his new eyes. We lingered on each summit that Saturday. There was no hurry.

On Sunday we hiked up the wonderfully rustic Doublehead Trail and walked where moose evidently roamed in great numbers (there were signs of them everywhere) over rock and root, with occasional glimpses afforded typically only to angels and birds, as we looked down on the soft, heavenly green and blue of spring trees and a deep lake. It was a perfect day and a perfect hike.

Atticus moved over those mountains as he always had. The only way one could tell that things were a bit off was the strange shaved areas about his legs, throat, and abdomen where they had poked, prodded, injected, and scanned him.

One attractive, well-scrubbed woman of means back in Newburyport saw him the day after his surgery and was so impressed by his haircut that she wanted to know what to ask for when she brought her dog to the groomer the next week.

"It's called the Catara-Thyroid Cut," I told her.

For all his walking, climbing, and sitting, there was something else about that weekend that moved me even more. It was something within Atticus, and it was evident in his encounter with an easily overlooked creature.

We were happily skipping down Mount Pemigewasset when we encountered the tiniest rodent I'd ever seen. It was sitting on a rock in the middle of the trail and was frozen with fright when my size-twelve hiking shoe nearly squashed it into mouse heaven. Not being an expert on the genitalia of mice, I couldn't say whether it was a male or a female, and it seemed like a rather personal question to ask, as I have discovered in my past dealings with sexually ambiguous humans. For means of convenience, I'll refer to *him* as Templeton. (Can you tell I'm a reader? A mouse and a dog come face-to-face on a trail, and each is given a literary name, thanks to E. B. White and Harper Lee.)

I stopped short, and Atticus sat nicely by as we took stock of Templeton and Templeton stopped quivering and appeared to be taking stock of us in return.

I snapped a photo of Atticus and Templeton together, then offered the little rodent a small square of cheese that was as big as he was. I was delighted when he accepted and took tiny bites while I held it.

In my clumsy attempt to get a better photo of Templeton and Atticus sitting facing one another, I frightened the mouse, and he ran off and found refuge in the most unlikely of places: between Atticus's legs. I say "unlikely" because miniature schnauzers are terriers that were bred for ratting. It's one of the reasons Atticus always chased the squirrels of Moseley Pines. So Templeton's choice of a safe haven was ironic to say the least. Under some other dog, Templeton would have ended up a nice snack, and even under the Atticus of old he would have been less than a mouthful of savory, crunchy fare.

The previous November on the Avalon Trail, Atticus stood above me as I struggled with my Lyme disease on a hike. He had a nearly dead mouse dangling from his mouth. I was strangely saddened to see him taking the life from a creature of the mountains and asked him to release it. As he did, it hit the snow and writhed in pain. I slid on a heavy glove and held the mouse in my hand so it didn't have to die on the cold snow while Atticus sat next to me looking down at it. We had a man-to-dog talk that day, centering on reverence for life, and I tried to explain to him that what he'd done was not cool and that I wished he wouldn't do it again. I reminded him that we were only guests in the mountains.

Now, had anyone encountered us that day, we would have been a strange sight: a man holding a mouse, talking to a dog about reverence. But that's the way Atticus and I went through life, and, strangely enough, it worked for us. We stayed with that mouse until it stopped moving and then laid it to rest.

Some may think that was a silly thing to do, since a dog like Atticus was bred for such things, but little did I know that our gentle talk that day would mean something to him. For not only did he not kill Templeton, he allowed him to find shelter beneath him and simply sat looking down on him in a curious manner for several minutes. Templeton evidently felt very safe, for he sat there nonchalantly cleaning himself after his meal. We all stayed that way for quite some time.

I wasn't really sure what to think of Atticus that day. I'd always known he was different, but it was one of those moments that surprised even me. When I relayed the story to my friend Parkie and told her about our talk the previous November, she noted that maybe it wasn't the talk—perhaps Atticus had been transformed by the kindness of all those people who'd believed in a little dog enough to send money so he could see again.

Whatever it was, Atticus had broken the chain. (Emerson said, "Whoso would be a man must be a nonconformist." Although "only" a dog, Atticus would have impressed Ralph Waldo.)

For generations the traits of Atticus's breed had been carried forth, and it was instinctual for him to go after rodents. And yet under the trees on the side of Mount Pemigewasset, he chose not to. He had accomplished what most people fail to do—change.

It was a simple but profound moment for us.

I thought about it for days. As always, our time in the mountains had me thinking about my father. Atticus had done something my father couldn't, or wouldn't, do. He'd changed who he was.

I would like to believe that my father had tried to change who he was.

Why else would he have embraced classical music and great writing? Or Jack and Bobby Kennedy and Hubert Humphrey and the change they wanted to see? Why else would he admire the great men of history? How else would he have been awed by the grandeur of the mountains?

He loved beautiful things and was moved by them. He knew what he wanted; he just didn't know how to get there. At least that's what I tell myself when I give him the benefit of the doubt. But I'll never know, for there were things he didn't talk about, and he remained forever a mystery. In his book *A River Runs Through It*, Norman Maclean summed up my frustrations with my father: "It is those we live with and love and should know who elude us."

In some ways his failure at finding happiness in life became my real quest. I would go to the places he wanted to get to. Mostly I made it, thanks, in part, to some bread crumbs he'd unknowingly dropped on his own journey, and to a most unique little dog.

Several days after our encounter with the little rodent up north, we returned to Susan Hayward for one of several postoperative checkups. At the end of it, we were given permission to start hiking again.

21

Dinner with Frank Capra

One minute.

That's how long it took me to like Maureen Carroll, the special-ist with whom Atticus had an appointment at Angell Animal Medical Center to look into his hyperthyroidism. She was confident, professional, attractive, accomplished, funny, she had a great smile with a hint of mis-chief about it, and she wore heels in a place where everyone else went for the comfort of tennis shoes. But it had nothing to do with any of that. I fell for her because of something she said: "Hello, Atticus."

Two words. It was that simple.

But they were two words I'd never heard Susan Hayward say. I can't remember Dr. Hayward ever talking to Atticus. But Maureen Carroll talked to him throughout our checkup. After all, he was the patient, and of course she talked to me as well.

Maureen Carroll got it, but so did everyone else we encountered that day at Angell, from the receptionist who checked us in, to the custodian who said hello, to Maureen's vet tech, Ann Novitsky. At one point Ann took Atticus out of the examining room to draw some blood and get a urine sample, but she carried him back in a minute later, saying, "I think he wants to be with you when we do this." Ann got it.

Angell is one of the best animal hospitals in the world. It's a huge place, bigger than some small-town medical hospitals and they deal with thousands of animals a year. Because of that, I was expecting we'd get lost in the shuffle. Our experience with Susan Hayward had been less than warm. She was a fine surgeon, and I was thankful she'd done a great job on Atticus's eyes, but I never got the impression she was totally invested in him.

I wanted something more. Maureen, Ann, and Angell gave us that.

They understood that Atticus was my family, but they also realized he was special on his own. In her notes to John Grillo, Maureen Carroll wrote, "Quite an amazing dog."

She read Atticus perfectly. She would later say, "He speaks English with his actions."

I told Maureen about the ultrasound and how the specialist never saw the tumors he expected to see. I asked her if there was a chance the blood tests were wrong and that Atticus didn't have hyperthyroidism.

"No, most likely not," she said. "We'll run some tests, and when we get the results, we'll have an idea of how to move forward."

We left the warmth of Angell and drove back to Newburyport under the darkness of night, knowing that it would take a week to get the test results. But even in facing the unknown, there was something about the people at Angell that made me believe that if we were in for a journey down a long, dark trail, we would have good company.

Atticus and I drove to Plum Island late that night and listened to the ocean's song. We sat on the beach and looked up at the stars. A week was a long time to wait.

I felt Atticus's little body as he leaned up against me and thought of the end of Sarah Williams's poem "The Old Astronomer":

Though my soul may set in darkness, it will rise in perfect light;
I have loved the stars too fondly to be fearful of the night.

Of course we weren't the only ones waiting for the test results from Angell. It seemed as though most of Newburyport was as well. In their kindness they were stars in the darkness.

Because so much money had come in for Atticus's medical bills, I told people we didn't need any more. That would change if the results showed us we had a lengthy, drawn-out fight on our hands.

But there was an existing fund-raiser planned, and it would go on. Paul and Paula Breeden and their son Matt owned Bottega Toscana, a quaint Italian restaurant less than a block down State Street from us. On our nightly walks, if the restaurant was still open, Atticus would stand on his hind legs and peer in through the glass door. If there weren't many customers inside, the Breedens invited him in, and he'd run back to the kitchen, where they'd give him a meatball. If it was crowded, which it was on weekends, people would look up from their dinner to see either Paul or Matt drop what he was doing to bring a meatball out to Atticus, who sat patiently waiting on the stoop.

The Breedens had offered to close the restaurant to regular business and hold a fund-raiser for Atticus. They'd charge twenty dollars for a plate of meatballs and spaghetti, salad, and bread, and ten dollars would go to the Friends of Atticus.

But what happens when you throw a party and no one comes?

It was held on a Tuesday and started at four in the afternoon. When the doors opened, Atticus sat outside waiting for people to arrive. No one showed.

At five o'clock a couple and their baby came in, but that was it. Forty-five minutes later, it was still empty. I felt terrible for the Breedens. They'd sacrificed a night of business for Atticus. I apologized to Matt.

"Hey, it was worth a shot," he said as he looked a bit sadly at Atticus sitting by himself. But just as Matt finished talking, the door opened.

By six it was busy.

By seven there weren't enough tables, and a line formed out the door. We had to make people leave after they ate so that others could come in. But no one wanted to leave!

By eight-thirty all the food was gone, but people kept coming. Everyone stayed, and the laughter and love rang throughout the restaurant.

Some had tears in their eyes when they greeted Atticus, but most were in great spirits. Some didn't come to eat, simply to drop money in the basket on the counter. Almost everyone was from Newburyport, although a few hikers made the hour ride from Boston to pay tribute to the Little Giant. Bartenders and waitresses working in other restaurants sent over portions of their tips.

There in the middle of all that joyous raucousness, surrounded by so many of his friends, sat a little dog. With his new eyes, he squinted up at people as one by one they approached and greeted him. They talked to him and petted him, and many snuck him a meatball.

It was an amazing night. He was George Bailey at the end of *It's a Wonderful Life*!

Eventually everyone left, and it was just Matt, Atticus, and me. We sat at a table, and my head was spinning. So much had happened. A little dog had touched a community, and they had come out to say, "We're here for you." We sat and talked about the night, and right then a police cruiser pulled up outside and its lights went on.

"Oh, boy, here we go," I said quietly. A cop rapped on the door, and I readied myself for the worst, because it was Newburyport and I was the editor of the *Undertoad*. We had just finished an uplifting night, but reality had come knocking.

Matt opened the door, and the officer walked up to where I was sitting, looked at Atticus in the restaurant, where he was in violation of the health code, and dropped some money in the basket.

He smiled and said, "Good luck, Atticus."

But Atticus didn't need luck. He had friends, and many of them. Or at least that's pretty much what Ann Novitsky said when she called me from Angell that night telling me there was no sign of the hyperthyroidism. The blood tests showed that Atticus was completely normal. It was as if it had never existed.

I couldn't believe my ears.

"But how can that be? I thought Dr. Carroll said the other tests were probably accurate," I told her.

"I know! I asked her the same thing," Ann said. She then said something about the power of friendship, or maybe the power of prayer. I couldn't really tell what she said—I was laughing too loud.

The American College of Veterinary Ophthalmologists has a trademarked motto: " . . . that light shall prevail over darkness."

It certainly had for us, in more ways than one.

22

The Promise

I'd like to tell you that we woke up the next morning and everything was perfect, but that wouldn't be the truth.

I woke up to relief and gratitude, and that lasted for a couple of days. Then came the crash. It was inevitable. From before the start of winter when I fought Lyme disease, to our successes and failures throughout the winter months, to returning to Newburyport, to Atti's blindness, we'd been on a roller coaster.

Once I learned that Atticus was going to be okay, I started to decompress. I collapsed into myself again. I felt the way I had when we first came back from the mountains in March: wasted, uninspired, as if I were just going through the motions. I knew my future wasn't with the *Undertoad*, but it was how I made my living and I needed to concentrate on Newburyport for the time being. It was difficult to do. In many ways I'd already broken away from the city and was ready to move on, but there was nothing to move on *to*.

Making matters worse, even though Atticus's eyes improved, I tore my calf muscle on a hike on Mount Carrigain. The only way to heal it was to rest it, so Atticus and I settled back into our Newburyport lives, and without the mountains we both languished.

That's when I made a most unlikely decision. I loved Newburyport, and it was clear that at least part of Newburyport loved me (and Atticus) back. The way people had come to Atticus's rescue proved it.

I needed to do something other than write the *Undertoad*, and I followed the advice of some people I liked and trusted when they suggested I run for mayor.

Now, that was a hoot to some folks. City hall's greatest critic wasn't just running for elected office, he was running for the most important office in the city. It gave people something to talk about. The response was what I expected. My critics attacked, my supporters loved it. And there were a few in the middle who didn't know what to think. But I knew I could count on many of their votes simply because they'd be curious about what I'd do as mayor. And I believed I would be a good mayor, since first and foremost I knew the city and would listen to its voices.

However, if I managed to get elected, I imagined myself as a one-term mayor. It would be two years and out. In order to do the job right, you couldn't be too much of a politician. There'd be tough decisions to make, and I'd step on some toes. I'd demonstrated in the *Undertoad* that I wasn't afraid to take a stand for something I believed in, but it was a good way to make enemies. I joked with some of my friends that I might become the first mayor of a Massachusetts city ever to be assassinated.

In order to get onto the ballot, all I needed to do was get the signatures of fifty registered Newburyport voters. I had those in the first two days.

I was confident I'd do well in the election. My five opponents lacked experience and visibility. Yes, I was controversial—anyone who takes a stand on the local issues is controversial—but I believed that would work in my favor in a field of mostly unknown candidates, because even the least educated voter would know who I was. The primary election would be in September. The two candidates with the most votes would face each other in November.

My campaign would be simple. There would be no team. Atticus and I would simply knock on every door in the city. I'd have a conversation with the voters, one by one. More than telling them what *I* was all about, I'd listen to what *they* had to say. It worked with the *Undertoad*, and I knew it would work running for office as well.

Early feedback was strong. People called telling me I could put campaign signs on their property. The editor of the *Newburyport Current*, a weekly newspaper, told me I was the strongest candidate in the early stages. I knew that the *Daily News* would never support me, but that was a blessing in disguise, since it was seen as part of the establishment and the average voter rejected the establishment. This was something that had festered in old Newburyport, and whenever the hoi polloi had their say, they liked to stick it to the powers that be.

The weekend before my nomination papers were due, Atticus and I went north and hiked the four mountains of Franconia Ridge. It was like seeing an old friend again. We took our time moving from Lafayette to Lincoln to Liberty to Flume. It was a pleasant summery day, with a breeze just strong enough to keep the bugs in check.

On top of Lincoln, we drank and ate, and Atticus went off and sat by himself. He gazed with his new eyes into the Pemigewasset Wilderness over the long green hump of Owl's Head, toward Galehead, the Twins, the Bonds, the Hancocks, and Carrigain. A slight updraft rose from the valley below and caught his ears, sending them flying. It did my heart good to see him that way again—the wind in his face, the joy of freedom.

Back in Newburyport a few days later, I announced that I was pulling out of the mayor's race. A local reporter was shocked and wanted to know why.

"Because I made a promise to Atticus," I told her. And I had.

I was going to sell the *Undertoad*, and we were moving to the mountains.

But there was one problem—no one really wanted to buy the *Undertoad*. It was not a moneymaker. It was my passion, and it had turned into my job, and I barely scraped a living out of it. My propensity to tell it like it was and refuse to shy away from controversy kept the major advertisers in town (banks, insurance companies, the local hospital) away. They all read the paper; most even subscribed. They just didn't want their business associated with it.

Ultimately, there were two parties interested in buying it, and they weren't offering much. One was a group of reputable businessmen from out of town. They hoped the *Undertoad* would give them a presence in Newburyport. But there was a problem: Our beliefs didn't line up.

I'd never adopted my father's conviction that Republicans carried the plague. I was an unenrolled voter but was admittedly far more liberal than conservative.

Although some questioned that, since over my last three years with the paper I'd let Peter McClelland, a retired schoolteacher, write an extremely conservative column. When some of my liberal readers threatened a boycott of the paper and some of the businesses who advertised, I pointed out that being a liberal meant I respected another person's right to print his or her opinion, even though it differed from mine.

In my last issue of the *Undertoad*, I wrote that I was proud of standing by Peter's right to express his views, but also that, being the editor, I had the last say. And it was a mischievous last say. One thing Peter routinely took aim at was gay marriage. He was vehemently against it. Because I considered Peter a homophobe, I surrounded his column with ads for gay businesses. I couldn't help myself.

The potential buyers would have liked Peter McClelland, but he might not have been conservative enough for them. They were to the *right* of the religious right. They loved George W. Bush, supported the war, didn't think women should have reproductive freedom, and believed there was something inherently wrong with gays and lesbians.

Unfortunately, the only other person interested in buying the *Undertoad* came with baggage—and lots of it. He was trouble. He was in his forties and had a lengthy police record. And when I say lengthy, I think he had nearly as many arrests as he had years.

I gave it a lot of thought, but it was clear I didn't have a choice in the matter, so I followed my conscience and sold the *Undertoad* to the convict. My father would have been proud.

Soon after paying cash up front for it—it was the only deal I'd accept from him—the new owner was arrested once again. There would never be another issue of the *Undertoad*.

Many deemed it a fitting ending. It wasn't that they disliked my paper. To the contrary, they considered it my creation and didn't think it should be in anyone else's hands.

I didn't get rich with the sale, but I made enough so that Atticus and I could pay off some debts and move to the mountains, and we wouldn't have to worry about money for close to a year. It would give us a start in our new home.

Our leave-taking was bittersweet. Not only was I saying good-bye to the *Undertoad*, I was leaving my adopted hometown and all our friends. There was once a time I thought I'd never leave the city, but the mountains had called, and Atticus and I were going.

I kept count during our last four weeks, and I'll remember it as "The Month of Forty-Three Good-bye Parties." I didn't want a big party. Instead I wanted more intimate get-togethers where I could spend time with each person I cared about. There were coffees and teas, breakfasts, lunches, and dinners. There were hugs, kisses, gifts, and cards exchanged. Some couldn't believe that Atticus and I were actually going to leave Newburyport. Others envied us.

On the day we left town, we'd said all our good-byes and I was ready to leave. We took one final loop around the city in my car. Our last stop was at John Kelley's gas station to fill the tank. John was old Newburyport.

"Well, you did it," he said. "You came to town, you had your say, you made a difference, and you did something I didn't think was possible."

"What's that?" I asked him.

"You got out without getting shot."

We both laughed.

Atticus and I were heading north to the mountains as we'd done so many times before. Only this time it was different. We'd given up Newburyport and were moving into an apartment in Lincoln owned by the same people we'd always rented a cabin from when we were hiking. As we started across the bridge spanning the Merrimack River, Atticus was looking out the window at the trees of Moseley Pines, and I couldn't help but be aware of the lump in my throat.

The *Undertoad* may have died in the hands of its new owner, but the city had a new set of scribes to document its trials and tribulations. Several blogs started up, following Mary Baker Eaton's lead, but again it was Mary in her Newburyport Blog who summed up my leaving: "It sounded as if when it came to Newburyport, that in the end, 'all passions were spent.' And Mr. Ryan left on October 1, 2007, for the White Mountains of New Hampshire." Mary was right—all my Newburyport passions *were* spent. In eleven years I made my mark, changed the city more than a little, and was leaving on my own terms. It was something to be proud of.

Atticus and I were ready for new adventures—and they were on their way.

Part III

Full Circle

*Thousands of tired, nerve-shaken, over-civilized people
are beginning to find out that going to the mountains
is going home; that wildness is a necessity; and that
mountain parks and reservations are useful not only
as fountains of timber and irrigating rivers, but as
fountains of life.*

—JOHN MUIR

23

A New Quest

One of my favorite places in the White Mountains is on top of Cannon Cliffs. It's about a half mile below the summit of Cannon Mountain along the Kinsman Ridge Trail. The cliffs sit above where the Old Man of the Mountain, the state's symbol, used to reside before he collapsed in 2003, the day after my father's car accident.

The Old Man was a famous rock edifice made up of several ledges, and if you looked up at it from the bottom of Franconia Notch, you could clearly see a man's profile. It was so *clear* that Daniel Webster once said, "Men hang out their signs indicative of their respective trades; shoemakers hang out a gigantic shoe, jewelers a monster watch, and the dentist hangs out a gold tooth; but in the mountains of New Hampshire, God Almighty has hung out a sign to show that there He makes men."

The Old Man was also Nathaniel Hawthorne's inspiration for his short story "The Great Stone Face."

The Old Man was the main reason we'd camped either in or near Franconia Notch when we were kids. And no matter how many times we saw him, the next time was just as striking as the first time. My father loved him, and we all did, too. My father also loved riding the tram to the summit of the mountain, and once on top we'd hike around. But we never made it down to Cannon Cliffs. I would have remembered that, for they are simply breathtaking.

From the top of the cliffs, the drop-off is precipitous. Combine the view down into the notch and up to the towering summit of Mount Lafayette, and the dimension is staggering. It's a place where you feel fully alive, yet insignificant in the big picture of things. You are high above the valley but dwarfed by living, breathing mountains. Whenever I stand on top of them, my fear of heights takes hold, and it feels as though gravity will suck me over the edge. My stomach lurches, and my legs shake. And yet such heights never deterred Atticus; they were but a vantage point for a better view.

On a relaxed day, when we weren't in too much of a hurry to get anywhere and we just wanted to hike to an awe-inspiring spot, the top of the cliffs was also a great place to take a nap. I'd use my backpack for a pillow, and Atticus would lie down next to me. We'd look at the views for a few minutes, then drift off to sleep. It's a particularly nice place for a nap on a breezy autumn afternoon, and during one afternoon in the last week of October that's what we were doing.

I woke up to see Atticus sitting closer to the edge than I like to get. He was looking intently up at the summit of Lafayette.

Seeing him do this always captivated me, but after the cataract surgery it had an elevated meaning. I thought of his eyes, of his thyroid problem that had disappeared, of those who'd contributed to him in our hour of need, of Angell Animal Medical Center—a great nonprofit that helps thousands of animals—and I made a decision. Since we were living in the mountains full-time and were in no hurry to do anything for the immediate future, I decided Atticus and I would take another crack at doing two rounds of the forty-eight in winter. Once again we'd use it for fund-raising, but our second Winter Quest would benefit Angell Animal Medical Center.

Angell loved the idea. I announced our efforts on our blog, and contributions started rolling in. Each peak was dedicated to a beloved pet, either living or departed. When people dedicated a peak, they sent along

a check made out to Angell, but they also sent a photograph, and sometimes even a written vignette about the animal. Each time we reached a
mountaintop, I'd post the photo of the pet it was dedicated to on our blog.

When the fund-raising was all set up, I thought about how different
our lives had become. It was the last week of October, and back in Newburyport the city was reaching the end of the mayoral campaign. The
following week the people of Newburyport would choose their mayor.
For the first time since 1995, I didn't have a thing to do with how it would
turn out—and it felt grand!

With afternoons spent on Cannon Cliffs or walking over the Southern Presidentials without a care in the world, I couldn't believe how
blessed Atticus and I were. Each day sparkled for us. We'd overcome
much, had learned a great deal along the way, and were experiencing the
tingling sensation that comes with new beginnings.

Atticus missed having a downtown where everyone knew his name,
but if we wanted that, we simply went hiking on a busy day, and there
were many on the trails who knew him. Our lives had reversed. We'd
gone from being very public at home and private on the trails to being
public on the trails and private at home.

Our apartment was a simple place, just a few miles from Franconia
Notch. It had a familiar feel to it. When I sat at my desk, I could look
through the trees bordering the Pemigewasset River where it was as narrow as a stream. The far bank was a tangle of trees and overgrown brush.
It had the look of a land that time had forgotten, a place where there used
to be life and the happy chatter of families. All that was left, however,
were a couple of rutted old dirt roads, some forgotten tires, some vestiges
of a campground that once was there, and the skeleton of a dead truck.

I didn't realize it the first time I looked across the river, but I knew
that place. That forgotten campground was one of my father's favorite
places to bring us. It was called Campers' World. He'd park the trailer
above the river, and when my brothers and I played on the river rocks, he
sat at a picnic table and wrote on his yellow pad. Those were some of the
most perfect days I ever knew. But they'd taken place thirty-five years

before. Campers' World had died an unceremonious death, and there was no sign to remind me that it used to be a place we loved. I smiled at how fate had delivered me to that place and took heart in knowing I'd be writing about a hundred feet from where my father had once written about the mountains and often dreamed about being a writer.

That was reason enough to call him for the first time in more than a year. I could hear the emphysema rattle in his voice, the weight of his age, how tired he was. We talked for thirty minutes, and by the end it was clear he needed to lie down. We were both happy I'd made the call.

Soon after, I made another phone call. I called Paige Foster and let her know about our new lives. I told her that Atticus was thriving. It was a warm and cheery conversation sprinkled with laughter.

Somewhere in the middle of it, I told her there was something I'd always been curious about. All the puppies on her Web site ran from $1,200 to $5,000. Why had Atticus cost only $450?

I considered him the best thing that ever happened to me and had no complaints whatsoever, but I was curious—had she thought he might have some health issues? And if so, was that why she'd contemplated keeping him for herself, as she'd once told me?

That wasn't it, she said. She'd given me a discount because she got the feeling that's all I could afford. If she'd sold him to someone else, which she said she wouldn't have done, he would have gone for at least $2,400. But she had a feeling he and I just needed to be together.

It wasn't my intent to accuse or offend, and while she said I hadn't, there was something in her voice that had me feeling I'd done something wrong.

Paige would follow our second Winter Quest by reading our blog and by watching her e-mail for photo updates of the little dog who'd once lived in Louisiana but had made a name for himself in the snowy mountains of New Hampshire.

After my conversation with my father, I got the impression he wished he were up in the mountains walking with me, living the life I was leading. I got the strangest feeling that Paige had a similar longing.

24

The Witch

If there was a word that summed up the beginning of our second winter of fund-raising, it was "snow."

From the very start of December, snow piled up, and when winter began, we sputtered to get going. We couldn't establish a rhythm, and because new snow continued to fall, we wouldn't have the opportunity to hike two days in a row until the third week. Winds were high, temperatures low. All in all, it was an ominous beginning.

On the first day of winter, we climbed the two Hancocks, and then we stuck with the smaller, easier peaks. We were already behind in the game. A year to the date since we'd survived the Bonds' blizzard, I wanted to add three peaks to our total, and I decided we'd do Tom, Field, and Willey, the three four-thousand-footers of the Willey Range.

The Willey Range had some history to it. It stood on the western side of Crawford Notch, and it was named for an ill-fated family that had been killed in 1826. When a landslide sent a thundering roar from the mountain above, the Willey family ran from their house, fearing that it was doomed. But that was a dreadful decision, because the mountain came tumbling down on everything *except* the house, which was left untouched.

No one survived. Six people were found dead outside, while three others were never found.

Numerous White Mountain artists captured the scene of the tragedy in their paintings, and Nathaniel Hawthorne used it as the basis for his eerie short story "The Ambitious Guest."

At the southern end of Crawford Notch, not too far from the original site of the Willey house, is Nancy Brook. It is named after Nancy Barton, who froze to death in 1778, legend has it, while attempting to follow her fiancé, who had abandoned her and absconded with her dowry. There have been many reports that her ghost still roams the area.

Who knows if the ghost of Nancy Barton still exists or if the accounts are just the fervid imagination of those who claimed to have seen her? I didn't believe in ghosts, but as I've said, I had my own issues with the mountains after the sun went down. And we were headed for the Willey Range late in the day.

As a boy I always slept on my side with one ear protected by my pillow, the other by my sheet and blanket, pulled high to cover and guard it from the horrid witch who determinedly haunted my dreams and hunted for such things as ears, eyes, and noses. When I slept, there was typically nothing visible of my face save for a small breathing hole close to but not revealing my nose.

Once, when I was very young, I dreamed that the witch was in my room, and when she wasn't able to get at my ears or my face, she decided to smother me by holding the covers over my head. Try as I might, I could not get her off, and I panicked. I panicked even more when I woke up to realize I wasn't dreaming. She was there, holding the covers down so tight I couldn't budge them.

I screamed, thrashed, and squealed until I was rescued by my father. However, he told me there wasn't any witch. I'd simply been so restless in my sleep that I'd turned my body completely around, with my head where my feet should be. The sheets were tucked in, creating the illusion that I was being held down.

I knew better; this witch was powerful *and* elusive.

She was so powerful, in fact, that I slept with my ears and head covered until I was finally sleeping with women, and even then in the middle of the night I would awaken with a start, look uneasily around the room, and sink lower into the bed so that my ears were covered and there was again an airhole for my nose.

I don't think I stopped sleeping that way until I was deep into my thirties, when I finally felt daring enough to confront both the witch and my fear of the dark.

The witch hadn't come around for the longest time, but there were nights I thought I'd hear her footsteps or hushed cackle or maybe her raspy breath, which smelled of death and rot. Whenever I sensed her, I was apprehensive, filled with unease but not nearly as paralyzed by fear as I used to be.

And yet as a grown man I sensed her lurking in the dark as we approached the summit of Mount Field. She waited until the sun was gone and the night had draped a thick blanket over the mountain before she made her appearance.

We had started our day later than normal to take advantage of the weekend hikers unknowingly breaking out the trail for Atticus. By the time we'd reached the summit of Mount Tom, the first peak, and looked over at Field about a mile and a half away and imagined the summit of Willey, another mile and a half from Field, I had an eerie feeling we would run into the witch as day ebbed to night. Don't ask me why.

I stood among the dead, blown-down trees and the small upstart saplings that have come to claim the top of Mount Tom, a seven-year-old in the body of a forty-six-year-old. It would be dark when we finished our hike if we continued over Field to Willey and then back again. I knew it meant that the witch would be out, close by, with her smell of death and rot reaching toward me like a bony finger.

I shrugged her from my mind, swallowed, and was on my way.

When we reached the top of Field, we encountered three gray jays. They are bold birds who can be found throughout the Whites, but they're more evident in the mountains right along Crawford Notch than they are anywhere else. They're so forward that if you hold your palm open with food in it, they will land on your fingertips and eat right out of your hand. They were there to say hello—or, more likely, "Feed us!" I played with them for a while and fed them granola, while Atticus watched them closely, making certain I didn't give away too much of our food. He and I then dropped down into the woods for the steep descent that led to the long climb up Willey. When we reached Willey, the light was fading. I took a few photos and then doubled back toward Field. In the open woods looking westward into the Pemi Wilderness, I could feel the approaching night. It was cold. Icicles formed on my hair as it brushed against the back of my neck. I stopped long enough to put on my hat.

On the ascent back up to Field, I could hear the witch; she was coming with the night. I could feel the chill of her presence growing stronger as the sky grew darker, the trees more shadowy. There was no wind, just a still presence in the air. Occasionally I would stop to catch my breath and notice the silence. It was *too* quiet. There was something behind the silence, and some faint noise came as I shuffled through the snow making my own noise. Whenever I stopped again, it seemed to stop also, just out of range, just out of hearing.

By the time Atticus and I reached the summit of Field again, the gray jays were gone and so was the day. Night was upon us. I retrieved one of my headlamps from my pack and pulled it on over my hat.

There we were on top of a mountain, night wrapped around us, and we were about three miles from the safety of the car. Below in the valley, lights twinkled in the Highland Center, an AMC lodge where outdoor enthusiasts stay. The thought of how cozy and comfortable the guests there were as they settled down for supper made me feel more like we were three hundred miles from any comfort.

Atticus has never minded the dark, and I'd worked on my fear the previous winter, doing my best to exorcise my childhood demons and evict the witch.

We left the summit and dropped into the snowy, silvery woods. The witch was near.

The snow was high enough that I occasionally hit my head on tree branches. They seemed to swing at me as I went by, especially since my headlamp was chasing the dark and casting lively shadows. We were on the steep Avalon Trail, where other hikers sometimes sit and slide down. I choose not to do this, because not only can it be dangerous, it also creates a luge run for those who hike it after it has frozen.

I watched each step, letting the teeth of my snowshoes bite into the solid, icy snow. Atticus, meanwhile, was gliding down the trail, straight-legged; his Muttluks served as four mini sleds. He was better at relaxing than I was when it came to glissading down a mountain. Try as I might, I always ended on my backside, so I decided to give it up.

I took my time negotiating the steep downhill.

In the dark the witch grew nearer, I knew this because I could feel her. I sensed something near us and called Atticus back, saying, "Behind me, please."

Then in the woods to our left, a boomlike crash sounded in the shadows of the tight trees and startled me. I turned to see if it was the witch, all the while knowing it was!

In turning, I lost my footing, and suddenly I was airborne, my feet higher than my head. When I landed, it was with a thud on my backpack, and in an instant I was racing down the steep luge run, gaining speed. I reached out but failed to grasp trees as I flew by. It would have been best if I'd just relaxed into it, but I fought it, and thus I was wildly out of control.

When the trail made an abrupt turn to the left, I didn't and instead went sailing through the air, landing in deep, soft snow.

Back, head, shoulders, knees, legs, arms. I was in one piece. I lay like that for a while, thinking of the absurdity of being in the woods in the mountains in a pile of powder, gazing up at the bottoms of evergreen trees.

Atticus caught up, climbed onto my chest, and stood there looking down at me.

In that ludicrous position, with a little dog on my chest, I decided that the time had come to put away the fears of my childhood. It was ridiculous.

I suddenly wanted to face the witch and get it over with. I wanted to tell her to go to hell. I'd had enough.

There was really nothing about her that should have scared me. After four and a half decades of life, I'd seen enough to know that the worst of it was much worse than anything the witch could throw at me.

When I got to my feet and back on the trail, I knew there was nothing else to fear. The bears were hibernating. And what of a moose? They used the trails often. What if we were to come upon one in the night? Clear thinking told me that a moose or any other creature of the night, even a witch, would probably be more frightened by the sight of a big man coming down the trail, snowshoes slapping loudly with each stride, sweat frozen to icicles on the fringes of my hair, red cheeks, a large pack on my back, and a bright, one-eyed light above my face. And then there was that little pixie next to me, he in his Muttluks with reflective strips that made him look like a light-footed demon of the woods.

Just what witch would mess with us?

Someone asked me once why I would hike, or at least finish my hike, at night, alone with Atticus on a mountain if I feared the dark, even the slightest bit. Good question. I guess I wanted to believe I was beyond such fears. But it's also because much of what I do with Atticus in the mountains is about being more than I have been in the past. It was about wanting to be a better me, about spitting in the eye of the witch.

And maybe there were times I thought I was out there rescuing the little boy who was trapped under the covers of his bed. The little boy whose mother had died and whose family had disappeared.

Whatever it was, I believed that when you eat a fear, it makes you stronger. Face the witch and she goes away. Make one witch go away and others will follow her.

As our descent back to the car continued, I actually stopped and turned off my headlamp and stood in the dark woods. No streetlights, no sounds from the highway, no sign of villages nearby. It was just me and Atticus and the mountain and the dense woods and the silent night. I stopped, took a breath, and relaxed.

Such release. Such peace.

Is it any wonder why many of those who were thought to be prophets throughout history found their peace wandering the desert, climbing mountains, or out at sea? It's the natural world that heals the soul.

Back at the car, I looked up at the dark outline of the Willey Range against the stars. The Willey family, the ghost of Nancy Barton, my witch. Whatever lingered in the night was no longer a concern of mine. I knew as I stood there that my fear would never return again.

25

Magic Is Where You Find It

We were falling behind in our attempt to climb ninety-six peaks. After the hike on the Willey Range, we were kept off the trails for another five days because of the constant snows. With more snow falling on a Friday night, I chose another late start for our Saturday hike up Mount Jackson. I chose Jackson because the weekenders were out in force with their snowshoes earlier in the day. They left the Crawford Path a flattened sidewalk cut through deep drifts on either side of the trail.

As we climbed, we encountered several others on their way down. The higher we went, the deeper the snow was on the side of the trail and the more magical the trees became, looking like creatures frozen in some distant dreamscape. I stopped often to take photos . . . and to catch my breath. As always, when I stopped, Atticus stopped, too. When I began again, so did he. Slowly, we made our way toward the top.

Within a half mile of the summit, we ran into Ken and Ann Stampfer, who were on their way down. We'd met them during our first year hiking, because they were friends of Steve Smith's. Soon they became our friends as well, and they adored Atticus as much as anyone I'd ever met.

Ken, ironically enough, was an ophthalmologist—for humans, not for dogs—but he became a constant source of information for me whenever

I had a question about Atticus's eyes. And Ann used to be a nurse, and she educated me on thyroid issues. During the week they lived near Boston, but each weekend they returned to their log cabin just a few miles down the road from where Atticus and I lived, in order to hike. In our first year up north, they became our closest friends and, in some ways, our salvation. In a place where we didn't know many people, it was good to know they were nearby.

And yet as friendly as we were, neither of us knew that the others were climbing Jackson that day. How strange it was to be in the middle of that snowy landscape, a couple of miles away from the road, and see their beaming faces come into view as they called out, "Atti!"

Atticus knew who they were immediately, even though they were layered in winter gear, and he abandoned his trundle and sprinted to greet them. We stopped and chatted for a few minutes before the winter chill caused each of us to begin shivering. Before parting ways, they informed me that there was no one else behind them.

I cannot tell you the pleasure such words elicited. A thrill ran through me from head to toe—I felt like a child who'd been locked in a toy store overnight.

I'm often asked, "Do you have a favorite mountain?"

"Any mountain where Atticus and I can be alone on top," I say.

And while that is true, there are some mountains that mean more than others, and it's not just because of the views. Each mountain has its own personality, and it triggers different things in me when I'm on it. As much difficulty as I have climbing any mountain, gifts are revealed along the way as I struggle upward, but there are some that are richer and have deeper treasures awaiting me. I can't say why some affect me more than others, but it's clear that they do.

Jackson is one such mountain. Whenever I'm up on the flat summit and look around, I feel as if I'm on top of a small table, and the world falls away at my feet. It stands on the lip of a near-cliff high atop Crawford Notch. To the west a sea of mountains reaches up and fades for as far as the eye can see, like waves on the ocean. To the south it's more of the same, though not as dramatic, since those mountains are not as close, but still they stretch ever onward. To the north and east, it's even more breathtaking, for Jackson is the shortest and southernmost peak in the chain of eight four-thousand-footers along the Presidential Range.

On a clear day, the view in every direction is awe-inspiring, but on Jackson the winter view to Mount Washington is astounding. It stands at the end of the spine, two thousand feet higher than Jackson's summit and clad in its brilliant gown of white.

When Atticus and I finally reached the top, the sky was a gorgeous charcoal gray, and there were no winds, so even though it was only twenty-five degrees, we were comfortable. Of course I was thrilled to have it to ourselves, and in my excitement I took photo after photo of views in every direction under that beautiful, brooding sky. I then picked up little Atticus, and we sat down for a spell. It's not too often you can do this on the top of a mountain in winter. We stayed there for quite some time, Atticus soaking in the views from my lap while I thought about how lucky we were to be up there looking at scenery some will never see. At such times my mind wanders, and both man and dog find ourselves in peaceful contemplation. It just seems to happen more often on Jackson than on most other mountains.

Beneath the graying sky, waiting for the storm that would strike in a few hours' time, long after we were home and safe, I let my mind drift back to a moment a year earlier. John Bartlett, a longtime reader of the *Undertoad*, was dying in Anna Jaques Hospital. I'd never met the elderly gentleman, but the '*Toad* had been delivered to his doorstep for as long as I can remember. (I know this because I delivered it; such was the glamorous life of a one-man newspaper.)

On one of the last days of his life, John Bartlett's son asked him if there was anything special he wanted. I took it as a great compliment that all he asked for was the latest edition of my paper. The son called me to inquire if he could get an early edition. I informed him it was just about ready to be sent to the printers and wouldn't be available for a couple of days.

When I heard the disappointment in the son's voice, I told him I would bring a draft of the *'Toad* to the hospital myself and share it with his father.

Later that day, after I read my paper to him, the elderly gentleman had a contented look on his face. He thanked me and told me that while he loved all the paper, his favorite column had become my letter home to my father, which of late had been filled with the mountain adventures Atticus and I had accumulated by the wagonload.

He confessed that he'd never stood on top of a mountain before, but he felt as if he had ever since I'd started writing about them.

"When you and Atticus are on a mountain, is it like you said?" he asked.

"How so?"

He closed his eyes and said in his halting voice, "You once wrote that sitting on top of a mountain and looking out at all that surrounds you is like looking at the face of God."

He had a good memory, for I had written that a year and a half earlier.

"Yes, that's exactly what it's like."

He then asked me if I would do him a favor. If it wasn't too much trouble, he wanted me to think of him the next time I was on top of a peak with Atticus. It was my pleasure to say I would.

Before I left, I told John that I'd heard he had recently celebrated his sixtieth wedding anniversary with his wife. I congratulated him on the accomplishment and noted that at my age it was a milestone I would never experience. "That's amazing. What is it like?"

John Bartlett—who would be dead within forty-eight hours, dry skin hanging off his bones, eyes barely open, lips dry and cracked and life just barely in him—well, he paused, and then the faintest smile appeared and he said, "It's a lot like being on top of a mountain."

On top of Jackson, under bruised skies with the day mostly spent, Atticus and I looked out toward Mount Washington, and I thought of old John Bartlett and our conversation.

Magic is where you find it; the only thing that matters is that you take the time to look for it. It can be the wonder in a little dog's face or the memory of an old man.

People continued to ask why I'd taken to hiking alone with Atticus. It was because such thoughts come to me on a climb or at the top or walking through the thick woods on the way down under a golden sun or bright stars. When there was no one to talk to, I found myself in a walking meditation. I was not a religious man, but if I were, the woods would be my church, the mountaintops my altar.

Not a hike goes by that doesn't leave me feeling richer for having done it. And when Atticus and I set out to hike ninety-six peaks in ninety days, I sometimes worried that by pushing for numbers in the name of reaching our goals I would sacrifice the magic each mountain offers.

I couldn't imagine I'd ever think the mountains mundane. They would continue to teach, inspire, and challenge me. In the coming weeks, they would help me construct the final pieces of a bridge to my father.

26

Death on Franconia Ridge

What I feared most that winter were the helicopters.

Whenever I heard one, the sound was as haunting as the cry of the banshee, and it foreshadowed doom. It meant that someone was missing or, worse, dead. The helicopters were search and rescue. They were a poignant reminder to respect the power of the mountains.

Because of that respect, I planned our hikes carefully by using my laptop to monitor trail conditions, weather reports, and the higher-summits forecasts religiously. Winter left little margin for error, especially for one as small as Atticus. If we were trapped on a mountain, I had a chance to survive because of my size. But Atticus couldn't just hunker down and wait for help. He had to keep moving to maintain his core temperature. It's one of the reasons that when we were slammed by the storm the previous winter on the Bonds, I hadn't emptied out my backpack and put him in there. He could have frozen sitting still for so many hours, even if I'd wrapped him in layers of my extra clothing. In the freezing cold, Atticus had to move to live.

I simply refused to play Russian roulette with the weather; Atticus was too important to me.

My conservative approach was why we were behind schedule, with only twenty mountains climbed a month into winter. The weather had been unkind so far, but I was hoping for a reverse of the previous winter, which had had very little snow in the beginning and then quick bursts of big storms hitting every two weeks.

It seemed to snow a bit each night. But that was down in the valleys. Up high it snowed far more than that.

One morning Atticus and I set out to climb Garfield, knowing that several people had done it the day before and left a well-trodden path that Atticus could take advantage of. There was the slightest dusting of snow outside our back door, like powdered sugar just barely gracing a fresh-baked cookie. When we reached the Garfield trailhead, it was the same fine powder, and yet up higher we pushed through a foot of new snow.

It was like that throughout the winter. Whether it had snowed in the valleys or not, the mountaintops always seemed to have a new supply. It was great for the ski industry, but bad for Atticus and me. When we did get to hike, it was mostly on smaller, individual peaks. What we needed was a break in the weather that would get us above tree line and allow traverses covering multiple summits. That would catch us up in a hurry.

We finally caught that break and headed to the four peaks on Franconia Ridge. The ridge was one of those hikes we saved for the best and safest days. It was a spectacular walk above tree line, but if the weather changed, it could also be a deathtrap. The ridge was one of those places folks talked about when they said, "People die up there."

It used to be that Mount Washington and the other high peaks of the Presidential Range were the mountains feared the most, and for good reason. The Mount Washington Observatory Web site keeps an ever-growing list of people—142 as of this writing—who have died on or near Washington since 1849. And yet it seemed that Franconia Ridge, particularly Lafayette and Lincoln, the sixth- and seventh-highest peaks, had been claiming lives as well in recent years.

We had a small window of opportunity before more snow came later that night, so Atticus and I took advantage of the calm before the storm.

We made our way up over the aptly named Three Agonies, where I struggled to keep up with Atticus, and he showed his trademark patience. Once past the Agonies and through the forest, we came out to Greenleaf Hut, one of the Appalachian Mountain Club's huts, which is closed in winter. We were met by an icy wind but sought shelter on the north side of the building. That's where I drank and ate, put on more clothing, and put Atticus's bodysuit on him.

It's a mile from the hut to the summit, and it's always difficult for me. I took it easy, moving slowly, stopping often to practice my climbing ritual of breathing heavily, swearing liberally, and praying for forgiveness—since I must have done something wrong to be in so much pain every time I climbed a mountain.

Above the hut I didn't need my snowshoes any longer and switched to MICROspikes, a new piece of equipment I'd acquired. They were a clever invention: strong elastic webbing that you could pull over the soles of your boots like rubbers. On the bottom was a crisscross pattern of chains and small, sharp teeth that cut into the ice. I had crampons for deep, hard ice, but my MICROspikes were just right for those days when I was dealing with ice but not necessarily an entire ice field. They were perfect, since the trail was no longer laden in snow. The winds had scoured the mountaintop and left a bony bed of rock and ice with only occasional patches of snow.

Along that remarkable section of desolation, where the rock is ages old, I was battered by the wind. It kicked flecks of snow and ice up like breaking waves, and they flew into my face every time a wave curled and broke again. Atticus was small enough to walk below the wind, taking shelter on occasion behind the large cairns marking the trail. He'd reach one and take cover. When he saw me approaching, he made a dash for the next one. He'd always been quite smart that way.

The wind was stronger than it was supposed to be, and there was a point when I thought about turning back, but I buoyed myself with, of all things, Tennyson. Each time the wind bared its teeth, I thought of the opening stanza of his poem "Break, Break, Break":

Break, break, break,
On thy cold gray stones, O Sea!
And I would that my tongue could utter
The thoughts that arise in me.

The waves of wind, ice, and snow thrashed the rocky top of the mountain, and me along with it. Toward the summit of Lafayette, it's a pretty barren place. On a summer day, it can be crowded and seem more like a subway station, with people coming and going or simply loitering for the views. But there was not another person in sight as we approached. There was no sign of life at all other than Atticus, and the sky was a muted gray with a dull sun that had turned its back on us.

While the wind shook me on my last approach to the top, I experienced a marriage of fear and excitement. The first thought was, *My God, what are we doing up here?* The second was, *I feel so amazingly alive!*

My words would never do it justice, but Tennyson's did: *"And I would that my tongue could utter | The thoughts that arise in me."* To be rendered speechless in that mysterious place, in those powerful conditions—just how often do any of us feel so overwhelmed, so out of breath with exhilaration? We work so hard to limit the variables in our lives. And yet on a mountaintop we have no control. We have only ourselves, and those were the times when Doug Cray's advice came into play once again: "Hold on to yourself, man." It was not unlike the storms I had endured in politics.

When faced with such wild experiences, as we were that day, I tried to take a minute to look around and say, "This is my life!" And I said it just like that, with an exclamation point. The sound of my own voice seemed to remind me that the adventure was worth having, and that I had chosen it, and it helped me tuck my fear away.

Such moments and challenges in life are all too fleeting and rare. The alternative is to be safe, but it's also numbing. Once Atticus and I discovered the mountains, I chose adventure instead, and life was richer because of it. It was as Kierkegaard had said: "To venture causes anxiety, but not to venture is to lose oneself. . . . And to venture in the highest sense is precisely to become conscious of oneself."

By venturing I had learned to relish my fear when things became a bit unpredictable.

I carefully placed my feet between rocks, testing the bite of the small spikes on occasional plates of ice. Before too long we had gained the summit, and while tired from the climb, we were exhilarated, too. On top of Lafayette, the mountain my father used to look at longingly from the observation platform on Cannon Mountain, the universe stretched out in every direction. There are higher places in the world, even higher in the White Mountains, but from the summit of Lafayette it doesn't seem that way, not with the Pemigewasset Wilderness dropping off to the east, Franconia Notch to the west, and the fading ridge that runs to the south. It is immense, widening and narrowing as it snakes along, and at times it reminds me of the Great Wall of China.

On that day, beside my little friend under a frowning sky, with no other sign of life around, it felt as if we were the last creatures alive on the world. That was part of the thrill of being up there. It was leaving the safety but predictability of home and experiencing life on the edge.

As always, I was inspired by the gumption and spirit of Atticus. He doesn't harbor my fears or concerns. Life is simpler for him. He just goes out and does things he knows he can do. When he reached the summit, he looked around and then sat down next to the sign to have his picture taken even as the wind whipped by him. We'd been there so many times through the past few years that he knew the routine. I always took his picture there.

Seeing Atticus like that, in circumstances both natural and wild, where some people would panic—I swear he gave me strength. He always had. I was never alone as long as he was nearby.

On that lonely and desolate morning, he gave me courage. By watching his calmness, his sense of belonging, even in the wildest of conditions, I gathered myself up, steeled myself, took some photos, and then moved on. We would be exposed above tree line, and the strong winds and freezing temperatures had me contemplating turning back, but by watching Atticus, my barometer, I decided against that. He was comfortable and willing to go forward—so we did.

We moved south along the ridge headed for Lincoln, but beyond Lincoln the sky was changing as the next storm front was coming in. High above, flat clouds were forming, but below, a wonderful undercast made it appear as though we were about to take a walk on the clouds. In the distance a fine line of blue between both layers of clouds mocked the dismal gray above and below.

My MICROspikes performed admirably, and I felt safe with them on. I carried my crampons and my snowshoes on my pack but needed neither, even as we climbed to the icy top of Lincoln.

Once we were there, the sky grew even more dramatic; the undercast was creeping beneath us like a long, bloated beast. It looked so thick and real that I felt as if we could step right off the ridge and walk across to the Kinsmans on its back. To watch it snake through Franconia Notch like that was magnificent and surreal. It had stolen some of our views of the valleys but offered up others even more astounding.

When we reached Little Haystack, the winds had died down and the storm was just taking shape. By this time the next day, it wouldn't be safe up there, but for the next several hours there was nothing to worry about. I decided to stick to our original plan, and we moved toward Liberty, descending into the woods for the nearly two-mile stretch of down, down, down, before a short but steep climb up. On Liberty it was just as icy and the sky even more forlorn. The wind had awakened and jeered us for our impertinence.

Our final peak of the day was Flume. Once there, we were stuck in a cloud, and neither Atticus nor I took much joy being there. Perhaps we were just exhausted, but we were feeling flat and uninspired.

That night Atticus and I heard the storm come in and knew it would be raging on Franconia Ridge, less than five miles away. Oh, how horrible it would be to be stuck up there in such a storm! We'd timed it perfectly.

Unfortunately that winter, two other hikers didn't. Three weeks after Atticus and I were up there, we heard the helicopters' haunting cry above our apartment.

Lawrence Fredrickson and James Osborne didn't pay close attention to the weather and made an attempt to climb Lincoln and Lafayette. A storm blew in, as was predicted, and they were stuck on the mountain overnight. The next morning the helicopters were out searching for them. It would take most of the day to find them.

Osborne would lose a leg. Fredrickson was not so lucky. He lost his life.

Several months after the tragedy, the *Nashua Telegraph* interviewed Osborne. He gave a horrific account. After spending the night in a tiny cave above tree line, the two men had tried to return the way they came. They were between Lincoln and Little Haystack when Fredrickson's eyes were stuck closed by frostbite. He had to continue with his hand on Osborne's shoulder.

Osborne talked about how they'd stumbled into the blinding snow while combating exhaustion. Both men were fighting for their lives, and Fredrickson couldn't keep up. Eventually he collapsed on the trail. Osborne urged him to get up, but hypothermia had taken hold already and he lay helplessly in the snow while winds raged above them.

They had almost made it back to the safety of the trees. Once there, they'd be out of the storm and might have had a fighting chance, but Fredrickson couldn't get up and Osborne didn't have the strength left to do anything about it. I can't imagine how difficult it must have been for Osborne to leave his friend behind, but he had no choice. He had to keep going in order to live.

Eventually Osborne passed out, and when he woke up, he was in the hospital. That's when he learned that Fredrickson had died.

The longer the helicopters searched over us, the more apparent it was that someone was in the gravest danger. I huddled under the blankets on the couch, praying for whoever it was up there and thinking, *There but for the grace of God go I.*

Because I watched the weather as closely as I did, Atticus and I did hike that same day, but we started at 4:00 A.M. and hiked Carrigain, which had far less exposure. The snow didn't start falling until we were off the mountain and nearly back at our car.

We returned to Franconia Ridge again a couple of weeks later to hike the four peaks. When we got to Little Haystack, I dropped a rose on the trail in memory of Fredrickson.

I recited Tennyson's "Break, Break, Break" on that second hike as well; the rest of it had significant meaning concerning what had happened between our visits.

O well for the fisherman's boy,
That he shouts with his sister at play!
O well for the sailor lad,
That he sings in his boat on the bay!

And the stately ships go on
To their haven under the hill;
But O for the touch of a vanish'd hand,
And the sound of a voice that is still!

Break, break, break,
At the foot of thy crags, O Sea!
But the tender grace of a day that is dead
Will never come back to me.

We would hear the helicopters again that winter, but thankfully there would be a different outcome. However, when spring came, a woman was killed while making her way up the Falling Waters Trail toward Little Haystack when a large rock broke free and came tumbling down the mountain, colliding with her head.

The deaths were stark reminders of why I took the precautions I did and how wild nature can be. It also gave me renewed respect for the times when Atticus had chosen not to hike. As I said before, simply by paying attention to my little friend's comfort level, I kept myself safe.

There had been many days that winter when he didn't feel comfortable hiking, and there would be many more. We were falling further behind, and while there was a chance we'd reach our goal, it was only a very slight chance.

27

My Last Letter Home

How does one describe the Bonds to those who have never been there? How do you capture the precipitous and awesome Bondcliff? The long, strong neck of trail that leads from the dramatic edifice up to neighboring Bond, which looms above you? The unmatched grandeur from a comfortable summit seat atop West Bond, which our friend Steve Smith so accurately dubbed a "scatter your ashes" kind of place?

Those are the challenges that faced me when writing about the Bonds so that my father could "see" a place he'd never been to. We still weren't talking, but I had continued to write to him on occasion.

I thought about genius loci, originally a Latin term for the pervading spirit of a place. It was not unlike the Abenaki Indian belief that there was something different about the mountains. They believed that protective spirits watched over the place. Out of reverence for the Great Spirits on the mountaintops, the Abenaki reportedly avoided the summits.

Genius loci can be found throughout the White Mountains, and yet to me no place feels richer with it than the middle of the Pemigewasset Wilderness, where the three Bonds hold court. It is the heart of the White Mountains.

Mount Washington and her neighboring peaks along the Presidential Range stand taller and more magnificent. Mount Lafayette and Mount Lincoln also stand taller, and the entire length of Franconia Ridge is spectacular. However, no mountains make you feel more primitive and wild than Bondcliff, Bond, and West Bond. And unlike the Presidential Range or Franconia Ridge, these are peaks that tourists don't get a chance to see from the road. In order to appreciate them, you have to get to them, which isn't easy. They are landlocked, so tucked away that most people don't even know they exist.

To get to Bondcliff, the southernmost peak, you can walk the nine miles from the Kancamagus Highway in the south or thirteen miles from Route 302 to the north.

In climbing the four-thousand-footers as often as Atticus and I had, I often tried to remember my initial visit on each mountain to assure that our hikes remained fresh. I attempted to peel back the experience of seeing them over and over again and recall the undiluted moment of awe that came with being on them the very first time. On the Bonds there is no need to do that. You walk among giants as you stand in the middle of the White Mountains and see towering peaks in every direction. Even if I saw the world from there a hundred times, it would not be enough.

With a calm day before yet another coming storm, my friend Mary dropped Atticus and me off at Lincoln Woods in the south, and we planned to reverse our past trips through the Bonds and finish at our waiting car up north at the end of Zealand Road.

We walked in darkness until the pale dawn arrived and were at the bridge to the wilderness area in an hour. Whenever I arrived at that point, I thought of how in mythology bridges represent a new world or a new life. And certainly, once you cross the bridge into the Pemi, it all changes. Maybe not the topography, but on the far side of the river it always felt as though Atticus and I had entered an otherworldly realm.

When we reached it that morning, the air was crisp and cold and I could see my breath. The morning was otherwise nondescript, but that soon changed when the sun rose high enough over the mountains to light up the bare January treetops, splashing them with a golden paint and making them appear to be as full of color as they are each autumn. It was a glorious display of color in a forest that seems black and white in the winter months.

With sunshine came warmth. Off went my hat, my gloves, and my heavier layer. I started sweating as if it were summer. Near the last brook crossing, the snow turned into a distasteful mashed-potato consistency and glommed onto the bottoms of my snowshoes. It made for slow and frustrating going, and I repeatedly used my trekking poles to whack the sticky stuff loose. It was a tedious exercise, and it went on for more than a mile until just below the entrance to the alpine zone. There the snow became more consolidated.

I was concerned about the ledge that led above tree line. It can be a challenge for Atticus in certain conditions because it is difficult to scale, but that day the snowpack turned it into a staircase for him, and he climbed up easily. When I emerged above tree line, Atticus was already taking in the astounding views, sitting peacefully on a flat rock. Even though we had many miles to go, I stopped and sat next to him. Together we looked all around us at mountains rising from north, south, east, and west.

On Bondcliff the perspective is different from anyplace else I know. Instead of miles and miles, I could see for mountains and mountains. In contrast I also saw the lingering scars left behind by the logging industry a hundred years before. In the winter when the trees are bare, you can see where primitive roads and railroad tracks once ran for loggers who raped the land without concern for anything but the almighty dollar. It is particularly noticeable on North and South Hancock. That great mass of mountain has so many old roads spiraling up and around it that it looks like faded graffiti or ancient hieroglyphics. For fifty years the mountains had been used and not appreciated.

In spite of those scars, I realized that with all mankind and progress has taken from the natural world, there on the Bonds you can also look around and see where man got it right.

White Mountain painters like Benjamin Champney and Thomas Cole painted the peaks as if they were a link between man and God, often equating mountains to cathedrals and valleys to Eden. Writers such as Hawthorne and Thoreau wrote short stories and essays that brought the legends and the land to life. Poets Lucy Larcom and John Greenleaf Whittier wrote lovingly of what the Creator had brought to New Hampshire.

It was the romantic translations of the landscape from these and other artists that helped fuel the efforts of environmentalists who were disgusted by what lumber barons were doing to a once-beautiful area. In the early 1900s, the Weeks Act was passed, reversing a fifty-year trend of selling off public land in the Whites to individuals for logging, and the land was returned to the public. The results of clear-cutting and fires were reversed and trees began to grow again. And paradise returned.

Sitting with Atticus on Bondcliff, I could see no sign of civilization except for a partial view of the ski slopes on Loon Mountain far off to the south. I got greedy and wished that I didn't even have to look upon those either. Without them the place would be untouched by the contemporary hand of man, save for the trails we traveled.

The other thing I noticed was how still the air was. There was no wind, no birdsong, no jets dully roaring above. I'd never been to a place so quiet in all my life. It wasn't eerie, it was serene. It was the calm before yet another coming storm.

On top of Bond, we felt the only breeze we'd get all day. But soon we were warmed by the trip to West Bond. The snow had drifted in places to the point where if I hadn't known better I would have thought no one had been out there for quite some time. That single mile took us an hour.

On West Bond the wind was gone again, and Atticus and I sat on a flat rock on the summit and took our time drinking in the views. It was one in the afternoon, and we were in no hurry to leave the best viewing point in the Whites. From there, Bondcliff looked even more dramatic than it does when you're on top of it. People who don't hike will see the pictures and see the backdrop of the cliffs and the sublime harshness and think it's not real. Sometimes, when looking on the cliffs from West Bond, I feel the same way.

We wouldn't see another person on the trails that day, and Atticus and I had the entire Pemi to ourselves. What a gift! And how I wanted to share it with one particular man.

It was so inspiring that I didn't want to leave the summit of West Bond. I took off my pack, pulled out paper and pen, and placed the backpack on the ground for Atticus to sit on. I started a letter to my father there and then. I wanted him to see what I saw, to understand where the dreams that he'd instilled when he brought us to the mountains during childhood had taken me.

I thought of my father and his ever-present yellow pad of paper forty years before, when he sat in our campground on the shore of the Pemigewasset River back in Lincoln. We played and he wrote. Now his youngest son sat alone with a little dog, miles from the closest person, high atop a mountain few will ever see, encircled by wilderness, and wrote him a letter.

> *Dear Dad,*
>
> *You would love it here, for it is a rare and most isolated place. Atticus and I are sitting on West Bond, surrounded by layers of mountains.*
>
> *In your younger days I know you enjoyed the poetry of the romantics, including Wordsworth. If you were here, I'm sure you would think of his poem "Upon Westminster Bridge":*
>
> *Earth has not anything to show more fair:*
> *Dull would he be of soul who could pass by*
> *A sight so touching in its majesty:*
> *This City now doth like a garment wear*
> *The beauty of the morning; silent, bare,*
> *Ships, towers, domes, theatres, and temples lie*
> *Open unto the fields, and to the sky;*
> *All bright and glittering in the smokeless air.*

That's what it is like in the middle of the Pemigewasset
Wilderness. Only the "ships, towers, domes, theatres, and temples"
were all nature-made and, thankfully, man-protected and preserved.
I'm a blessed man to be on this adventure with Atticus, and when we
sit high atop a peak I often find myself remembering the stories you
used to read to us in bed. Now, so many years later, Atticus and I
have become the very characters I loved as a child. We are Huck and
Jim, Frodo and Sam—on a great quest. It's as if we've walked out
of the pages of one of those books you read to us.

Whether you know it or not, it's all a result of seeds you planted
in my childhood.

We have not always gotten along, but I wanted you to know
there are things I dearly appreciate, and when Atti and I are up here,
you're often with us.

Well, it's getting cold and late, and we should get going. To
paraphrase Frost, we have "miles to go before we sleep." About
thirteen, to be specific.

Love,
Tom

I tucked the piece of paper into my backpack so that I could retype it when we returned to my apartment. Little did I know that it would be the last letter I ever wrote to him.

From West Bond the journey to Guyot is relatively short, but once again the drifting snow made for slow going, and it took us another hour. But Guyot, even on a cloudy day, was well worth it. On those bald mounds, there is a perspective that almost matches the Bonds themselves. In winter it's like walking on the moon. The vast, gentle roundness of Guyot lends contrast to the jutting surrounding peaks of Franconia Ridge, Garfield, and South Twin.

On the back side of Guyot, the trail was packed down. I was thankful for the efforts of whoever had done it. But by that time I was tired. It took another hour to get to Zealand, and my energy was dwindling with the light of day. However, Atticus was as bouncy as if it were a five-mile hike. I fed him throughout the hike, giving him handfuls of food about fifteen times during the long day, and it kept him fresh.

From Zealand we cut across the Lend-a-Hand Trail and to Hale, and that last thirteen hundred feet of elevation gain took all my strength. Night had fallen, and I had nothing left when we made our way down to Zealand Road for the last 2.7 miles back to the car. I shuffled mindlessly along and appreciated why many hikers refer to marathon hikes as "death marches."

It was the second-longest hike we'd ever done, and my body felt it. However, as tired as I felt after five four-thousand-footers and twenty-five miles, it was a small price to pay for such a day. In spite of our impressive total during that fourteen-hour hike, we were dropping further behind in our totals for the winter, although at least we were starting to get some longer hikes in. Soon we'd have a run of better weather, but would it be enough to get us back on track?

28

Those Eyes, Those Beautiful Eyes

We were far behind the preceding year's total of mountains hiked, and I cannot tell you how frustrated I was. There was either too much snow, too much wind, too much ice—or a combination of all three. Some trails were impassable, under more than ten feet of snow. The Wildcat Ridge Trail was one of them. The snow was so deep it touched the lowest branches of the trees. It was impossible to even crawl beneath them.

As much as I wanted to believe that we still had a chance to reach our goal, I knew we didn't. And yet we weren't quitting.

On the day we hiked both Whiteface and Passaconaway, the sun was so bright and the snow so white that I had to put on my sunglasses. I worried about Atticus's eyes. They'd been sensitive to bright light since he had his surgery, but he seemed to be doing fine.

The slabs of rock along the Blueberry Ledge Trail were filled with snow, and I struggled mightily to get up each one. Atticus would stand just above, having been able to walk on top of most of it, and look down on me. He patiently stopped and waited, an expression of concern on his face as I turned red and sweat ran down my face. After I caught my breath, he'd take off, climb to the top of the next ledge, and wait once more. This went on for several steep but short climbs. However, on the next-to-last ledge he didn't stop. I called out his name, and he didn't come.

I called again, louder, but he was nowhere to be seen. I feared he'd been attacked by an animal or fallen off one of the ledges. I called out to him again.

Shit, what's happened to him?

I was so tired I literally couldn't stand and fell to my knees to regain my strength. I forced myself up to the last ledge, and he wasn't there either. By this time I was panicky. My heart was racing, my head was spinning.

I looked straight ahead and then up at the little bump of rock in front of a cliff. Had he fallen off? I started frantically bellowing his name. I turned to take off my pack, and when I did, I finally saw him. He was on the highest rock, the one with the most unobstructed view. But he wasn't looking down at me; he was sitting looking out toward the glistening lakes to the south.

Amazing. Only a view like that could keep him from me, I thought.

Watching him, I had to smile, my Little Buddha, with his precious eyes. He found such peace in these mountains. Bookstores are filled with stories about how animals help us to get where we need to go, but could it be, I wondered, that our roles were reversed? At times like this, I thought that perhaps I was the one bringing *him* where he most needed to be.

Instead of climbing up to join him, I sat where I was to take in the best view of all: Atticus.

We weren't going to make our goal. We wouldn't even be close, but watching Atticus like that made my winter complete.

Well, maybe not quite complete. The mountains weren't done with me yet.

The weather wreaked havoc with our plans, and we were kept off the trails for more than a week. When the storms finally let up, the conditions couldn't have been more different from those on Whiteface and Passaconaway. We set out for Crawford Notch before dawn, and I parked near the Gateway to the Notch where great rocks lay snug against the road on either side. It is so dramatic that Herman Melville once compared it to the entrance to Dante's Inferno.

We hit the trail to Jackson early enough for me to wear my headlamp and for Atticus to disappear beyond its beam of light into the blackness. Yet another storm was coming, and I wanted to make it down before it hit. My MICROspikes cut into the crisp trail, giving me all the traction I needed. There was a time when such a walk would unnerve me, but no longer. I welcomed being enveloped in the dark, feeling like a well-kept secret.

Once we were beyond the first jutting climb up out of Crawford Notch, my breath caught up with me, but I struggled with my breathing throughout the hike. In the previous two weeks, I had lost any semblance of a hiking rhythm. Before the last major band of weather came, we had hiked eight of the previous ten days, but that seemed like ages ago.

I was struggling. My breathing and my stride were off, and I stopped often. When I moved, I moved too quickly, no rhythm. I relied on my trekking poles more, because my legs were weak, and I pulled myself up the mountain with them.

Somewhere along the way, a gray morning broke and lazily filtered through the trees. Night was more tolerable. At least in the darkness, the light from the headlamp cut through the unknown and was definitive. But in the gray light, we were walking through a shroud. The higher we climbed, the icier the trees became. They were somber specters looking down upon us, eyeing us with suspicion.

We stopped just below the summit, where the two French Canadians had laughed at Atticus the previous winter. I gave Atticus some treats, shoved some more into my bib, took off my MICROspikes, and replaced them with crampons. I put on my heavier jacket, pulled on my hat and gloves, and left my pack behind as we started the last climb of the day.

I don't enjoy crampons, because you have to take extra care when walking on them—more than a few people have stabbed themselves in the leg with their long spikes—and I didn't miss using them, considering all the deep snow we had to contend with during the past few months, but they were a comfort on the steep and icy pitch to the summit.

Atticus first made for the trail sign and sat as he usually does, but when he didn't see me take out my camera, he made for the summit cairn. How eerie to lurch about on high in the murk of a thick cloud, in still-but-comfortable air. At the cairn Atticus nudged my leg, so I offered him a treat, but he didn't want it and nudged me again. This meant he wanted me to pick him up, and so I did, and together we looked off into the gray abyss toward where Washington would normally be.

We stood there for a while, in the middle of a cloud, and I realized we had the same view my father now had.

The preceding week my sister Nancy walked into his house and found him lying facedown on the carpet, furniture strewn about, the signs of a fall.

Heart attack.

The ambulance brought him to the hospital. He was in intensive care, then moved to pulmonary care, and during the weekend he was moved to a nursing home. He wouldn't be returning to his own home.

Atticus and I visited him two days before we hiked Jackson. It was the first time I'd seen him in more than a year.

When we walked into the room, it was difficult to recognize him, that once-strong man, a giant—sometimes benign, angry more often than not. He had a leg and an arm flung over the side rail of his bed. He was confused, tormented; he looked at me with terror and pleading. He seemed to recognize my face but couldn't place it. His voice was fragile and filled with fear.

"Get me out of here," he said.

Atticus and I spent five hours with him. For all but maybe thirty minutes, he didn't know who I was. My brothers and sisters and I weren't surprised; this had been coming for a long time. He'd mostly given up trying a couple of years earlier, when he'd stopped taking his medication regularly, stopped eating right, and kept smoking.

I put him in a wheelchair, and Atticus and I took him down to the lounge, which was empty.

"Hello, Jack."

He nodded suspiciously.

"How are you doing?"

"How do I look like I'm doing?" he said with an exasperated tone.

I asked him several questions, but he was addled. He wanted to know where his mother was. When I told him she was dead, he was clearly surprised. I asked him about his family. He was still confused. I asked who his favorite daughter was.

"Grace?"

"Grace is your sister, Jack."

"I have a daughter?"

"You have three daughters and six sons."

"I do?" He looked bewildered. "Do I have a wife?"

"You did. Her name was Isabel. But she died in 1968."

He thought for a moment and looked sad.

I asked about each of his children, starting with the oldest and working down to me, the youngest.

I'd say, "What can you tell me about Joanne?" and he'd tell me bad things about Joanne and why he didn't like her. I asked him about John. He did the same thing. The only one he spoke highly of was Eddie, who had been his caretaker before moving up to New Hampshire.

Then I came to me. "What can you tell me about Tommy?"

"He's the biggest prick of them all."

"I heard something similar," I said. "But why do you say that about him?"

"He could care less about me."

"I don't think that's true at all, Jack. He loves you very much, but sometimes he might not like some of the things you do."

He shook his head. "I'll never see him. He won't come to see me."

"Oh, I heard he was here to see you."

"I don't believe it," he said. "He wouldn't bother."

"Maybe you were sleeping. What can you tell me about Tommy?"

He thought for a moment. "He's married."

I was surprised. "He is?"

"I told him not to marry her," and he shook his head with disgust.

"Why did you tell him that?"

"I told him not to marry her because she's black. That's why he won't talk to me."

"What's her name?" I asked.

"I can't remember. He doesn't bring her around me."

He thought for a bit. "They have a kid."

"I didn't know that," I said.

"A boy. He's half white, half black. Mulatto."

"What's his name?"

"Atticus."

Atticus, who was sitting near us, looked up when he heard his name.

After all those questions, we took my father back upstairs, and I asked the nurse if he could have some ice cream. My father loved ice cream. He kept several varieties in the freezer and ate it every day.

"He hasn't had dinner yet," she said.

"Yeah, so?"

"We don't allow them to have ice cream until after dinner."

I couldn't believe it. She actually looked like she enjoyed what she was saying.

"You're not serious," I said.

"I'm very serious. It ruins their appetites."

"So tell me," I said, doing my best to be respectful, "how will you feel if you live to be eighty-seven and some nurse tells you to eat your dinner before you can have ice cream?"

"Sorry, no ice cream until after dinner," Nurse Ratched said.

"Can I speak to your supervisor, please? Or better yet the director?"

Nurse Ratched returned a few minutes later and thrust something they give diabetics instead of real ice cream into my hand.

My father, who watched appraisingly throughout the exchange, was happy to be getting ice cream. But when I opened up the little container, it didn't look the least bit like ice cream. And judging by my father's face as I fed him a spoonful, it didn't taste like it either.

"How is it?" I asked him.

"Tastes like shit."

Atticus and I left and went to the grocery store, and I bought a half gallon of ice cream. When we returned, I fed him some. After the first few spoonfuls, a veil had lifted.

My father, who hadn't realized who I was since I'd been there, saw Atticus sitting on the floor in front of him and out of the blue said, "You're a good dog, Atticus." And Atticus moved closer.

"He's a good dog," my father said.

"Yes, he is," I said.

"Better than you deserve," he added.

Ah, he'd finally realized who I was, and I laughed. From that moment on, he was clearer, and we talked and he was friendlier, but he grew tired.

My brother David showed up, and we talked for a bit. He told me that a few days earlier my father had been really confused, and when David had shown up to see him, my father had said, "Good, you're here. Now get Eddie and Tommy and get me out of here." We didn't quite know what he meant by that, and David suggested he was just really gone. Perhaps he was, or maybe there was something else going on.

I drove home that night and tried to hike Jackson the very next day, but I couldn't. The weather was fine, but I wasn't. And so Atticus and I got up early, before the storm came in, and tried again.

That's what I was thinking about looking off into the cloud while I held Atticus.

I said some prayers and thanked my father. For all his sadness and pain, he'd passed many things on to his children. I loved the mountains he'd given me. But more than that, he'd also passed something else on to me, the best part of who he was. The part of him that had once been a dreamer. For whatever reasons, he'd let his dreams die, or he'd covered them up and didn't want us to see them. I would never understand that part of him, just as Jack Ryan would never understand that a father is never a failure as long as his children continue on, even if it is with but one or two lessons or traits once carried by the father.

We also differed on something else: what happens after death.

When he looked into the belly of a cloud, the same kind I saw that morning, the same kind he saw around him as he neared the end, we saw two different things. He saw nothing. For him the world was closing in on him, empty, cold, a dead end. He'd always believed that once he died, that would be it. Nothing would follow. For me . . . well, I liked to think different. I liked to think that clouds, no matter how dense, how seemingly immovable, were all the more reason for faith and that something else awaits us. To that end I held on to something C. S. Lewis had written: "Has this world been so kind to you that you should leave with regret? There are better things ahead than any we leave behind."

There is much I don't know. However, I believe those mountains have a mystical power to them—the genius loci. They bring us closer to death, hence closer to life. They are fierce and wild, but life-affirming at the same time.

Looking off into the gray mist with tears rolling down my cheeks, I felt Atticus licking my face. A smile was born out of the sadness. Love was near, even in the darkness.

If only . . . if only there were some way to bring that mountaintop home to a man who was at the doorstep and ready to walk through, some way to ease his struggle, bring him to the mountains, and give him something to hold on to.

As Atticus and I made our way down from the summit, I tried my best to bring the mountaintop home with me to ease my own pain. Mount Jackson had been our fifty-ninth peak of the winter, far below what I'd hoped for when it all started. But the number meant very little when compared to the wealth of experience the mountains had given us.

29

Mount Washington

On the last day of winter, Atticus and I finally made it to Mount Washington. The weather had been horrible, and I didn't want to chance it. But the sun was out, the temperature warm, and there was not even a trace of wind.

Although it was a workday, the trails were crowded. We made our way up the Jewell Trail, to where it goes above tree line and intersects with the Gulfside Trail. We stopped there to take a break, and a large group of eighteen hikers were coming up the trail behind us. When they saw Atticus, most of them calmly greeted him by name. By that time it wasn't out of the ordinary to see the little black-and-white dog with the funny eyebrows on a mountain in winter. A few of the others were very excited and while approaching got out their cameras to take his picture as he stood on a rock above them and watched them.

While most of the crowd went left on the Gulfside and headed for Mount Jefferson, Atticus and I climbed up the shiny ice toward Mount Washington. It was so hot that I wore only a T-shirt, and the glare was so severe that I could feel a sunburn coming on.

We moved carefully, me wearing crampons and Atticus taking his time over the ice. We ran into two more people who recognized Atticus, then saw a fellow off in the distance setting up his tripod. When we drew closer, he said, "Would you mind if I got a picture of you two?"

On the summit we stopped for lunch, but soon a party of three thirty-somethings were standing near us. They were all trying to make cell-phone calls but weren't having much luck. Then one of them pulled a satellite phone from his backpack and said, "This will work!"

When I heard him yelling to whoever was on the other end of the phone—"Hey, you'll never guess where I am!"—I knew it was time to leave. We had come to the mountains to get away from just that kind of thing. In contrast, at the closed Lake of the Clouds Hut, a half mile below the summit of Mount Monroe, there was a man sitting with his back to us. The hood of his jacket was pulled up, and he was holding a newspaper and a pencil. Atticus startled him when he walked by, and the man looked up. He was thin and weathered. He wore glasses and had a tanned face. I guessed him to be in his sixties. His coat was a mess: faded orange with long strips of gray duct tape covering large sections of it, placed where the worn fabric had ripped through.

He was working on a crossword puzzle and deep in thought.

Imagine that. Coming off Washington, standing at the base of Mount Monroe, the fourth-highest peak in New England, encountering a man in such worn clothing that if he were in downtown Boston he would pass easily for a street person. He was sitting on a rock working on that puzzle as if he were waiting for a bus.

He was absorbed in what he was doing, so I respected his privacy as I readjusted my crampons, took off my pack, fed Atticus, and swallowed some honey. When we were getting ready to set off for Monroe, he asked about Atticus. A few questions turned into a wonderful conversation.

His name was Richard, he was seventy-eight years old, and he climbed Washington because he and his wife had climbed Washington every year. I asked where his wife was, and he told me she had died a year earlier. He told me she was one of the first women ever to hike all the Adirondack four-thousand-footers in winter. She was originally from

Switzerland. They'd shared a love of the mountains and gotten married long ago. They had two children.

Richard and his wife had made the move from New York to the White Mountains twenty years earlier. Even though he was alone, he liked where he lived and said he would never leave. He loved the mountains and climbed them whenever he could, but he didn't bother with lists anymore. He also appreciated snowmobilers.

"Most people don't like them," he said. "I like them because I can use my mountain bike on the groomed trails."

As for his coat, he told me it was at least fifty years old and that his wife had always wanted him to get rid of it, but he refused. His crampons were just as old, if not older, he told me. They had leather straps, but he kept the spikes sharp. His wooden ice ax was equally ancient.

He proudly showed me his mittens when he took them out of his backpack. They were oversize, made of wool, and liberally patched with duct tape. His wife had wanted him to get rid of those also, but he reminded her they'd once saved her nose, so she suggested he keep them.

"We were up on Mount Marcy in the winter, and I was having a conversation with a man when he pointed out that my wife's nose was turning white," Richard said. "So I just held one of my big mitts up over her nose and continued my conversation. She got to keep her nose."

My conversation with Richard was enlivening and just the opposite of what I'd experienced on top of Washington.

Of course, it had me thinking about my father and wondering how different things would have been had my mother not dropped a cigarette in her hospital bed. The other thing I noticed was how freely Richard talked about his life and his wife and how much he loved her. In some ways I knew more about him than I did about my own father.

As we walked over the last few mountains of the winter, my thoughts drifted back to Atticus and me. We were finishing with sixty-six mountains, thirty fewer than what I'd planned and hoped for. But in a winter with a record snowfall of more than 250 total inches, I'd come to terms with the things I could and could not control. I had Atticus and the mountains themselves to thank for teaching that to me.

Over the last two winters, we'd climbed 147 peaks, stayed safe, raised thousands of dollars for two great causes, and transformed our lives. Not bad for a little dog and a middle-aged, overweight newspaper editor with a paralyzing fear of heights who supposedly never belonged in the mountains in winter.

30

Good-bye

With winter over, Ken and Ann Stampfer invited Atticus and me to join them on a hike. After three months of "having" to climb only four-thousand-footers, it felt good to do something not on a list. It was my first time on the Boulder Loop Trail, and I enjoyed it immensely, from the gentle climb, to the views, to the small, twisted trees on the ledges etched against the rich blue sea of sky.

As I sat down to write about the hike the following night in my journal, Atticus knew that something was different. He always sat within sight of me, often in contact with my foot or a leg. But on that night he was right by my side.

I was sitting on the couch with my legs up, and he was stretched out, not at my feet as he usually was when we were on the couch but lying parallel to me, his body in full contact with mine, his head against my hip. I could feel his heart beating. He wanted to be close, just as he had when he was blind and feeling lost. But this was different from that last time. Back then he was looking to be held; this time around he was looking to hold me.

It was Monday, and my father's wake was scheduled for Wednesday down in Medway, with the funeral on Thursday. The wake and the funeral meant nothing to me. What did mean something to me was the last time I'd seen him.

It was Saturday, and he was lucid, smiling, happy to see Eddie, David, and me when we arrived at Milford Hospital together. And it was just by chance that we were together. Atticus and I had arrived from Newburyport at the same time my brothers arrived. When the four of us walked in the front door, the receptionist took a look at Atticus and said, "I'm sorry, we don't allow dogs."

"How come?"

"We just don't. It's against the rules."

"He's always been allowed in hospitals," I said with a smile.

"I'm sorry, it's not allowed."

When I said, "Okay, can I see the rules, please?" my brothers took a step to the side, and Eddie looked as if he wanted to crawl away.

I told them I'd be up in a minute, and they escaped.

After I talked with the receptionist a bit, I brought Atticus back out to the car. I took it as compliment that when I entered the room and Eddie told my father they wouldn't allow Atticus in, he said, "Oh, that's too bad." And I could tell he meant it.

My father was different that day. He'd gotten rid of all his anger and pain in the nursing home, and he was lighter.

At one point during the visit, David pointed out that it was Easter weekend and that some of our brothers and sisters would be in the area. He told my father to be ready for visitors. I joked that since so many members of the family would be dropping in on him, it would be a great weekend to kick the bucket. He laughed at this. His humor had returned. Although my brothers didn't seem to think it was funny.

Eddie told him that the doctors thought he was getting better and he would be out of the hospital soon and back at the nursing home. My father simply shrugged and said that it didn't really matter where he was. He then said, "What's next? What's after all this?"

I took comfort in that, for he'd always said there was no tomorrow after death, no next chapter. He seemed resigned to that fact, but on his last afternoon, with the sun splashing in the windows and his eyes bright, he seemed to sense, or at least maybe hope, that there was more to it all than just the closing of a book.

I also took comfort in my father's last words. They occurred just after midnight while two nurses and a doctor were with him. One of the nurses was yelling at him to "Breathe . . . breathe . . . breathe!"

My father's response was precious and typical of Jack Ryan. The last words he ever spoke were, "Why? Am I giving birth?"

He loved joking with those he didn't know well, especially women, especially pretty women. I'm sure he was happy that two nurses were with him when his heart gave out. And I took solace in knowing he wasn't alone.

He once joked that he thought for sure he would die in the spring, after a long, dark, and cold winter, when young women wore less clothing and he was more distracted while driving by them. I always thought he would die around that time of the year as well, but for a different reason: It was between the end of Patriots season and the beginning of Red Sox, and he had little to care about.

In the weeks to come, I thought about the time David had arrived to visit my father and he'd said, "Good, you're here. Now get Eddie and Tommy and get me out of here."

As it worked out, the rest of my brothers and sisters never got to see him. David, Eddie, and Tommy arrived together, and my father was getting out of there.

I'm not sure why he chose the three of us. I believe it was because we were the three who were near him the most after he crashed his car, but more than that, Jack Ryan had a plan. David was the responsible, stalwart one. He'd handle the money and pay for the getaway. Eddie was the golden son with a good heart. He would take care of my father. As for me, I was the younger version of him, but the one who didn't give up on his dreams, the one who was bold enough to *drive* the getaway car.

After that accident when I was filling in for David and Eddie, I showed up on occasion to take my father to a doctor's visit. On the way home one day, I asked him if he wanted to drive in and see the new high school.

"They won't let us drive up there," he said.

But I drove him up, and we watched them working for a couple of minutes before a man with a hard hat came up to the car. He looked in and saw a middle-aged man, an old man, and a little black-and-white dog.

"Can I help you?" he asked.

My father looked a bit nervous.

"We're just watching," I said.

"I'm sorry, but you can't be here," he said.

There was the slightest tinge of disappointment on my father's face, and I looked at the construction worker and said, "Do you know who this is?"

"Um . . . no. I'm sorry, I don't," he said.

"You're obviously not from around here, are you?"

"No, I'm not."

"This is Francis Burke, former superintendent of schools."

"Oh, I'm sorry, I had no idea. Do you want to get out of the car and take a closer look?" he asked.

My father was tired and shook his head just enough so I could see it.

"No, we're fine here," I said.

After I drove my father home, he had the silliest grin on his face and said, "That was kind of fun."

Yep, I was with David and Eddie because I would be driving the getaway car.

I did not learn of his death until I returned from our hike along the Boulder Loop Trail with Ken and Ann Stampfer, later on Sunday. In hindsight it was just as well, as I spent much of the day telling them about my visit in the hospital with him and his better qualities. I noted that while he'd never climbed a four-thousand-footer, he'd loved being in the mountains and he'd taken us up Cannon and Wildcat on their gondolas, and Washington by way of the auto road and the cog railroad.

He'd taken us on many shorter hikes to lower elevations. The Boulder Loop Trail wasn't around when he was last in the mountains, but he would have loved to take all of us kids. When we reached the ledges with the views to the south and west, he would simply have stood there and absorbed the wonder, and it would have shown on his face. That's one of the reasons I so loved the White Mountains—the magic reflected in my father's face when he was up there. He was different when he sat and gazed out at the views. He was humbled and inspired. He was peaceful.

To know that I got to bring him back there through my words and my photos made me smile. And I knew that I wouldn't have done any of it without Atticus. In having Atticus along, I was able to bring my father back to a place he loved.

On our Easter Sunday hike, Atticus led Ann, Ken, and me up the trail, and when he sat down on the ledges at the highest point and cast his eyes toward Passaconaway and the Tripyramids to the south, I saw that look come over his face, that peaceful, blissful look that said everything was right with the world—that look he'd almost lost the year before. After all those mountains, after all those years with Atticus, I finally realized where I'd seen that look before and why I was so transfixed by it. It was when I was a boy, standing next to my father, and I saw him gaze happily out at the mountains.

I didn't want to go to the funeral. It meant nothing to me. I'd said my good-byes to my father, and I knew that a bit of him would be with me whenever I hiked. Like Max, he would live in the mountains forever, at least for me. But I ended up going, because it would mean something to my brothers and sisters.

Atticus was not allowed in the church. I'm sure he didn't mind, other than for the fact that he wouldn't be able to keep his eye on me. But the weather was cool enough that I cracked the windows of the car and left him there. Through the years, he'd spent more time in the car than I had. I was hardly ever in it when he wasn't, but he was in it plenty when I wasn't. So he was comfortable.

At the cemetery, however, I let him out of the car, but first I took him to the woods in the back corner so he could stretch his legs and go to the bathroom. When we came over to the grave, I looked at Jack Ryan's four surviving brothers and sisters clustered together, along with their families. Then I saw something I'd rarely seen: all my brothers and sisters standing together. Some were even holding each other. Behind them stood their families. I hadn't planned it, but I realized while watching both groups that Atticus and I were off on our own toward the foot of the grave. I'm not sure how my brothers and sisters felt about that, or if they even noticed, but that's the way it seemed things were supposed to be.

31

Heartache

If you live to be a hundred, I want to live to be a hundred minus one day, so I never have to live without you.
— *POOH'S LITTLE INSTRUCTION BOOK*

After our winter came to an end and my father passed, Atticus and I settled into a quiet existence, and not much happened as spring became summer and summer grew old. By September we had moved to the other side of the mountains and were living in Tamworth, just a few miles from Whiteface and Passaconaway.

We were still climbing mountains, just not as many of them and without the same intensity. Oftentimes we'd simply go for long walks around the bucolic countryside. It was upon returning from one of those walks that I received news from the Massachusetts Society for the Prevention of Cruelty to Animals (MSPCA-Angell) that Atticus and I were being honored at their annual Hall of Fame dinner. The two of us were receiving the Human Hero Award for our fund-raising efforts the previous winter.

The award was given every year "for exceptional devotion, compassion, and bravery on behalf of people and animals." It was one of four awards MSPCA-Angell gave out. The others were the Young Hero Award, the Animal Hero Award, and the Humanitarian Award. The ceremony was to take place at the John F. Kennedy Presidential Library in October.

Six days before the event, when foliage was at its peak, Atticus and I went for a walk. I'd never seen a more picturesque day: stunning blue skies, trees like flames in the late-afternoon sun, comfortable temperatures, a gentle breeze. We walked, as we often did, toward the trails that led to Whiteface and Passaconaway, but we weren't planning on a hike, just a relaxing stroll. We approached an old yellow farmhouse that sits quaintly in the valley at the foot of the mountains, and Atticus looked for his friend. She was a tall, leggy Newfoundland with a threatening bark that disappeared as soon we got close. She'd bark loudly, then invite him to play. However, she wasn't there that day. But two other dogs were.

They had the bodies of Australian cattle dogs but were blond. They barked but kept their distance—at first. When I turned to look at a footbridge to the left, I heard a horrifying yelp. One of the dogs had come out of nowhere and struck in an instant, latching onto Atticus's throat.

Atticus had never been a fighter. He'd never even been a barker, and when other dogs barked at him, he didn't know what to make of it. I considered one of his greatest gifts his gentle innocence and his belief that all living creatures were just as temperate as he was. I often had to remind him, "Not all dogs are friendly, Atticus."

The attacking dog wasted no time in going for the kill. Its grotesque snarls rang in my ears, as did Atticus's stunned and helpless yelps. She lifted him off the ground, whipping him around by his throat. His legs flew helplessly about like a rag doll's. By the time I reacted, Atticus was limp in her mouth. Her growls were savage when her eyes met mine.

I charged her, and she dropped him in a heap. She then bared her teeth at me and approached. I yelled loudly and readied for her attack. At the last second, she thought better of it and backed up a few feet, continuing to eye me and show her teeth.

It had happened so fast that I was stunned and couldn't believe it. *Not this way*, I pleaded. *Please, not like this.*

I turned back to Atticus, and he was stirring, but barely. He struggled to get up. I went to him but kept an eye on the attacking dog, and she was approaching again. I stayed between the two of them as I moved toward Atticus. He stumbled, started to fall, caught himself, and then slowly started to walk back the way we'd come. A few more steps and he was walking somewhat more normally. I caught up to him, and he looked a bit confused as he limped along.

"Atticus, stop, please. Let me see."

When I looked into his eyes they were distant and dazed. He let me run my hands over his body, checking for wounds. The muscles of his back and shoulders were tight and tender to the touch. When I ran my hand under his head, I felt blood pooling in my palm. There was a large hole in his throat, and I could see inside.

I pulled myself together and picked him up and carried him back toward the car. I could hear him breathing heavily. I walked faster. His eyes appeared tired. I held him tight and ran. He put his head against my chest, and I could feel blood seeping through my shirt.

In emergencies I can rise to the occasion, and I handled it well. However, as strong as I was, Atticus was even more so. Just before we got back to the car, he wanted to get down. At first he took a crooked step, and then he trundled down the dirt road, from time to time shaking his head back and forth, but looking mostly calm. However, when we got into the car I feared he was going into shock. I took off my shirt and wrapped it around his neck.

I called the nearest vet. She was working at the Sandwich Fair and couldn't see us. I called a friend, and she suggested the North Country Animal Hospital, but that was more than twenty miles away, and it was after hours. Luckily, they had twenty-four-hour emergency service. But it was late on Friday afternoon of Columbus Day weekend, and traffic going into North Conway was a mess. I held Atticus and was afraid he was getting worse, but there was nothing I could do. We were locked in bumper-to-bumper traffic.

When we arrived, we were met by Christine O'Connell, a young vet. She gave Atticus a shot—general anesthesia—and I stayed with him through the surgery.

Dr. O'Connell sewed the wound closed, found other punctures in Atticus's neck, and cleaned them and sewed some of them as well. She then inserted a long drainage tube. The dog had shaken him so fiercely it had loosened the layers of skin around the bite holes, and sacs of loose flesh were already pooling with nasty bacteria-filled fluids. She told me that Atticus was another shake or two from death, and as horrifying as the attack had been, we were very lucky.

"He'll be all right, won't he?" I asked.

"You're going to have to watch him closely," she said. She told me to check for signs of a collapsed lung. They would appear within twelve to twenty-four hours. If he was breathing heavily during the night or if his gums went blue or his upper back felt like bubble wrap—all signs that air wasn't getting to his lungs—I was to rush him back to the hospital. She would insert an air tube into his chest, stabilize him, and I'd get him into Angell as soon as possible.

He slept soundly, having been heavily medicated.

I had stayed as strong as I could, but when we got back to Tamworth, I started to come off my emergency high and felt the impact of the attack. He'd never been injured while climbing hundreds of mountains, but there he was now, so vulnerable and in pain after a senseless attack.

My mind raced that night. I asked myself what I could have done differently as the attack played out in my mind in slow motion again and again. Of course I felt I'd let my friend down. I was usually good at seeing such things developing and stopping them before anything bad occurred. But everything had happened so quickly.

I held him as carefully that night as I'd held him when he was a puppy the first day we met. I moved my hands slowly over his body, loving him with my touch, wanting him to feel it.

As I cradled him, I could feel his full weight falling onto me, and I saw those grotesque tubes sticking out of both sides of his throat, the dried bloodstains on his hair.

I wept.

I prayed.

I pleaded.

It was to be the longest night of my life.

Dr. O'Connell had told me to check on him every ninety minutes. I didn't dare sleep. Instead I stayed up throughout the night. With Atticus on my lap, just as he'd been after his cataract surgery, I typed out an e-mail that night, and the Friends of Atticus woke up again.

It didn't take long for e-mails to start coming in, and by the next morning the phone wouldn't stop ringing. People offered to help in any way they could, some offering money. I was thankful but told them prayers would be better.

The hikers on Views from the Top and Rocks on Top sent an endless stream of encouraging e-mails, and a Newburyport blog told its readers, "Pray for Atticus."

Carter Luke, the CEO at Angell Animal Medical Center, was made aware, and emergency staff was notified that their "hero" might need their help and to be ready for him. And radio station WYKR in Wells River, Vermont, just across the New Hampshire border, ran regular Atticus updates, as did the *Northcountry News* Web site. I wrote a column for them called "The Adventures of Tom and Atticus," and readers knew of the little dog's exploits and loved him. Steve Smith wrote about the attack in his hiking column in the weekly newspaper the *Mountain Ear*.

Friends left messages, but I didn't call any of them. I didn't have it in me. Instead I sent out regular e-mail updates.

The next morning Atticus woke up in great pain and had a difficult time walking. I carried him outside so he could go to the bathroom. He moved his neck stiffly around as if checking himself for damage, and I'm sure he could sense those tubes sticking out of his throat. When his eyes met mine, they were soft and sad. I sat on the grass next to him, and he leaned his body against me.

He had made it through the night. But he wasn't in the clear yet, and we had work to do. I remembered what Paige Foster had said when Atticus went blind: *He needed the mountains.* I wasn't about to hike with him in this condition, and yet I wanted him to feel better. And I wanted him to feel safe again.

The first thing we did was drive over to the house where he was attacked. We sat in the car for a while and watched the dog watching us. Atticus looked at me as if wondering what my next step would be.

"Stay here, please," I said as I got out of the car and closed the door. I could see those tubes and the dried blood on his fur. I could see his eyes going from the dog to me. It barked at me, and I called for the woman who lived there to come out. She'd met Atticus and was always friendly to us, but when she came to the door, she looked at me curiously, as if I were trespassing.

"What do you want?" she asked, eyeing me up and down.

I pointed to Atticus, who was watching us intently from the window. I didn't even have to finish telling her what had happened. She saw the blood and the tubes, and tears welled up in her eyes. She grabbed hold of my arm like she needed help to stand.

She told me the two dogs belonged to a friend and that she was watching them for the weekend. She was out when the attack had taken place. That's why we hadn't seen the Newfoundland. He was with her. Whenever she looked over at Atticus, fresh tears filled her eyes, and she apologized again and again. "I really don't know what to do."

"I just wanted you to know what happened," I said. And that was true, but it wasn't the only reason for us to go to her house. I didn't tell her this, but I wanted Atticus to watch me approach the dog. At first the dog appeared as if it wanted to attack again, but I was firm and looked it in the eyes and said, "Sit!"

It did. Then I told it, "Lie down." Reluctantly, it did that as well.

In the car, Atticus was watching intently. I wanted him to see I wasn't afraid. I wanted him to know I would make sure nothing like that would happen again. I wanted him to know he was safe.

When I got back into the car, Atticus, who always rode in the passenger seat, stood up and put his front paws on my thigh and looked into my eyes. We stayed like that for a moment before I put my hand on the back of his head and gently rubbed his ears. He pushed his face against mine. Paige's voice came to mind: *Y'all will work it out.*

Atticus couldn't climb a mountain—he wouldn't be able to do that for a while—but he could be outside. Our next stop was to go to the Brook Path just down the road. It's a lovely trail that follows a gentle, meandering brook through a fairyland of mossy rocks and thick trees. I carried him along the path for about a quarter of a mile until we came to a bend in the stream, and we sat down together. His face was still sad, but ever so slowly, over the next few hours, he started looking around. The song of the rushing water, the call of the birds, the gentle swirl of colorful leaves falling down around us, the smell of good earth—it all helped. I wanted him to be where he could get strength and feel peace and quiet. I wanted him to be in nature.

We sat together for three hours. Sometimes he turned and sat motionless with his back to me and gazed at the stream. Occasionally he turned toward me and looked me deep in the eyes as if asking, *Why?*

A bird landed on a low branch to watch us. We watched it come in closer, just three feet away from Atticus. The two of them looked at each other. They stayed that way for about a minute. When the bird flew away, Atticus came to me and pushed his nose against my arm. It was his way of saying, *Let's go.*

There was *one* phone call I returned late in the afternoon the day after the attack. It was to Paige. I wasn't quite sure why she was the one I called back. I suppose it was because part of me, deep down inside, always felt that Atticus was partly hers. She'd never said anything to make me feel that way, but I could sense they were connected. She had followed us closely for six and a half years. There were days we talked, days we e-mailed, and she often checked our blog. Besides, no one knew us the way Paige did.

She was concerned and loving on the phone and started out right away telling me what I needed to do. I loved that about Paige. She felt she could fix anything bad that ever happened to Atticus. I listened to her attentively for several minutes. When I told her what we'd already done that day, she was silent for a bit and then said, "Tom Ryan, wherever did you learn to take care of that little boy so well?"

"I had a good teacher, Paige."

We talked for several hours that afternoon. Strangely enough, after the first twenty minutes, it was not about Atticus anymore. Instead we spoke about our own lives. I was lying on the couch, and Atticus pushed up next to me, and I held him close.

Over the next couple of days, the Friends of Atticus sat and waited. We all did. I wasn't the only person who had wept. I wasn't the only person who was praying.

32

The Great Art of Sauntering

Six days after that vicious attack, Atticus walked the red carpet heading into the John F. Kennedy Presidential Library as if nothing out of the ordinary had happened.

Knowing him as I did, I should have trusted that a gaping hole in his throat wouldn't be enough to keep him down. He stepped into the building as if he'd been there a thousand times before. That little dog who was banned from the Newburyport post office and city hall was not only welcomed at the John F. Kennedy Presidential Library, he was honored.

The good people of the MSPCA couldn't have been kinder to us, and especially to him. I think after seeing the photos of what he looked like after the attack, they expected a different Atticus.

Thoreau once wrote, "It is a great art to saunter."

Watching Atticus step into that august building was watching great art. People greeted him by name, told him he looked good, wished him a good evening, and he sauntered as if he truly belonged there. It was like he was back on the streets of Newburyport again.

Eventually we made our way down to the "VIP room" where the heroes of the night were gathering, along with some of the sponsors of the event. Again Atticus walked in as if he owned the place: not with an air of arrogance but with comfort and ease. He sauntered in, his little bum swaying in a carefree manner, surveyed some of the smaller dogs in their jeweled collars and sparkling leashes, and stopped directly in front of singer Emmylou Harris, the big star of the evening. She was on hand to get the Humanitarian Award. He stopped right in front of her and caught her eye. How could he not?

I picked him up, and introductions were made, and we chatted for a while, Atticus sitting up in the crook of my arm, Emmylou occasionally rubbing his belly or his chest, the photographer taking photos and more photos.

From that exclusive room, Atticus and I made a break for it, seeking out the manicured lawn against the sea with the view over to Boston. Outside, we talked with the caterers and the security people and heard their stories, and they smiled at the little dog who greeted them as if they were stars like Emmylou Harris. When we went back inside, a couple of folks were in panic mode looking for us. It was time to mingle with the rest of the attendees in the main lobby. There were many dogs at the cocktail reception, pretty dogs, some shaped as perfectly as if they were backyard topiaries, all well behaved, all leashed. Atticus wove through them, no leash, no collar, feeling free—sauntering.

There was plenty of money in the place, lots of old Beacon Hill money, and yet everyone was as nice as could be. Then again, I was with a carefree little dog, one who was always at home anywhere.

It was as it had always been for Atticus. Everyone knew his name. I grabbed an extra chair and pulled it up to the table for him. Nearly all the dogs that were in the cocktail reception in the lobby were put in another room during the dinner.

Speeches started, food came, and we people-watched. Atti and I shared some chicken and then were visited by Dr. Maureen Carroll. We shared a warm hug and a long chat, then went to talk to Ann Novitsky, her vet tech. We'd only met Maureen and Ann twice before that night, but it was like visiting old friends.

It became time for the presentation of awards. Heather Unruh, News

Center Five coanchor, introduced the first hero, Amanda MacDonald, a remarkable teenager. She had done incredible work gathering signatures for a ballot question intended to put an end to greyhound racing in Massachusetts. She read her speech with poise beyond her years.

I was told we were up next. Great . . . how does one follow such an impressive kid?

I'm a writer, but I decided not to read a speech. I figured I'd just wing it. While the introduction was read, photos from some of our hikes flashed on the large movie screen behind Heather, and people loved them. At one point the audience gave such a joyous gush of oohs and ahhs at a photo of Atti on North Kinsman with Franconia Ridge in winter white behind him that Heather stopped reading the introduction, turned around, looked up, and said, "I've been stumped by a dog."

I carried Atticus onstage, just as I always held him on a mountaintop. When I turned toward the audience, I was blinded by the bright lights. There were people out there—I just couldn't see them. I knew that the movie screen above and behind was showing a larger version of the two of us, and I was wondering if the audience could see the wetness in the corners of my eyes. The weight of the past week came leaking out. My legs shook, and so did my voice.

I'm not really sure where I started, but after thirty seconds or so it was easy. There were people to thank, jokes to make, talk of Atticus and what he'd been through, praise for Angell and the doctors and the vet techs and fund-raising people.

At one point while I was telling the story of my friend Atticus and his blindness, he laid his head on my heart, and the audience melted. It's one of the few things I picked up from them. Later a woman asked me, "Did you train him to do that?"

"No," I said. "He does what he wants to do."

Carter Luke would later tell me his staff at MSPCA-Angell and he referred to Atticus putting his head on my heart as "The Moment."

The next two presentations went to Boston Police Department dogs and Emmylou Harris. Then it was over.

A week before, I had held Atticus with a hole in his throat and wondered if he would live. My, how things had changed. When the awards ceremony ended, we couldn't make it through the crowd. Maureen Carroll told me she'd laughed so hard she nearly peed. Others told me they'd cried. When we made it to the hallway, Atticus met his public and posed for photos. Each time someone walked by with a centerpiece of flowers, Atticus stopped them by putting his front paws on their thighs so he could smell the sweet scent. He had a way of getting his point across. On a night of a lifetime, it was time to stop and smell the roses.

One man asked me, "Is Atticus the perfect dog?"

I was surprised by the question, and I took a moment to think about it. I quickly cataloged our six and a half years together and said, "No. But he's the perfect dog for me."

During my speech I forgot to mention three individuals who would have loved the night.

My father: He who adored the Kennedys and Boston politics and anyone on Channel Five News would have loved it, if only for the setting. When my brother David gave my father's eulogy, he said that Dad always wished for but never received a standing ovation and wondered what that was like. At the end of the eulogy, we all stood up and clapped for him. I would have gladly given Jack Ryan the standing ovation Atticus and I had received. I was hoping he was watching from wherever he was.

Paige Foster: What a proud night for Paige. Atticus was with me because Paige gave him up. She once told me she was going to keep him, but instead she gave him to me. Because of her kindness, so much had happened in my life. Imagine having bred more than a thousand puppies and giving up the only one you were going to keep, and having him be honored this way.

Maxwell Garrison Gillis: If it weren't for Max, there wouldn't have been an Atticus. Max changed everything. He opened my heart, and when he departed, he left it open and in walked Atticus. But in all honesty, a bit of Max did make the journey with us, and a bit of him remained behind. I brought along a small vial of his ashes and sprinkled them inside JFK's sailboat, *Victura,* which sat outside on the lawn.

When we returned to Tamworth after our big night, I looked forward to getting back on the trails. But first we'd have to see Dr. Christine O'Connell again. She was pleased with the way Atticus had healed, and she smiled when she told me she'd received fan mail for taking care of him.

I didn't know much about Christine other than the fact that she looked very young and she'd been there for us when we needed her. I asked, "How long have you been a vet?"

"I was a vet tech for several years before I became a vet."

"But how long have you been a vet?"

"Only a few months," she said.

I'm not sure how I would have felt had I known that before she went to work on Atticus's throat, but I was glad that things had worked out the way they did. She had gumption, and I liked that about her. I was also happy to know that we had someone to turn to in the mountains in case we ever needed anything. We'd always return to Angell for Atticus's major medical needs, but Christine would be our regular vet from that point on.

33

Paige

Just as Paige was the only person I called back when Atticus was attacked, she was the first person I called the morning after our big night at the John F. Kennedy Presidential Library. I recounted the entire evening, and she hung on my every word. She giggled and laughed. She asked me to repeat things and wanted every detail. It was as if she never wanted to forget any of it.

Oh, how she was filled with joy at how the little dog she'd bred had gone from being an only puppy in the hills of Louisiana, to an instant celebrity in Newburyport, to a legend in the White Mountains, to being honored as a hero. When I told Paige that the award was as much hers as ours, she was humbled; I could hear the sadness in her voice. "Without you, Paige, none of this would have been possible. I have you to thank for so much."

In the coming weeks, we e-mailed regularly, and on the Monday before Thanksgiving we had a conversation that revealed more than I ever could have imagined. Paige, who had always been warm, supportive, intuitive, and above all mysterious, began telling me the story of her life—and how Atticus came to live with me.

She was a willowy, ethereal woman, tall and slender, with long legs, and she loved being outside. She was tough and hardworking, and yet, as she put it, she could be "as delicate as fine china."

Six months before Atticus was born, Paige was riding her bicycle along a country road and was hit by a car. She'd struggled to regain her health, but nothing had worked. Mentally, physically, and emotionally, she limped through life. She'd lost her center, and nothing felt right. Then, on a March night, something unusual had happened. One of her dogs had been due to give birth. Paige had a way with animals and had worked with them her entire life, starting on her parents' farm, and she could predict how many babies an animal would have. She figured the mother dog had four puppies in her, but when the moment came, she was stunned to find only one tiny black-and-white pup.

She'd never been wrong like that before.

She held this little creature in her hand, cleaned him off, weighed him, and on the way to bringing him back to his mother she stopped in her tracks. There was something different about this little baby. She wasn't sure what it was; she just knew it deep down in her heart.

Over the next six weeks, she devoted much of her time to him, and, curiously, in that same period she began to heal. "There was something about him that reflected who I was," she told me. She'd often carry him out back into the woods and sit his tiny body on her lap and let him look out on the world and tell him she didn't know how it was going to happen but that he was going to have the most extraordinary life.

Paige, who had lovingly bred more than a thousand puppies and sent each of them off into the world, had decided that for once she would keep one. He was the only thing that made her happy. You see, she was locked in a very unhappy marriage.

Life had not been kind to Paige. It began when she was seven years old and her grandfather started touching her. It would go on for years, and no one had wanted to believe what he was doing. As with many children who are sexually abused, Paige often ended up with other people who weren't kind. I suppose that's how she ended up with a much older husband who treated her miserably.

"Tom, that day you called to ask if I knew something was wrong with Atti and that's why I charged you less . . . well, it hurt. You wondered why I only charged you four hundred and fifty dollars. If I hadn't been married at the time, I would have given him to you for nothing.

"I had no intention of selling Atticus to anyone, but then you contacted me out of the blue, and I could hear how heartbroken you were, and I figured if Atticus had helped me as much as he did, he would be able to help you, too.

"The morning I sent him off to you, I sat in the airport parking lot and cried my eyes out. I cried and cried until there was nothing left, because I didn't want to give him up. He was all I had!"

I was speechless.

"Later that same day, when you had Atti in your arms and you called and thanked me, I could hear how happy you were, and I knew I'd done the right thing.

"Then you kept on calling and wanted to do right by him. I always give the same advice to everyone who buys a puppy from me, but it seemed like you were the only one who would do whatever I told you to do. It made me so happy to see you two grow together. And how everyone in Newburyport took to him—I just loved that."

In the days that followed, we talked endlessly, and Paige revealed more and more.

"Whenever I sent out a baby to live with a new family, I felt as if I was standing on a beach and sending each one off in a little boat to sail across the ocean to a life where they would be safe, happy, and loved. I always wanted to know so much about their new lives, because they were living my life for me—a life I'd never have. I'd send them off and stand there looking out over the water and say sadly, 'But not for me.' But none of the people kept in regular contact with me except one. That was you. You told me *everything,* and without knowing it you let me live through the life you and Atti had."

I often listened to Paige in silence during those phone conversations with tears running down my cheeks.

"Then when you started hiking mountains with Atti . . . you have no idea what that meant to me. When I was a little girl, I would tell my mother that there would come a day when I would run two thousand miles away and go live in the mountains and no one would find me. And there the two of you were—two thousand miles away in the mountains.

"When you sent me photos of him sitting on top of a mountain looking out like that, I sat at my computer and traced my finger over the screen and imagined that I was living that life, and I could feel what Atti was feeling. You often took my breath!"

She talked of when I'd called her about Atticus going blind. "It was as if you were saying, 'Please, Paige . . . please help me. Help me fix him.' And I would have done anything, Tom. My heart just melted. I never told you, but I called my vet down here and I was going to drive up and get Atti and bring him back and have his eyes fixed, and when he was all better, I was going to bring him back to you. But then I heard how everyone wanted to help and how nice they were. I just couldn't believe it. So I didn't say anything, and I was so happy when everything turned out good. But I was always right here for you and Atti. And if anything ever happened to him, you would have had a new puppy within days, and you wouldn't have had to pay a cent."

There wasn't much Paige and I didn't share. We opened our lives up to each other. One day I felt guilty after I got mad at her. It was when she was telling me about her husband. She never referred to what he did as abuse, but that's what it sounded like to me. I asked her, "Why did you stay, Paige? Why did you put up with it?" For she was still married after nearly twenty years. She was tied to him through debt and was two years into a three-year escape plan.

I didn't yell, I was just short, and I was angry because I wanted Paige to be happy and because I knew what it was like to be abused. But when she started crying, I would have crawled through the phone to her if I could have. In between sobs she said, "Why did I stay? Why did I stay? I stayed because no one ever gave me an instruction book, Tom! I didn't know how to get out. Life's not easy, you know!"

I apologized, and Paige did, too, and we continued to talk day after day.

All the while as her story unfolded, I couldn't believe what she had done for me. It was astounding. This little dog, this amazing woman, the gift they gave me. The life they gave me.

One day the subject of our first conversation came up. It was after she had shown me photos of all her other puppies and I hadn't been interested in any of them. She said she had one last puppy, but he was "different." I mentioned how I fell in love with Atticus because he wasn't like the other dogs. They were all perfectly posed, but not him. He could have cared less about impressing the camera.

"Tom Ryan, you have to remember that I didn't want to give him up, and I wasn't sure I was going to send him to you, so when I took his photo, I didn't pose him like I did with other babies. I was half hoping you wouldn't be impressed. But you saw through that and didn't care how he looked. I had a lump in my throat after that, because I knew I was going to lose him."

There was one last question I had for her. I'd always been curious about her first piece of advice on raising Atticus: *Carry him everywhere you go, and don't let anyone else hold him that first month.*

"That worked so well. I tell everyone who gets a puppy that they should do it. Where does it come from, Paige?"

There was a pause on the other end of the phone, as if she were wondering whether she really wanted to tell me, and then in a soft, vulnerable voice she said, "That's the way I always wanted to be loved, Tom."

34

Home

When I think back to the night that Atticus and I were honored as heroes at the Kennedy Library, I think the good people at the MSPCA only got it half right. There *was* a hero on that stage, but it wasn't me.

In *The Hero with a Thousand Faces*, Joseph Campbell wrote, "A hero ventures forth from the world of common day into a region of supernatural wonder: fabulous forces are there encountered and a decisive victory is won: the hero comes back from this mysterious adventure with the power to bestow boons on his fellow man."

That wasn't me. It was Atticus. He ventured forth again and again from "the world of common day," he faced "fabulous forces." And as Campbell pointed out, the journey was not complete until the hero returned to "bestow boons." And boy, did he ever. He brought inspiration to everyone who followed his journey, but none more so than me.

Four decades into my life, I made a decision that changed everything. I adopted an unwanted dog and gave him a home. He, in turn, gave me one. In his brief time with me, Max opened my heart and left the door open for Atticus. I owe much to one dog who died and even more to another who lived. Max sent me on my way, but it was Atticus who led me home again, who taught me about love, about the kindness of my fellow man, about daring to dream and finding a way to love my embattled father—who, while he never understood this, will always live, as long as his son carries his dreams for him.

While it was never planned this way, it is wonderfully ironic that Atticus was named after my favorite literary hero. In *To Kill a Mocking-bird*, the attorney Atticus Finch takes on the lost cause of helping Tom Robinson. Atticus is tested as never before. It's not a stretch to say that my little Atticus went to even greater, more heroic lengths in saving his Tom.

Perhaps Atticus was different from the very beginning—as Paige said—and that's why he selflessly led me over all those mountains when he was going blind, because he knew there was something in me that needed to do that. Or maybe what made Atticus special was Paige's selflessness in giving up the one thing she never wanted to give up to a stranger who needed him more than she did. Then again, it could have been that he was allowed to be who and what he wanted to be, for he was raised first by Paige and then by me as we both wished we'd been raised . . . and loved. No matter the answer, I was taught to be more selfless by both Atticus and Paige, and I turned from a life where I wrote about the limits of mankind and instead chose a life without limitations, where middle-aged, overweight men and little dogs can do the most remarkable things together—even in some of the most dangerous conditions in an ancient mountain range.

Someday, if I outlive my family and friends and most of my good sense and I end up in a nursing home as my father did, those who take care of me will surely think me mad when I tell them of one little dog and the adventures we shared, 188 mountains climbed in three winters, and a night on the stage of the JFK Presidential Library.

How lucky we have been, this man and dog, to have the experiences we've shared, and how many lifetime memories we've accumulated since we met. I cannot imagine a world without Atticus in it, not now, not while the adventures keep coming.

As for our next adventure, Atticus made me believe that love is the answer to nearly everything, and I was ready to give it another try. Seven years after I had picked him up at the airport, he and I were returning there—to pick up our date. Paige Foster was flying up from Louisiana. She was finally going to those mountains two thousand miles away from the life she knew, and she would see the views her little dog had seen, then lost, and finally found again.

Neither Paige nor I could predict how things would work out between us. But that's the thing about adventures—you're invited to take a chance without knowing the outcome, and all that matters is that you say yes. Getting together for a first date after all those years was fitting. Because the fact was, Paige had taught me more about love than anyone I'd ever known. She taught me how to love completely and selflessly as she held my hand in bringing up Atticus.

There was something else fitting about our giving love another chance together. I was seven when my mother died and I lost my innocence, while Paige was seven when her grandfather stole hers. We'd been forced out of the Garden at the same age, and we'd found our way back again. It was Paige who put it best: "We are two seven-year-olds who lost our way a long time ago, and we are coming home, brought together by a seven-year-old dog we both love."

In telling the story of my friend Atticus M. Finch, I often think of that wonderful line from Antoine de Saint-Exupéry: "Perhaps love is the process of my gently leading you back to yourself."

For that's what that little dog did. He led, I followed, and in the end I became the man I dreamed of being when I was a little boy.

So they went off together. But wherever they go, and whatever happens to them on the way, in that enchanted place on the top of the Forest, a little boy and his Bear will always be playing.

—A. A. MILNE, *THE HOUSE AT POOH CORNER*

Acknowledgments

I was once asked if Atticus was the perfect dog. "He's perfect for me," I said. That's the way I feel about Brian DeFiore, my agent. He recognized this story for what it could be and helped me grow it into a book. In the process he made me reach to become a better writer. Where Brian left off, Cassie Jones, my editor at William Morrow, took over. Atticus's breeder, Paige, once thanked me for letting Atticus be who he wanted to be. "You didn't train the Atticus out of him," she said. I'm thankful for Cassie's enthusiasm, insight, and guidance. More than anything, I am blessed to have an editor who not only didn't edit the writer I was out of me but, like Brian, helped me become a better one. There are numerous others in the William Morrow/HarperCollins family I'm grateful for. Seale Ballenger, the head of publicity, has been a friend from day one (and Atticus gives a shout-out to Maddie and Petey), and I also appreciate the strong support and efforts of Jessica Deputato, Liate Stehlik, Lynn Grady, Jean Marie Kelly, Shawn Nicholls, Shelby Meizlik, Megan Swartz, Mary Schuck, Nancy Tan, Maureen Sugden, Lisa Stokes, and Nyamekye Waliyaya.

When I went looking for an artist to create a map of the White Mountains, I never realized I'd find one less than a mile from my front door.

Kathy Speight Kraynak's masterful pen-and-ink drawing ended up far better than my imagination had envisioned it.

I started my writing career in Newburyport as the publisher and editor of the *Undertoad*. The lessons Ed Metcalf, Doug Cray, John Battis, and Carol Buckley offered up were a great education for a budding scribe, and they're still with me. Tom O'Brien and Sue Sarno were among those who gave me my Newburyport education. My Newburyport family includes the always supportive Peter Jason Riley and Bob Miller.

Paul Abruzzi, the manager at Newburyport's Jabberwocky Bookshop, is not only a grand friend; his generosity and advice helped me take the step from newspaperman to author.

Steve Smith and Mike Dickerman will tell you that when they wrote *The 4,000-Footers of the White Mountains*, their objective was to produce a guidebook. But to me it was a treasure map that helped me find the pieces of my fragmented life and put them back together. Many a new hiker finds him- or herself falling asleep with their book on the nightstand. Thanks to the hours I spent at Steve's Mountain Wanderer store in Lincoln, New Hampshire, I met others who shared a love of the mountains. Two of them, Ken and Ann Stampfer, turned out to be our White Mountain family. Their love and friendship sustained me when I moved north.

What does a newspaperman do when he leaves his newspaper behind? He finds a new one. Or in my case, I was fortunate the *Northcountry News* and *Mountainside Guide* found me. I didn't realize that when Bryan and Suzanne Flagg first invited me to write "The Adventures of Tom and Atticus" in their pages I would be writing much of the outline of this book.

Atticus appreciates Marianne Bertrand and her staff at Muttluks for their generosity and for making sure his paws are always protected with their invaluable hiking booties.

I send my love to my aunt Marijane Ryan and my sister-in-law Yvette Ryan. They've been my biggest cheerleaders, and both read my manuscript religiously, offering guidance and helping me to steer clear of pitfalls.

Special thanks go to Romeo Dorval; Lisa Dorval; David and Emmett Hall; Constance Camus; Peter and Julie McClelland; Laura Lucy; Marie Bouchard; Christine Vallerand; Laini Shillito; Sue Little; Tom Jones; Jeff Veino; Aaron Lichtenberg; Manford Carter; Joe Carter; Leeane Galligan; Leigh Grady; Kevin, Cal, and Ruby Bennett; Christine O'Connell at the North Country Animal Hospital; the Friends of Atticus; and Sarah George—my sister from another mother.

I cannot say enough about the staff at Angell Animal Medical Center and MSPCA Angell in Jamaica Plain, Massachusetts—particularly Atticus's vet, Maureen Carroll. Kathleen Santry, Diane Wald, and the rest of the good souls in the fund-raising office were instrumental in assisting us when we raised money for animals in need. All you need to know about MSPCA Angell is that the first people to contribute were members of its staff. Imagine working at a place you believe in so much that when you get paid you turn around and give it back some money. It's just one of the things that make MSPCA Angell an extraordinary place.

Last, if it were not for life-saving emergency surgery by Drs. Stuart Battle and Bob Tilney of North Conway's Memorial Hospital, I wouldn't have lived to finish the book. It was their good work and the incredible care of my ICU nurses, Maureen Murphy Ansaldi and Doug Jones, that kept me alive during septic shock. (And yes, the hospital was good enough to let Atticus stay with me every day, even in ICU.) I'm forever grateful.

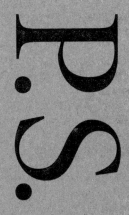

About the author

2 Meet Tom Ryan

About the book

3 An Interview with Tom Ryan
by Jessica Lahey

Insights,
Interviews
& More . . .

Meet Tom Ryan

Courtesy of the author

TOM RYAN IS THE FOUNDER of the Newburyport, Massachusetts, newspaper *The Undertoad* and served as its publisher and editor for more than a decade. In 2007 he sold the newspaper and moved to the White Mountains of New Hampshire with miniature schnauzer Atticus M. Finch. Over the last five years, Tom and Atticus have climbed more than 450 four-thousand-foot peaks.

After raising thousands of dollars for Angell Animal Medical Center in Jamaica Plain, Massachusetts, the pair was inducted into the Massachusetts Society for Prevention of Cruelty to Animals Hall of Fame as corecipients of the Human Hero Award. Tom currently writes the popular "The Adventures of Tom & Atticus" column in the *Northcountry News* and *Mountainside Guide* and the blog The Adventures of Tom and Atticus. He and Atticus live in the White Mountains of New Hampshire. ◡

An Interview with Tom Ryan

by Jessica Lahey

I HAVE ALWAYS BEEN A SUCKER for a good coming-of-age story; tales of adventure, trials, and spiritual epiphany fuel my mind, my soul, and my teaching. These are our stories; the tales of humankind's journey through the world, into the wilderness, and back home again. These are the stories I tell my children and my students. Stories of heroes who step out of ordinary lives and, despite the obstacles in their path, achieve the extraordinary.

When my copy of *Following Atticus* arrived in the mail, I dropped my briefcase on the floor of my mudroom, sat on the nearest chair, and opened to the introduction. The first passage I read was Tom's description of Atticus, a lone figure atop Wildcat Mountain: "He is Frodo Baggins, he is Don Quixote; he is Huck Finn. He is every unlikely hero who ever took a step out of the door and found himself swept up in adventure."

When I read that passage, I knew. I had found a kindred spirit. Two, actually.

Heroes are not necessarily the stuff of summer blockbusters and caped crusaders. Sometimes, they are just a man and his small dog doing what they know is right. Doing what they are meant to do.

Tom writes that *Following Atticus* ". . . is not the end of a book but merely a chapter." In the following interview, ▶

An Interview with Tom Ryan *(continued)*

I ask Tom about the new direction his life has taken since the book's release, the obstacles he and Atticus have encountered in the world beyond the White Mountains, and the paths these two unlikely heroes have explored in search of their next chapter.

Jessica Lahey lives, writes, and teaches middle school in Lyme, New Hampshire. You can follow Jessica's adventures in teaching at www.jessicalahey.com and in the *New York Times*, where she writes about teaching and parenting.

Q: *You two clearly love the White Mountains, and the solitude they provide. Was it hard to leave the Whites in order to go on the road to promote* Following Atticus?

A: It was more difficult than I thought it would be. Atticus and I lead a simple but wonderful existence in the White Mountains, and I missed it while we were on the road. However, it was so exciting as a first-time author to have a book tour, and I felt honored to be able to bring the White Mountains on the road with us, since I talked about them so much at each event. In the end I considered going on the road with Atticus just one more adventure.

Q: *You wrote of your admiration for Atticus's balance and composure in the face of potholes and frost heaves in the roads of Newburyport. How did Atticus* *handle the figurative "bumps" in the road during your book tour?*

A: Although I often tell people that Atticus is happiest on top of a mountain, he really appears to be most at ease wherever we are together. We did our book tour our way. We drove. And in doing so it gave us more alone time and allowed us to set up each day in a manner that would allow us to get out on plenty of walks and have freedom other authors might not have in flying from one city to the next. And taking care of Atticus on a book tour is not unlike taking care of him on a mountain. Seeing to his needs, it only reaffirms the friendship we share. It's just another way of following Atticus.

Q: *You and Atticus seem uniquely suited for each other. You wrote, "I chose the puppy that didn't look like the others. In my mind I suppose I went with the one that didn't fit in because I felt like I didn't fit in either." Do you still feel this way or have the writing and hiking offered a new place for the two of you to fit in?*

A: I definitely still feel the same way. It's the nature of any writer or adventurer to be on the outside looking in. The hero's journey, as described by the mythologist Joseph Campbell, is a solitary quest. Its appeal is universal and there are many parallels, but the journey is distinctive. Each journey, each adventure belongs ▶

to the individual alone, and that's what brings spice to life and creates a more interesting world. I feel Atticus and I were on a path that was distinctive for us. And it wasn't just hiking the mountains, but it was where those hikes took us in life. That was a journey only he and I could take.

Q: *One of your goals for the founding of your Newburyport newspaper* The Undertoad *was to "shine the light in the dark places," in order to improve one little corner of the world. Do you think that the process of writing about surviving "the shipwreck" of your childhood with an abusive and indifferent father helped shine a light on that particular dark place?*

A: After my last issue of *The Undertoad* was published and Atticus and I moved to the mountains, a friend asked me, "Do you think that maybe somewhere in the back of your head you tried to fix Newburyport, your home, because as a child you didn't have the ability to fix the dysfunction?" I'd never thought of it that way, but I suppose there's truth in that, just as there's truth in what you're getting at with your question. So yes, I would say that by writing about "the shipwreck" and writing about moving forward and forgiveness, I was able to put the abuse and the confusion of my childhood behind me. It's said that you shouldn't write a book unless you learn something in the process. In writing

> " Each journey, each adventure belongs to the individual alone, and that's what brings spice to life and creates a more interesting world. "

Following Atticus I discovered just how much forgiveness I had within me, and my love for my father came through more clearly than it ever had.

Q: *A review of* Following Atticus *from the* Appalachian Mountain Club Outdoors *quoted you as saying that* Following Atticus *"is not about the dog, and it's not about the mountains." What do you believe the book is about?*

A: It's about life, and growth, and redemption. It's about getting lost and finding your way back home again. It's about the journey inward, not the one to the top of the mountain. It's about friendship and discovery. And above all it's about love. I debate this from time to time with other hikers. They say the purpose of climbing a mountain is to get to the top. For me it's more about where the hike takes me—and that has more to do with feelings and experiences than simply checking a mountain off a list as a typical "peakbagger" would do.

Q: *People have noted that you don't speak for Atticus in the book. Why is that?*

A: I'm glad you asked this question. Those who haven't read the book have sometimes asked, "Does Atticus have a voice in the book?" And my answer is always the same—no, he doesn't, he's a dog and dogs don't speak. I think it would be presumptuous and ▶

> ❝ In writing *Following Atticus* I discovered just how much forgiveness I had within me ... ❞

> ❝ It's about getting lost and finding your way back home again. ❞

An Interview with Tom Ryan (*continued*)

disrespectful of me to pretend to know what he's thinking. We do have our own way of communicating where he uses his actions to let me know when he's happy or content or nervous. But to pretend I know what he's thinking, well, I just wouldn't do that. I respect him too much for that.

Q: *In describing the Newburyport locals, you used the analogy of "crabs in a bucket—when one climbs up, the others try to pull him down." The novelist Paulo Coelho has used this same analogy to describe writers and the business of writing. Have you received any feedback from other writers since the release of* Following Atticus, *and what have the other "crabs" had to say about your success?*

A: I think this is a touchy subject. (*Laughs.*) But I think it's true of certain personalities in creative fields. A good friend of mine is a wonderful painter but she tells me she never shares her works in progress with other artists because some will try to undermine her. I think it's a lot like anything else in life. There are big people and small people. Big writers and small writers. A big writer will help you take steps forward and isn't threatened by your possible success. A small writer won't reach out to help and they'll turn their back on you.

There's a scene in the movie *Midnight in Paris* that touches on this perfectly. A budding writer, Gil, goes back in time and meets Hemingway and asks him if he'll read his manuscript. The Hemingway character says, "I hate it." Gil says, "You haven't even read it yet." And Hemingway answers: "If it's bad, I'll hate it. If it's good, then I'll be envious and hate it even more. You don't want the opinion of another writer."

Q: *You've described the White Mountains as both your escape and your homecoming. Why do you think they have such a pull on you?*

A: I'm sure it's because of my father and his love of the White Mountains and all our family vacations up there. I saw a different side of Jack Ryan in the White Mountains. Gone was the anger and the frustration, replaced by a sense of wonder and awe.

I also think it was the first place I looked at as a child and saw the power and beauty of nature and felt that same sense of wonder and awe my father exhibited and that made us equals.

And of course there were the legends that come with the White Mountains that I learned as a child. They lent an air of magic and made the mountaintops and valleys feel like a fantastic world one could only find in a book.

Q: *Your account of that first winter ascent of Mount Tecumseh was haunting—total darkness, wraithlike trees, and an overwhelming sense of sadness pervades that scene. You* ▶

> "I saw a different side of Jack Ryan in the White Mountains. Gone was the anger and the frustration, replaced by a sense of wonder and awe."

wrote that you felt the trees were delivering a message. What were they saying to you on that cold, dark night?

A: We have a tendency to let ourselves get distracted from what's most important in our lives by the mundane. Perhaps we're just too busy, or maybe we're afraid to face things we mask in denial. But while climbing a mountain that superficiality is wiped away, at least for me it is. It's a Zen moment and I suppose up until that point I hadn't really dealt with how my father was aging and how he wouldn't always be there. Fear has a way of shocking you into what's most important, and being on my knees in the dark underneath those trees I was paralyzed. Something else took over and brought my thoughts back to my father.

Q: *You describe a ritual you have at the summit of each mountain, "I'd pick him up as I had when he was a puppy, and he'd sit in the crook of my arm, and together we'd look out at the views. Whenever we did this, the only thing I heard from him was a contented sigh. At that moment I always said, 'Thank you,' but I was never sure who I was thanking." Have you figured it out? Do you know whom you thank?*

A: I haven't figured that out. I think about it often, especially after I put it in words, and when I return to a mountaintop with Atticus and find myself saying the same thing, almost as if it's a prayer, I now contemplate who that is addressed to. At different times I think it's addressed to Atticus, my father, Paige Foster (Atticus's breeder), or maybe it's to God. I don't really know. What I do know is the overwhelming sense of gratitude I feel.

Q: *You recount your pride in Atticus, your "ineluctable hero," particularly when he led you to safety through blinding snow and wind on Mount Lincoln. How does Atticus continue to lead you through your life?*

A: I have pointed out that by keeping Atticus safe by not exposing him to dangerous elements or conditions kept me safe as well. But it's more than that. I know that I raised Atticus in part as I wished I'd been raised, and in seeing to his needs and seeing to it that his life is full and rewarding and filled with love I'm sure there's a bit of me that's still tending to myself. In taking care of him and seeing to it that his life is full, my life is just as full.

Q: Following Atticus *received a 2012 Nautilus Book Award, which "recognizes books and audio books that promote spiritual growth, conscious living, and positive social change." What sort of growth or change did you hope to bring about in yourself or the world with this book?* ▸

An Interview with Tom Ryan *(continued)*

A: It was a pleasant surprise to win two silver medals in the Nautilus Awards. As far as what change I "hoped" to bring about . . . none, really. I've been interviewed many times and people ask me why I wrote the book. It's simple. I'm a writer and a storyteller. It's what I do and who I am. And when I looked back on the life that Atticus and I have led and the friendship we share together, I realized I had a story to tell. What others take from it is up to them. I'm just glad they do take things from it.

Q: *You profess to live by Ralph Waldo Emerson's words: "The good of going into the mountains is that life is reconsidered." When you stand on the Whites these days and reconsider, how do you feel about the direction your life has taken?*

A: I love it. How could I not? I live in one of the most beautiful places in the world. I'm living a dream by writing for a living about things I love. And I get to continue discovering new experiences with Atticus, a truly remarkable friend and dog.

Everyone has their own dreams. Mine just turned out to be a writer, writing about the mountains I find enchanting. By making a leap of faith into this simpler and wonderful life, I can't feel anything but blessed.

Q: *You write of the "genius loci," or spirit of a place you seem to find throughout the White Mountains. Where are you finding the "genius loci" these days? What are your sacred spots?*

A: My favorite summit is usually wherever Atticus and I can be alone and soak our surroundings in. And fortunately for us there are many places throughout the White Mountains we can hide out. But if you're looking for specific places, I'll tell you we spend a lot of time on the Moat Range, in Evans Notch on the New Hampshire and Maine border, and on a multitude of supposedly lesser peaks because of the solitude and the vistas afforded.

Q: *With the success of* Following Atticus *comes a lack of privacy. Do you long to be the anonymous "Mike" and "Sparky," or have you found a way to make peace with the public persona of "Tom and Atticus"?*

A: "Mike" and "Sparky" are alive and well. We just can't use that one any longer. Nevertheless, I am an expert at finding hiding places and private places. It's the nature of our life in the White Mountains to be local celebrities and when we run into people on the trail they typically know who we are, so we often find trails where no one else is hiking. It's also one of the reasons we hike at night. No one is out then.

Q: *You have reached so many of your goals—you've climbed the forty-eight* ▸

An Interview with Tom Ryan *(continued)*

four-thousand-foot peaks, raised a huge amount of money for charity. What are your goals today?

A: Funny, but in the mania to achieve things I realized what my true goal was and that was to find a simpler life, a quiet and peaceful life. And each day I do my best to strive for that. But another goal has to do with helping animals. There's public ways of doing this by lending our names to events and causes but I have a vision of a simple cottage by a river in a valley with mountain views and a little barn full of animals that are unwanted because of age or disability. And, of course, Atticus is by my side throughout it all.

Q: *If the last words of* Following Atticus *are "not the end of a book but merely a chapter," what comes next? What would the title of the next chapter be?*

A: Good question. So many possibilities.
The best stories are those that don't seem to end, they are the ones that turn into a new beginning.
For me, my adventure started when I left the path I was on by adopting Max, an elderly unwanted dog with no prospects for the future. By bringing Max into my home it gave me a home. When he died less than a year and a half later I wanted to continue to cultivate the life he gave me and that's why Atticus came into my life. Max and Atticus have taught me much about myself, about

66 The best stories are those that don't seem to end, they are the ones that turn into a new beginning. 99

what's important, about friendship, love, and life. And so it's only fitting that now that Atticus is ten years old we close the circle.

The other day one of our Facebook friends let me know about an unwanted fifteen-year-old miniature schnauzer, William, who had been dropped off at a kill shelter and wanted to know if I could help find him a home. Now Atticus and I live a simple and happy life, and there was no need to complicate things by bringing an unwanted dog into our lives for what could be the last year of his life. And yet, just as I did with Max at the very beginning, I inexplicably wrote back, "I'll take him."

With the help of the New Jersey Schnauzer Rescue Network, Atticus and I drove down to Connecticut to pick up William yesterday. And just as plain old Max wouldn't do and his name grew into Maxwell Garrison Gillis, plain old William wouldn't do either. I now share my life with Atticus Maxwell Finch and William Lloyd Garrison. I think the spirit of Max is smiling at me from the great beyond—and, of course, he's smiling at Atticus and William, too.

Bonus question: One of the best things about the publication of Following Atticus *has been the remarkable friendships developed among our readers on the* Following Atticus Facebook *page. We chose one question from a Facebook friend to answer here:* ▶

An Interview with Tom Ryan *(continued)*

Catherine Harnden Howell: *If you could choose anyone, living or dead, human or animal, to accompany you on one of your mountain hikes, who would that be?*

A: Catherine, there are two, and in many ways they *have* hiked with Atticus and me. The first is my father, who would have loved this entire adventure—from the first summer to the race against the weather in the winter quests, to the life we have in the mountain. And the other is Maxwell Garrison Gillis, Atticus's predecessor. As you know, Max now has a place in White Mountain lore. He never got to see these peaks I was inspired to do with Atticus, but his ashes are sprinkled on each one of them. But still, it would be great to see my father's face just as I did when I was a child and he gazed upon the mountains. And it would be magical to have Max see the places he ultimately sent us to. When it came to climbing the White Mountains, these two inspired me more than anyone else. I wanted to reconnect with my father; and not only did I want to give Atticus the childhood joys I never had, I wanted to give him the life Maxwell Garrison Gillis never got to lead. 〜

Don't miss the next book by your favorite author. Sign up now for AuthorTracker by visiting www.AuthorTracker.com.